MICHAEL'S EVIL DEEDS

"He reminds me of those impossible characters one reads about in magazines, who detect crime for the pleasure of it." FRONTISPIECE. *See page* 40.

Michael's Evil Deeds

BY E. PHILLIPS OPPENHEIM

WILDSIDE PRESS

INTRODUCTION

Meet E. Phillips Oppenheim

Edward Phillips Oppenheim (1866-1946) was an Englishman, born in London, the son of a leather merchant. For twenty years he worked in his father's business, while beginning to publish novels. His first, subsidized by his father, barely broke even, but before long he was successful, enough so that a rich admirer, also in the leather business, bought out the firm and put Oppenheim on salary to support his writing career. Oppenheim soon hit his stride and became a bestseller, one of the most popular writers of his generation. He produced one hundred and sixteen novels and thirty-nine collections of short stories. At least twenty-one films were produced from his work, mostly in the silent era, including three versions of his most popular work, *The Great Impersonation*.

Oppenheim's specialty was the fast-moving, glamorous suspense thriller, written in a breezy, easy-to-read style. He was the epitome of the "entertainment" writer of his day, without any pretensions of literature. His stories are filled with high society people, spies, diplomats, and political intrigue, without much actual detection, so, it has been remarked, his relationship to the formal mystery story is slight. One difference between Oppenheim and many other writers who described glamorous high society was that he had actually been there. Once he was successful, he had a yacht and a villa on the French Riviera, where he spent his winters and moved in elite circles.

In his most famous work, *The Great Impersonation,* a German and an Englishman, who could be identical twins, meet together in Africa and note their uncanny resemblance. Then the German plots to make the Englishman disappear and steal his identity in order to carry on an espionage mission. The trick of the book is that the reader follows the man's return to England without ever knowing *which* man has returned. Is it the Englishman or the German impostor? Even those closest to him don't know.

Oppenheim was widely admired in his day. John Buchan, the author of *The Thirty-Nine Steps* called him "My master in fiction."

—Darrell Schweitzer
Philadelphia, Pennsylvania

MICHAEL'S EVIL DEEDS

CHAPTER I

THE UNDISCOVERED MURDERER

MICHAEL

The duel — or shall I call it, perhaps, vendetta — between Norman Greyes and myself — known under many aliases but christened Michael Sayers — commenced on the morning of the third of November, some years ago, when I left my suburban home at Brixton to catch my usual train to the city, and found myself confronted upon the pavement with the immediate chances of life or death.

I will admit that I was taken by surprise. Every man at Scotland Yard was known to me by name and reputation, and I was perfectly convinced in my own mind that there was no one in that much abused but, from our point of view, admirable institution, capable of penetrating the secrets of my daily life and discovering in me, the reputed Thomas Pugsley, leather agent of St. Thomas' Street, Bermondsey, and Number 138, Woollerton Road, Brixton, the most accomplished and daring criminal of modern times. I knew at once,

when I saw the police sergeant, with his two plain-
clothes companions, crossing the road towards me, that
some one else was taking a hand in the game. Even
at that moment, when I had little time for observation,
I saw the well-remembered figure of a man emerge from
behind the curtains of Number 133, opposite, and it
took me exactly ten seconds to realise that henceforth,
after I had escaped from this present dilemma, I
should have to move my pieces with greater circum-
spection across the chessboard of life. I recognised
him the instant he appeared before the window. There
were a few streaks of grey in his black hair, but his
keen, grey eyes, his forceful mouth, his long, lean face
were all unchanged. He was the one man in the old
days whom we had all feared, the man whose retirement from the Force we had celebrated with a small but
very select little dinner at the Café Royal. My old
hatred of him blazed up as I realised the voluntary
nature of his return to the career which he had abandoned. I made up my mind then that if ever the time
came when I should be the arbiter of his fate, this man
should have no quarter.

The street was a short one, and within fifty yards of
a bustling thoroughfare. Nevertheless, at that early
hour there were not many people about, and, as it afterwards transpired, witnesses of the spirited few seconds
which followed were almost non-existent. It has always been my principle that the best form of defence is
prompt attack. Whilst the inspector, therefore, stood
with his mouth open ready to inform me that he held a
warrant for my arrest, I shot him through the right

shoulder blade. He staggered and would have fallen
but for his two companions. Before they had propped
him up against the railings and recovered from their
surprise, I was round the corner of the street and in
an empty telephone booth in the adjacent post-office.

I have always maintained that the Telephone Company is an unjustly abused institution. On this occasion, at any rate, my defence of them was justified.
Within thirty seconds of asking for Number 1000
Hop, I was speaking to the warehouseman whose duty
it was to dust and keep in good order my samples of
leather, which, to tell the truth, were rarely used. My
few rapid words of instruction spoken, I turned my
attention to those ingenious devices which, although
savouring a little of the trickster, have on more than
one occasion assisted me in preserving my liberty. I
turned my overcoat, which, in place of a sober black
garment, now became a covering of light grey tweed
with a belt behind. I rolled my trousers up to the knee,
disclosing very well cut brown leather gaiters. I left
my black bowler hat in the telephone box, replacing it
with a tweed cap; removed with a little pang of regret
the most wonderful dark moustache which the hand of
artist had ever fashioned, adjusted a pair of spectacles,
and made my exit.

There was some commotion in the street outside, and
the freckled young lady behind the counter paid scant
attention to me.

" The telephone service doesn't get any better, " I
said pleasantly. " It's taken me nearly ten minutes to
get two numbers. "

She accepted my complaint with equanimity. Her attention was still on the street outside.

" What is it?   A fire " I asked.

She shook her head.

" I don't know, " she answered. " Did you pay for both your calls? "

I assured her that I had done so and made my way into the street. There was a little crowd in Woollerton Road, and a motor ambulance came dashing by. I strolled along the broad thoroughfare until I came to a taxicab. I hailed the man and hesitated for a moment, glancing up at the sky.

" Is it going to keep fine? " I asked the driver.

He considered the point for a moment.

" Don't fancy there's much more rain about, guv'- nor, " he replied.

" Then drive to Streatham Hill Station, " I directed.

From Streatham Hill I travelled to London Bridge by the electric railway, and from London Bridge I took a taxi to Waterloo. From Waterloo I caught the ten-forty train to Brookwood, and from the hotel there, where I paused for some slight refreshments, I engaged a taxicab to drive me to " Linkside," the country retreat of a certain Mr. James Stanfield, situ- ated on the fringe of Woking Golf Links. William, my man-of-all-work, was digging in the garden, and wel- comed me with the bucolic indifference of his class. Janet, his niece, admitted me promptly to the house and received my unexpected visit with that respectful lack of curiosity, which was a heritage of her earlier train- ing as parlourmaid. She lit the fire in the little sitting room, and listened to my few remarks with imperturbable pleasantness. Yet on that morning, perhaps more than any other in my life, I felt a shadow of uneasiness concerning Janet. I watched her in silence, stooping over the fire, a young woman with a figure whose perfection her ill-fitting corsets and clothes failed altogether to conceal, pale of complexion, with introspective, queer-coloured eyes, close-lipped, and with a mass of well-brushed, glossy brown hair. When she stood up, a little flushed with her exertions, she faced me for a moment, waiting for orders. I am not a susceptible man, but it struck me for the first time that the girl was more than ordinarily good-looking.

" Nothing has happened during my absence, Janet? " I enquired.

" Nothing at all, sir, " she replied.

" Nobody called? "

" There was a rate-collector, " she said. " He wanted to know your address in London. "

" Did you tell him? "

" I do not know it, sir, " she reminded me quietly.

I removed my glasses and polished them. I am an expert physiognomist, but the girl's impassivity baffled me.

" I will leave it with you before I go away next time," I promised. " Please put me out a grey tweed golf suit and stockings."

" Shall you be requiring lunch, sir? " she asked.

" I will lunch at the Golf Club, " I told her. "I shall dine at home. "

" Is there anything particular you would like for
dinner, sir? "

" I leave everything to you, " I replied.

She left me silently and without further remark.
When I went upstairs, a few minutes later, my bedroom
as usual was spotlessly neat, my golfing clothes laid
out without any single omission. I discarded my somewhat heterogeneous articles of attire, donned my golfing habiliments with some care, and made my way to
the links. In the passage of the clubhouse I met the
Secretary.

" Are you wanting a game this afternoon, Mr.
Stanfield? " he asked.

" I should be glad of one, " I replied.

" There's a man just come down, " he went on,
" four handicap. You will find him in the luncheon
room. "

I made my way there. Seated at a table alone was
Sir Norman Greyes, the man who had watched for my
arrest, a few hours ago, in Woollerton Road, Brixton.

NORMAN GREYES

I resigned my position at Scotland Yard early in
the autumn of 19 — for two reasons. First, as a pro-
test against an act of gross injustice which, although it
did not affect me personally, was still bitterly resented
by the majority of my fellow workers; and secondly
because, through the unexpected death of a distant
relative, I succeeded to a baronetcy and a sufficient in-

come. I spent the best part of three years in travel,
nearly half of which time I was in the United States.
On my return to London I found myself, much against
my will, hankering after my old profession. It was
very clear to me that my old department had lost the
mastery it had once attained over the criminal world.
The problem of several cold-blooded murders and various large and daring robberies remained entirely un-
solved. In the intervals of my country life, I began
to study these from an outsider's point of view, chiefly
from the columns of the newspapers, but also to some
extent from hints and information supplied to me by
my friend Inspector Rimmington, who had been one
of my colleagues in the old days and now held the post
which I had vacated. Gradually I came to a certain
conclusion, a conclusion which I kept largely to myself
because I felt sure that no one at the Yard was likely
to agree with me. I decided that the majority of
these undetected crimes were due to one person, or
rather to one gang of criminals presided over by one
master mind. Purely from the inherited instinct of
my long years of service in the Police Force, I set myself the task of hunting down this super-criminal. In
November, 19—, I began to believe that I was on the
right track.

There were three crimes which I became convinced
had been committed by the same hand. The first was
the great robbery of jewels from Messrs. Henson and
Watts's establishment in Regent Street, and the murder of the watchman, who was shot dead at his post.
No trace of even a single article of this jewellery had

ever been discovered. The second crime was the robbery of a number of bearer bonds from a messenger
in a railway carriage on the London, Chatham and
Dover line. The messenger was also shot, but recovered after six months' nursing, although he could never
give any coherent account of what had happened to
him. The bonds were disposed of in South America at
a considerable loss. The third was the robbery from
Lord Wenderley's house in Park Lane of a great collection of uncut jewels, and the serious wounding of
Lord Wenderley himself, who was attacked in the dark
and who neither saw nor heard anything of his assail-
ant. There were other crimes which I thought might
be connected with these, but these three, for various
reasons, became linked together in my mind as the out-
come of one man's brain. I set myself the task of
discovering this one man, and the day came at last when
I really believed that I was in a position to lay my
hand upon him. There is no necessity to detail the
whole train of circumstantial evidence which finally
brought me to a certain conclusion. It is sufficient to
say that after watching him for three weeks, I became
convinced that a man by the name of Thomas Pugsley,
carrying on business in Bermondsey as a leather agent,
and living apparently the most respectable of lives at
Brixton, was in some measure connected with these
crimes. I discovered that his leather agency business
was prosecuted without energy or attention, that his
frequent absences from London were not in neighbour-
hoods where his wares could be pushed, and that he was
often away for a month at a time, with his whereabouts

unknown even to his landlady. The latter was a
highly respectable woman at whose house he had lived
for the last two years, and who I honestly believe was
ignorant of her lodger's antecedents, his habits and
business. By taking rooms in the neighbourhood, I
easily discovered all that she knew and one or two
circumstances which lent colour to my suspicions. I
placed these before Rimmington and it was decided to
make an arrest.

A more clumsy piece of business than this intended
arrest was never planned or carried into effect. The
inspector placed in charge of the affair by Rimmington, with his two subordinates, arrived at Brixton an
hour later than the time fixed upon, accosted Pugsley
in the street, and were very soon made aware of the
class of person with whom they had to deal. Before
the inspector could get out half-a-dozen words, he was
lying on the pavement with a bullet through his
shoulder. His companions dragged him on to the
pavement and set him up against the railings. Then
they turned to look for Pugsley. There was not a
trace of him to be discovered anywhere. The amazing
skill and cunning of the man was amply demonstrated
on that morning. By some extraordinary means he
seemed to disappear from the face of the earth. The
books of his business, when examined, showed that he
had done scarcely any business; his warehouseman was
an honest but stupid fellow who knew nothing except
that his master took numerous trips, he thought
abroad, to obtain fresh agencies. There was enough
money in the bank to pay all liabilities, but so far as

Thomas Pugsley himself was concerned, he seemed to
have walked off the edge of the world.

The morning which witnessed, however, the shooting of the inspector and the remarkable disappearance
of the man in whom I was so deeply interested, was
memorable, so far as I was concerned, for another
noteworthy incident. Absolutely disgusted with the
result of my six months' labours, I determined to wipe
the whole thing from my memory and travelled down
to Woking with the intention of playing a round of
golf. I was introduced by the Secretary to a resident
of the place whose name was James Stanfield, and we
had a round which ranks amongst the best I ever played
in my life. Stanfield was a silent but by no means a
gloomy person.. He appeared to be about forty years
of age and an absolute golf maniac. He played every
shot with the most ridiculous care, but I must confess
with also the most wonderful precision. His drives
were never long, but they were long enough for him to
escape trouble, and in the approximate eighty shots
which he took to complete the course, I cannot remember one that was in any way fluffed or foozled. He
beat me at the seventeenth hole, and it was whilst we
stood together upon the eighteenth tee that the incident
happened which was to bring still more excitement
into the day. On our right was a small plantation of
shrubs through which wound the path which my partner pointed out to me as leading to his house. Our
attention was attracted by the continued barking of a
small dog which had wandered from the adjacent foot-
path. I had the curiosity to walk a step or two into

the plantation to see what was the trouble. My companion, however, who was a little on my left, was the first to discover the cause of the dog's excitement. At a little cry from him I hurried to his side. Stretched upon his back, with extended arms, and a small blue hole in his forehead, we found the body of a man. He was dead but still warm, and by an extraordinary chance I at once recognised him. He was one of the two plain-clothes policemen whom I had seen in Woollerton Road that morning, foiled in his attempt to arrest the man who had been passing under the name of Thomas Pugsley.

JANET SOALE

Just before midday on Thursday, the third of November, my master made one of his unexpected reappearances. I was not surprised. Only the night before I had dreamed of him, and it seemed to me impossible that with my passionate prayers going out day by day, he should stay away much longer. When I first saw him turn in at the gate, I was filled with wild excitement. If he could have seen me at that moment, he would have known and understood everything. By the time he had reached the front door, however, and I had let him in, I had regained my self-control. I must have seemed to him just the ordinary well-mannered, well-conducted parlourmaid.

He changed his clothes and went off presently for his round of golf. When I went to his room to brush and

press the clothes which he had taken off, I found, however, that he had placed them in a drawer and apparently locked it. The discovery, coming on the top of
many others, gave me food for thought. I resolved to
watch the next morning's newspapers. It was becoming more and more clear to me that there was something in my master's manner of life which he was anxious to conceal from the world. I was the more convinced of this when I saw that in the top drawer, which
he had opened to take out a tie, he had concealed a
small revolver, loaded in all six chambers. A merchant
with offices in the City and a country cottage for golf
does not carry a loaded revolver about with him. My
heart beat with excitement as I picked it up and
handled it. I forgot my master's indifference. I
ignored the fact that, although I am well enough to
look upon, and that my face and figure have won me
more admirers that I could count on the fingers of both
hands, he has never cast a second glance in my direction. I still had faith in myself if I chose to make the
first advances. I have never made them to any man,
but I have an instinct. I believe that he is cold and
unresponsive from habit. I believe that if I could
make him understand the fires which are burning me up
night and day, he would throw off this mask of coldness
and mystery, and give me that place in his life which
I crave.

I was loitering about his room, looking still at that
closed drawer, when to my amazement a man entered —
a thin, weedy-looking person, with sunken cheeks and
a straggling, sandy moustache. I am not easily

frightened, but it gave me a turn when he closed the door behind him.

"What do you want?" I asked sharply. "How dare you come up here?"

He looked at me earnestly. It was obvious that my first thought was a mistaken one. This was not one of the admirers whom I found it difficult sometimes to keep at arm's length.

"Young woman," he said, "I am a police officer. You seem to be a sensible girl. Answer the questions which I ask, do not obstruct me in the course of my duty, and you will be rewarded."

I looked at him in silence for several moments. I do not think that I changed colour or showed anything of the terror which sat in my heart. My master was in danger. All the time I stood there, I was thinking. How was I to help? How could I help?

"Your master returned here an hour or so ago," this man continued, "and has now gone off to play golf. I want the clothes which he wore when he came down."

"How do you know that he changed?" I asked.

"I saw him come in and I saw him go out," was the quiet reply. "This is his bedroom, is it not?"

"It is," I admitted.

"Then the clothes must be here. Where are they?"

"I do not know," I answered. "I was looking for them myself. I was just going into the bathroom next door to see if he had left them there."

He stepped back and entered the bathroom. He was only gone for a few seconds, but I found time to take the revolver from the tie drawer and to slip it into my open pocket.

" The bath has not been used, " he said a little shortly, when he came back. " I should like you to stay with me whilst I search these drawers. "

I made no objection, and he made a hasty search of the contents of the first two. When he came to the bottom one and found it locked, he gave vent to a little exclamation.

" Have you the key of this drawer? " he demanded.

" No, " I answered. "My master has taken it with him. "

He made no bones for what he did, nor offered any apology. With an instrument which he carried in his pocket, he forced the lock and bent over the contents of the drawer. He was a man addicted, I should imagine, to silence, but I heard him muttering to himself at what he found. When he stood up, there was a smile of triumph upon his lips.

" What time do you expect your master back? " he enquired.

" I do not know, " I answered. " He was lunching at the golf club and playing a round afterwards. About five o'clock, I should think. "

He walked to the window and stood looking out over the links. I, too, looked out. In the far distance we could see two men playing.

" Do you know the links? " he asked.

" Very well, " I told him. " I have lived here all my life. "

" What hole are they playing now? "

" The seventh."

" What green is that just opposite? "

" The seventeenth. "

" Where is the tee for the eighteenth? "

" Just out of sight underneath the trees. "

He nodded, apparently well content. His eyes lingered upon me. I saw a look in his face to which I was
perfectly well accustomed. He had discovered that in
my quiet way I was good-looking. He came a little
nearer to me.

" Are you very fond of your master? " he asked.

" I see very little of him, " I answered. " He gives
no trouble. "

" Do you know that you are rather a pretty girl? "
he ventured, coming nearer still.

" I am always very careful of strangers who tell me
so, " I retorted, taking a step backwards.

He laughed.

" You'll give me just one kiss for this? " he begged,
holding out a pound note. " You're an intelligent
girl and you've told me just what I want to know. "

I looked at him curiously. If it were true that I
was an intelligent girl, it was scarcely a compliment
which I could return. For a police officer he must
have been a hopeless idiot.

" I don't allow any one to kiss me, " I objected,
pushing the pound note away.

" You must put up with it just for once, " he insisted.

I scarcely believed that he was in earnest — and for
the first time in my life a man kissed me upon the lips.

I can find no words even now to describe the fury which was born in my heart against him. I feared even to speak, lest my passionate words might carry some warning to him of the things which were in my heart. He seemed perfectly indifferent, however, and in a few minutes he strolled out and made his way across the garden to the little spinney. I took up my master's field glasses and satisfied myself that he was still a long distance away. I waited for a quarter of an hour. Then I took another path which led into the plantation and made my way cautiously to where the man was standing with folded arms, leaning against a tree. I drew nearer and nearer. I am light-footed and I have even been called stealthy. It was part of my early training as a parlourmaid to make no noise when I moved. So I stole to within a few yards of him, unperceived and unheard. I am not an emotional person, and my mind was quite made up as to what I meant to do. It was curious, however, how slight things left vivid memories with me during those few seconds. It was a queer, gusty November day, with tumbled masses of clouds in the sky, and a wind which bent the tops of the sparse trees and brought the leaves rustling down the muddy paths. A bird was singing just overhead, and I remember that in those strained moments I found myself translating his song. He was singing because he was glad to be alive in this wood full of dying autumnal things. Very soon there would be company for the creeping and crawling insects to whom winter meant death. And afterwards! I had a vivid little mind-picture of a crowded court-

house, of the judge who might try me and the jury
who might pronounce my fate. For a moment I
shivered. Then I thought of that loathsome caress.
I thought of my master and I smiled. If he knew, he
would thank me. Some day he would know!

I was so close that I think my victim felt the breath
from my lips or the sensation of my approaching body.
He turned quickly around and I saw his eyes wide-open
with apprehension. He would have shrunk away but
he semed paralysed, and as he stood there I shot him
through the forehead. He swayed on his feet, his
mouth open like the mouth of an insane man. His
eyes rolled, he pitched and fell forward on his face. I
listened for a moment. Then I took the path back to
the house. I had finished what I came out to do.

MICHAEL

My round of golf with the man who was the declared hunter of my life and liberty afforded me no
apprehension whatever, although I must confess that
the first sight of Norman Greyes seated in the club
luncheon room, only an hour or so after he had witnessed the abortive attempt to arrest me, was something of a shock. I came to the conclusion, however,
that his presence here was accidental, and in no way
connected with that harmless and respectable inhabitant of the neighbourhood, James Stanfield. I played
golf steadily and with success. It was not until that
startling discovery close to the eighteenth tee that my

equanimity was seriously disturbed. As we looked down upon the dead body of the plain-clothes policeman whom I had last seen in Woollerton Road, we both recognized him. No hint of anything of the sort, however, escaped from my lips.

After the first few seconds of stupefaction, Greyes naturally took charge of the affair. He set the caddies to search all around for a weapon, and begged me to summon my gardener, or any one who might be of assistance. I called for Soale in vain, however, and remembering that he had asked leave to visit his brother at Mayford, I abandoned the quest. Subsequently, one of the men working on the course appeared, and we carried the body into my tool shed. Greyes locked the door and telephoned for the police and doctor.

"You will excuse my apparent officiousness," he said, "but I once had some connection with Scotland Yard."

"There is nothing to excuse," I assured him. "I am only too thankful that you happened to be here. Do you think that it is a case of suicide?"

"I have reasons for doubting it," he replied, "apart from which, if it were suicide, the weapon would have been found. As the event happened so close to your house and actually on your path, Mr. Stanfield, you will not mind, I am sure, if I ask your servants a few questions."

"I shall be only too pleased," I told him. "My staff is rather limited as I am only here occasionally. My gardener is out for the afternoon, so there only remains my maidservant."

I led the way into the house. Janet was busy in the kitchen but came at once at our summons. As usual, she was wonderfully neat, and her manner, although reserved, was perfectly open.

" We want to know, " my companion asked, " whether there have been any callers at the house this afternoon? "

" None, sir, " she replied, " except the boy with the chicken I ordered for the master's dinner. "

" Have you seen any one about the place? "

" No one, sir. "

" Did you hear anything which might have been the report of a pistol? "

" Nothing at all, sir. "

" Have you been outside the house yourself? "

The girl shook her head.

" I have had no occasion to go out, sir, " she replied. " I have been busy in the kitchen. "

Greyes nodded and dismissed her after a few more unimportant questions. Soon a police inspector arrived, and the doctor. I let them visit the scene of the crime alone. As soon as they had gone, I went upstairs. I looked in my tie drawer for the small revolver. It had gone. I looked in the bottom drawer, which I had left locked, for the clothes which I had worn when I had made my escape. The drawer had been forced open and they, too, had disappeared. Then I realised that I was faced with a problem. Some one had penetrated my defences. I had been — I probably still was — in danger. I went down to the study and summoned Janet once more to my presence. When she arrived, I took a seat between her and the door. I made her face the window. Down in the straggling plantation, the police inspector was still talking to Greyes.

" Do you know anything about this affair which you did not tell Sir Norman Greyes? " I asked her.

" Yes, sir, " she replied.

I looked at her thoughtfully. She was very straight and shapely in the grey twilight. Her eyes met mine without flinching. I have been an indifferent student of women's looks, but I realised then that they were a very beautiful though rather a cruel colour, greeny-brown of a light shade, with delicate lashes and finely cut eyebrows. There was a passionate curve to her lips which I had never before noticed. Her neatly braided hair was brown and lustrous.

" You had better tell me everything, Janet, " I enjoined.

" Soon after you had gone out, " she said, " the man who lies in the outhouse came here and asked me questions about you. He made his way into your bedroom. He was anxious to see the clothes in which you had travelled down. He opened the bottom drawer of your wardrobe and found them. "

" There was a revolver in the top drawer, " I remarked.

" I had discovered that and hidden it, " she replied.

" And after he had found my clothes? "

" He went down to the plantation to wait for you. "

" Did he say what he wanted? "

" He had told me that he was an officer of the police. "

" And then? "

" I went down the other path, and I made my way across the spongy turf to where he was standing. When I was so near that there was no chance of missing him, I shot him dead. "

I am a man to whom courage is second nature, and I have seen death trifled with, and have trifled with it myself, like the juggler with his ball, but I have never heard it spoken of with more indifference. Outside, the figures of the detective and his companion were still visible in the little wood. The body of the dead man was only a few yards away. I leaned forward and looked at the girl, striving to get past the almost cynical impenetrability of her speech.

" Why did you do this, Janet? " I asked.

" He did what no man in the world has ever dared to do before, sir, " she replied.   " He kissed me — upon the lips!   I wonder that I did not kill him where he stood! "

" Had you no other reason except this, Janet? " I persisted.

" I wished to save you, sir, " she answered.

" To save me from what? "

" From the Law. "

" You think that I was in danger? "

" I know that you were. "

" Who or what do you think I am? "

" A great criminal, " she answered.

I was staggered, for it was plain to me now that I

must have been at this girl's mercy many a time. She
went on slowly.

" I have always believed, " she continued, " that you
were leading a double life. The few visitors you have
had have come at night, and secretly. Whenever you
have arrived here and Mr. Stanfield has recommenced
to play golf, there has been a tragedy or a great robbery in the newspapers on the following morning. I
always felt that some day or other this would happen.
Now that it has come, I am glad. "

" You realise that you have killed a man in cold
blood? " I persisted, determined to try her to the
limit.

" I am glad that I have, " she replied.

" For a domestic servant, " I said, "you have a
wonderful sense of your obligations. "

" You need not scoff at me, " she complained. " I
am a woman, a dangerous woman but a clever one. I
was not brought up to be a servant. I am fit to be your
companion. That is my hope. "

" I have never trusted a woman in my life, " I told
her.

" You will trust me, " she declared, in a low tone.
" You will remember what I have done for you to-day.
I am the woman who was made to complete your life.
You had better realise it and make use of me. You
will not regret it. "

She came a little closer to me, and though women
have never been more than the toys of my idle moments,
I felt the passion of her strike into my heart. My
senses were aflame. I saw life differently. Her voice

became softer and more sibilant. She was like some beautiful animal. Her eyes were appealing but inhuman.

" You shall marry me, " she continued. " I have a fancy about that and I insist. Then think of the benefit. If disaster should come, I shall never be able to give evidence against you. But there will be no disaster. I know how clever you are. I, too, have brains. My master, say that this means something to you. I have given you proof of my devotion. Repay me. "

I took her into my arms. There was a savage fire about her lips which warmed my blood, a fierce delight in her strange-coloured eyes which amazed whilst it enthralled me. This modern Borgia seemed to have fastened herself on to my life. The figures of the men in the little wood grew more shadowy.

" Where is the pistol? " I whispered, holding her away from me for a moment.

" Where no one will ever find it, " she answered.

" And the clothes? "

"Burned. I run no risks when your safety is in question. "

The searchers came back to the house half an hour or so later. I was busy rebinding the handle of my putter. Janet was in the kitchen, preparing my dinner. Greyes accepted a whisky and soda. He looked tired and a little dejected.

" Any luck? " I asked him, under my breath, as he prepared to take his leave.

He shook his head.

"So far as circumstantial evidence is concerned," he admitted, "I am afraid we shall be in a bad way. A more brutal murder I never remember. A young man, too, with a wife and three or four children, simply out to do his duty. If——"

He stopped short, swallowed a little sob in his throat, and turned away.

"I hope that you will give me another game of golf some day, Mr. Stanfield," he said, as he prepared to take his leave.

"With great pleasure," I assented.

NORMAN GREYES

Yesterday the inquest on poor Richard Ladbrooke, after having been twice adjourned, resulted in a verdict of murder against some person or persons unknown. The verdict itself is a terrible reflection upon our present criminal methods. It pulls at the strings of my conscience with sickening intensity. Ladbrooke had found a clue which he confided to no one. He had travelled down to Woking in search of the missing man Pugsley — or Michael Sayers, as I believe him to have been. He must have been murdered there either by Pugsley himself or some confederate, yet not one of us has been able to lay our hands upon a single shred of evidence. I have been unable to tear myself away from the place. I have had several games of golf with Mr. Stanfield, and I have dined with him once at his house — a very excellent dinner and wonderfully cooked. He is desirous of offering a small reward for

the apprehension of the murderer, but at present I
have not encouraged him. I do not want a crowd of
people stirring up the waters. I have not said as much
to any one — not even to him — but I am making it
the object of my life to lay my hands upon the so-called
Thomas Pugsley. The day I find him, the mystery of
Ladbrooke's murder will be solved. And I shall find
him!

CHAPTER II

NORMAN GREYES TELLS THE WHOLE STORY

On the evening of my return from the Riviera after a three months' holiday, I was accosted in the lounge of Marridge's Hotel by a middle-aged man of inconspicuous appearance, who had been seated in a corner alone. It was some few seconds before I could recall him to my memory, but curiously enough a crowd of unpleasant associations gathered themselves together in my mind even before I recognised him.

"You haven't forgotten me and our golf down at Woking, Sir Norman?" he asked.

I knew all about him then.

"Mr. Stanfield, isn't it?" I said. "No, I haven't forgotten."

I was a few minutes early for my party, and I accepted the offer of a cocktail from my golfing acquaintance, while I waited.

"That was an extraordinary interruption to our first game," he remarked. "I never fancied my little house much afterwards. I gave it up, in fact, within the year."

" I heard you had left, " I told him. "Have you
still your model domestic? "

" She left me soon afterwards, " he replied regretfully. " You had no luck in your investigations, Sir
Norman? "

I shook my head. The subject was still a sore one
with me.

" I had no luck at all, " I confessed. " I came to
certain conclusions which carried me a little way along
the road, but all the clues ended abruptly. Yet I don't
despair. I always have the fancy that some day or
other I shall solve that mystery. "

The waiter brought the cocktails and we raised our
glasses.

" I drink, then, to that day, Sir Norman, " my companion said.

" I am with you, " I declared heartily.

We talked idly of various matters for a few moments
— principally of golf, which I had been playing regularly in the South of France. There were several
dinner parties being given in the restaurant that evening, and some very beautiful women were in evidence.
One in particular attracted my attention. She was
tall and, though slim, beautifully made. Her complexion was perfect, although a little colourless. Her
strange-coloured eyes had a nameless attraction. Her
hair, beautifully coiffured, was just the shade of brown
which appealed to me. She bowed to my companion
as she passed, and joined a little group at the farther
end of the hall. The last thing I noticed about her
was her wonderful string of pearls.

"That is a very beautiful woman," I remarked.
"Do you know who she is?"

"A South American widow — De Mendoza, her name is."

"You know her?"

"My humble apartment is on the same floor as her suite," my companion replied. "She is gracious enough sometimes to remember the fact that we meet occasionally in the lift."

My friends arrived, and I made my adieux to my erstwhile golfing acquaintance. Somehow or other, my meeting with him had left an unpleasant impression behind it. It had forced my thoughts back to the humiliating recollection of the fact that the murderer of Richard Ladbrooke still remained undiscovered, and that the man who had called himself Pugsley had walked away from detection under our very eyes and never been heard of since. Amongst my fellow guests was an official of the Home Office, and our conversation naturally drifted into the subject of social order.

"Your connection with Scotland Yard having long since ceased, Sir Norman," he remarked to me, "you will not be over-sensitive as to facts. The epidemic of crime which was raging about two years ago seems to have broken out again with exactly the same results. There are four undetected murders and five great robberies up to the debit of your late department. Your people believe that the same person is at the head of it who planned all those robberies eighteen months ago and escaped arrest by shooting the inspector."

I affected to take only a casual interest in the information, but as a matter of fact I was considerably moved. If the man who had last concealed his identity under the name of Pugsley, but whom I strongly suspected to be the notorious Michael Sayers, had really come out into the open once more, life would certainly possess a new interest for me during the next few months.

We were a party of six that evening — a celebrated criminal lawyer and his wife, my friend from the Home Office, with his wife and sister-in-law, and myself. The criminal lawyer, who was our host, heard scraps of our conversation and leaned forward.

" You did well to leave Scotland Yard when your reputation stood high, Sir Norman, " he said. " A new era of crime has dawned and the struggle is no longer equal. It isn't the riffraff of the world to-day who take to murder and burglary. The skilled and conscienceless scientist has taken their place. The criminal of to-day, in nine cases out of ten, is of higher mental calibre than the detective who is opposed to him."

" The struggle should be the more interesting, " I remarked vaguely.

It was a fancy of mine that my continued interest in my profession should remain as little known as possible, and I talked for some time on indifferent subjects to the lady who was seated by my side. We admired Mrs. De Mendoza and her gorgeous rope of pearls. My host intervened.

" It is women like that, " he commented, " who

choose to deck their bodies with jewels of fabulous value, who encourage crime. Roughly speaking, I dare say that necklace is worth eighty thousand pounds. For purposes of theft, it could probably be disposed of for fifty thousand. What a haul for the scientific thief! If it is really true that Pugsley is once more at work, what an opportunity!"

"A woman must be very brave," my hostess declared, "to run such risks."

"The jewels are probably in the hotel safe most of the time," I suggested. "I don't suppose she goes out in them."

Our host smiled.

"I can imagine Pugsley finding a few minutes in the hotel quite sufficient," he observed. "He or his successors, whoever they may be, would think little enough of human life by the side of, say, fifty thousand pounds. The modern maxim of the thief seems to be all or nothing. By killing at sight they certainly increase their chances of escape."

That closed our conversation upon the subject. We sat about in the lounge and drank coffee and liqueurs, danced for a time and smoked a few cigarettes. The party broke up as the lights in the lounge were being lowered. I was the only one of our little gathering remaining in the hotel, and I was talking for a few moments to the head porter, who was an old acquaintance of mine, when a man made a somewhat hurried entrance through the swing doors and seemed on the point of proceeding to the office. As he saw me, however, he hesitated and, turning aside, addressed me.

" Excuse me, but are you Sir Norman Greyes? " he asked.

I admitted the fact.

" Can I ask you to give me five minutes of your time on a matter of urgent business? "

I looked at him with some surprise. His voice and address were good, and in appearance he differed in no respect from the crowd of diners who frequented the place. He drew a card from his pocket and handed it to me.

" It is an absurd hour, I know, to trouble you, " he apologised, " but I can explain in a very few minutes if you will give me the opportunity. "

I stepped underneath one of the electric standards and looked at the card —

MR. STANLEY DELCHESTER

and underneath was the name of a famous insurance company. I motioned him to follow me into the deserted lounge and invited him to take a chair. I must say that he wasted no time in stating his business.

" Many years ago, Sir Norman, " he reminded me, " when you were officially engaged at Scotland Yard, you saved our firm a great loss in the matter of the Hatton Gardens emerald theft. "

" I remember it quite well, " I admitted.

" We understand, " my visitor continued, " that you have now resigned from the Force, but we hoped that you might be inclined to undertake a small commission for us. It came to the ears of our Chief quite

unexpectedly that you were staying here, and he sent
me after you at once. "

" I can at least hear what the business is," I replied.

" There is staying in this hotel, " the insurance
agent proceeded, "a Mrs. De Mendoza, the reputed
widow of a fruit merchant in Buenos Ayres. She is the
fortunate possessor of a very wonderful pearl necklace,
which she has insured with our firm for a hundred
thousand pounds. Our acceptance of the policy was a
grave error which we recognised almost immediately
afterwards. We know nothing of the lady, and under
those circumstances it is against our business policy
to accept the risk. We have done our best to protect
ourselves, however. Since the policy was issued we
have kept in constant touch with the lady and in daily
communication with the hotel detective. By to-night's
post, however, we had a message from the latter to say
that he was at home ill, and that during his absence
his duties would be taken over by the night watchman.
The policy has only one more week to run, and will not
under any conditions be renewed. We want to know if,
for any fee which you care to name, you will do your
best to guard the necklace for us during that week? "

"Have you had any intimation of thieves working in
this neighbourhood? " I asked him.

" None whatever, " he replied. " I will be perfectly
frank with you. It is not an ordinary robbery of
which we are afraid. For some reason or other, our
enquiry department has formed a dubious opinion of
Mrs. De Mendoza herself. "

" I see, " I remarked. " You are afraid of a bogus
theft. "

" Precisely! Directly we received the letter from
the hotel detective, we rang up the manager here. All
that we could learn was that the illness was altogether
unexpected, and that the man had been compelled to
go home at a moment's notice. In reply to our request
that a trained detective might take his place, the management assured us that they considered nothing of
the sort necessary. No robbery of jewels had ever
taken place from this hotel, and they considered their
night porter fully competent to watch over the interests
of their guests. "

I considered for a moment.

" Sir William Greaves, our manager, desired me to
suggest a fee of two hundred guineas, " my visitor concluded.

" I will accept the commission, " I promised.

The next morning I interviewed the manager of the
hotel, to whom I was well known. He showed some irri-
tation when I spoke of Mrs. De Mendoza's necklace
and her nervousness concerning it.

" To be quite frank with you, " he confessed, " although Mrs. De Mendoza is a good client and pays her
accounts regularly, I am inclined to be sorry that we
ever let her the rooms. "

" Why? " I asked.

" People with valuable jewellery should accept its
possession with a certain resignation, " he replied.
" This is the last hotel in London where a jewel rob-

bery would be likely. The lady herself, I understand, takes every possible care and caution. She wears her necklace nowhere except in the restaurant and lounge, and every night it is deposited in the hotel safe. I cannot see that she has the slightest cause for anxiety, nor do I understand the nervousness of the insurance company. However, you may rely upon it, Sir Norman, that every facility will be given to you in your task. I would suggest that you pay a visit to the lady herself."

The idea had already occurred to me, and later in the day I sent up my card to Mrs. De Mendoza and was at once invited to enter her sitting room. I found her writing letters, simply dressed in a black negligée and wearing the pearls. I was struck once more by the extreme elegance of her bearing and figure. As she turned and invited me to seat myself, she stirred in my memory a faint suggestion of reminiscence. I was not sure even then, however, whether it were a real person or a picture of which she reminded me. She listened to the few words with which I introduced myself and smiled deprecatingly.

"It is true that I am very foolish," she admitted, "but then I have always been a person of superstitions. I have owned my necklace for some years, and I have had it with me in quite lawless places. I have never, however, felt just the same amount of apprehension as I do at the present moment."

"That certainly seems strange," I replied. "The servants at this hotel are more carefully chosen than at any other hotel in London, and the guests are in nearly every case old clients."

She shrugged her shoulders.

" Apprehensions such as mine, " she said, " are not based upon reason. However, I must confess that I feel more comfortable now that the insurance company has engaged your services. Would you not like to examine the pearls? "

She came over to my side, and, without unclasping the necklace, let it rest in my hands. The pearls were all marvellously matched, all of considerable size, and with that milky softness which she pointed out to me as being a proof of their great perfection. As we stood there, necessarily close together, a wisp of her hair touched my forehead. Something in the timbre of her low laugh as she brushed it back, induced me to look up. There were qualities about her smile and the peculiar expression of her eyes which gave me a momentary thrill. I understood at once why men turned their heads always to look at her. Notwithstanding her reserved appearance, she possessed that strange gift of allurement which Helen of Troy might have bequeathed to Mademoiselle de Vallière.

" Do you admire my pearls? " she asked softly.

I let them slip from my palm.

" They are very wonderful, " I admitted.

She moved slowly away. I breathed more easily as the distance increased between us. She looked over her shoulder unexpectedly and I believe that she realised my sensation. The slight frown passed from her forehead. She was obviously more content.

" Tell me how you propose to guard my treasures, Sir Norman? " she enquired, as she sank into an easy-chair. " Shall you stand behind my chair at dinner, disguised as a waiter, and lie on my mat at night? It gives one quite a shivery sensation to think of such espionage! "

" Believe me, " I assured her, " I shall not be in the least obtrusive. I understand that you send your pearls down every night to the hotel safe. "

" I have always done so, " she answered. " Do you think it would be better to keep them up here? Will you promise to sit in this easy-chair, with a revolver on your knee, all night, if I do so? "

" Not for the world, " I declared. " The hotel safe is much the better place. "

" I am glad to hear your decision, " she said, with a slight smile. " I should sleep very little if I thought that my pearls were near me — and that you were sitting here, on guard. The idea would be disturbing. "

" One cannot guard against miracles, " I observed, " but I think you can make your mind quite easy about the necklace. If you should need me at any time, the number of my room is four hundred and thirty-two. "

" On this floor? "

" On this floor. "

" Tell me, " she asked a little abruptly, as I rose to take my leave, " who was the man with whom you were talking last night in the lounge — a slim, middle-aged man with a very hard face? I am always seeing him in the lift. "

" A man I know scarcely anything of, " I replied. " His name, I believe, is Stanfield. I once played golf with him down at Woking. "

" Stanfield? " she repeated. " Was it in his grounds near Woking that a murder was committed — a policeman was found shot there? "

I nodded.

" I was playing golf with Mr. Stanfield at the time, " I told her.

" And the murderer was never discovered? "

" Never ! "

" I wonder you didn't take an interest in the case yourself, " she remarked.

" I did, " I told her.

She made a little grimace.

" My fears for my necklace are reawakened, " she declared. " Surely it ought to have been an easy task for a clever man like you, one who used to be called a really great detective, to discover the murderer? "

" It is beyond my powers to bring him to justice, at any rate, " I replied. " There are many criminals walking about to-day, of whose guilt the police are perfectly well aware. They cannot be arrested, however, for lack of evidence. "

" How thrilling! " she murmured. " Will you ask me to dine with you one night and tell me some of your adventures? "

" I shall be charmed, " I assented. " Meanwhile, — "

She accepted my departure a little unwillingly. I am not a vain man, and I felt inclined to wonder at a certain graciousness of attitude on her part which more than once during our interview had forced itself upon my notice. I decided, however, that she was just one of those women who are born with the desire to attract and dismissed the matter from my mind.

About seven o'clock, a note was brought into my room:

> Dear Sir Norman,
>
> A lady and her husband who were dining, have disappointed me. Can you, by any chance, be my guest? If so, let us meet at eight o'clock in the lounge.
>
> Hopefully yours,
>
> BLANCHE DE MENDOZA

I scribbled a line of acceptance. I felt, as I descended into the lounge that evening, a premonition that life for the next few hours was going to be very interesting indeed.

At eight o'clock precisely, Mrs. De Mendoza came into the lounge. She was wearing a white lace evening dress, with an ermine wrap which hung loosely around her, disclosing the pearls underneath. Her entrance made a mild sensation. Mr. Stanfield, who was seated in his accustomed corner, drinking his cocktail, watched our meeting and departure into the restaurant with obvious surprise.

" The little man was there again who stares at me so much — Mr. Stanfield, I think you called him? " she remarked, as we took our places.

I nodded.

" I dare say he was surprised to see us together, " I said. " I asked him who you were, on the night of my arrival here. "

" Why? "

" For the same reason that a great many other people ask the same question, " I replied.

She made a little grimace.

" You are determined to pay me no compliments this evening, and I am wearing my favourite gown. "

" I admire your taste, " I assured her.

" Anything else? "

" You are the best-dressed and the best-looking woman in the room. "

" Too impersonal, " she complained.

I turned the conversation to the subject of the necklace. The pearls were collected for her, she told me, by her husband, some in India, some in the Malay States, some in Paris, some in Rio. She spoke of him quite frankly — a prosperous fruit-broker who had achieved sudden opulence.

" It was quite as much a change for me as for him, " she remarked. " I was a typist in Buenos Ayres before we were married. I have known what it is to be poor. "

She answered all my questions without reserve, displaying later on much interest in the recounting of such of my adventures as were public property. I began to feel that I had been mistaken with regard to her, that she was really exactly what she seemed — a very wealthy woman of adventurous type, suddenly released from matrimonial obligations and a little uncertain what to make of her life.

We took our coffee in the lounge afterwards. In the background, my golfing friend, Mr. Stanfield, was seated, smoking a cigar in a retired corner, and having the air of studying every one who passed.

" He is quaint, that little man, " my companion remarked once, as he glanced over towards us. " He reminds me of those impossible characters one reads
about in magazines, who detect crime for the pleasure
of it, and discover hidden treasures in absurd places. "

" He is, as a matter of fact, " I told her, " a retired
city merchant with a passion for golf — at least, that
is what the Golf Secretary at Woking told me. "

The music was seductive, and presently we danced
once or twice. In the ballroom, however, my companion
showed signs of renewed nervousness. The fingers of
one hand were nearly all the time straying around her
neck, as though to assure herself that the necklace was
still there. Presently she drew me away with an
apologetic little laugh.

" I am quite mad, " she confessed, " but I have a fit
of nerves to-night. I am going upstairs early. Do you
mind? "

" Of course not, " I told her. " Let me see you to
the lift. "

" I am going to ask you to do more than that, " she
said, as we crossed the hall. " I am going to ask you
to come up to my sitting room and escort my maid
down to the office when she takes my necklace there.
As a reward, you can come back afterwards, if you will,
and have a whisky and soda with me. "

" I shall be very pleased, " I acquiesced.

I rang for the lift and we ascended together to the
fourth floor. She handed me her key and I unlocked
the door of her charming little salon. She pointed to
the evening paper and an easy-chair.

"Please make yourself comfortable for five minutes, " she begged, looking back from the threshold of
the inner room. "I shall just let Annette help me out
of my gown. Then I will give her the jewel case and
she shall call for you. "

She nodded and disappeared. I stood for a moment looking after her. The door was closed softly.
I heard her call to her maid in the further apartment.

Those next few seconds seemed to beat themselves
out in my brain, charged with a strange and almost
amazing significance. I am convinced that I acted from
impulse. There was nothing definite in my mind when
from behind that closed door I conceived the sudden
idea which prompted my action. I crossed the floor
of the sitting room and opened the door which led on
to the corridor. There was no one in sight, and it
seemed to me that fewer of the electric lights were lit
than usual. I stood there, every nerve of my body
rivetted upon an attempt at dual listening. I listened
for the return of Mrs. De Mendoza, and I listened for
the opening of either of her doors. Presently, what I
had divined might happen came to pass. The door of
her bedroom, in a line with the one behind which I was
lurking, opened. I peered through the crack. Annette,
the maid, a trim, dark figure, had crossed the threshold.
She stood for a moment, listening. Then without even
glancing towards the sitting room, she walked swiftly
along the corridor and turned to the left towards the
lift and staircases. In a couple of stealthy strides I,
too, had reached the corner, and, peering round,
watched her movements. To my surprise, she passed

the lift and turned the other corner of the corridor towards the staircase. As soon as she was out of sight, I followed. As I reached the farther angle, every light was suddenly extinguished. There was a little gurgling cry, the sound of a heavy fall upon the soft carpet. In a second or two I was on the spot. I could dimly see where Annette was lying, gasping for breath, apparently half-unconscious. By her side lay the jewel case, open and empty.

I did nothing for a moment towards raising any alarm. I bent over the girl and satisfied myself that she was not shamming,—that she had, in effect, been subjected to a certain amount of violence. I glanced at the transoms over the doors of the bedrooms opposite. There were three of them between where I was and the turn to the lift. Suddenly the farthest door was opened, softly but not stealthily. A figure ap- peared and, leaning down, threw a pair of boots upon the mat. I suppose that I was dimly visible in the semi-gloom, for the man suddenly left off whistling and turned in my direction.

"Hullo, there!" he called out.

I drew from my pocket the little electric torch which I had been keeping in readiness, and flashed it upon him. It was my friend Mr. Stanfield, in striped yellow and white pyjamas, a cigarette between his teeth, his feet encased in comfortable slippers.

"What the devil are you doing out there?" he demanded. "And who's turned the lights out?"

"Better turn them on and you may see," I replied. "There's a switch close to your door."

He found it after a second or two's fumbling and stared at us in amazement. The maid, with her fingers still to her throat, had recovered sufficiently to sit up, and was leaning with her back to the wall, ghastly white and moaning to herself. The empty jewel case told its own story.

" Jerusalem! " Mr. Stanfield exclaimed breathlessly. " A robbery! "

" Ring your bell, " I directed.

He disappeared into his room for a moment, leaving the door open. Presently he reappeared.

" I've rung all three, " he announced.

" Then the wires have been cut, " I answered, pointing to the register lower down, which had not moved. " Go to the lift and see if you can get any one. "

He was gone for about half a minute. I leaned down towards the girl, who was beginning to cry.

" Did you see who attacked you? " I asked.

" No! " she sobbed. " All the lights went out suddenly. Some one came up from behind. I never heard a sound — just the clutch at my throat and the choking. "

" Why did you not wait for me or go down by the lift? " I demanded.

She looked a little puzzled.

" I never go by the lift, " she replied.

" Why not? "

" Fred, the second-floor valet, generally meets me on the floor below, " she explained reluctantly, " and — "

" I see, " I interrupted. " But didn't your mistress tell you to wait and go down with me? "

The girl seemed surprised.

"My head is queer," she admitted, "and I can't remember much, but madame said nothing to me except to tell me to hurry down."

The silence of the corridor was suddenly broken. Mr. Stanfield reappeared, followed by a little army of servants and the manager.

"Send every one away except two men whom you can trust," I begged the latter. "Mrs. De Mendoza's necklace has been stolen."

There was a murmur of consternation and excitement. The manager selected two of the servants and dismissed the rest. He posted one by the lift and one by the staircase. I explained in a few words what had happened.

"Do you think the thief has got away?" he asked.

"One cannot tell," I replied. "I want to know about these three rooms."

He glanced at the numbers.

"The furthest one is occupied by Mr. Stanfield," he announced. "The other two are empty."

"You are sure that this one," I asked, pointing to the door close to where we stood, "is unoccupied?"

"Certain," was the confident reply. "Take my keys and see for yourself."

I was on the point of doing so when Mrs. De Mendoza appeared. She was clad in a wonderful light-blue wrapper, and the touch of excitement seemed to add to her beauty.

"My necklace!" she gasped. "Don't tell me that it is gone!"

" Madam, " the manager began, " I regret to
say —— "

" What were you doing, then? " she cried, turning
to me. " Do you mean to say that it was stolen whilst
Annette was with you? "

" Annette was never with me, " I replied. "She left
your bedroom with the jewel case, without coming near
the sitting room."

" Is this true, Annette? " her mistress demanded.

" But why not, Madame? " Annette faltered. " You
said nothing to me about going into the sitting room. I
did not know that monsieur was to accompany me. "

" The girl is telling a falsehood, " Mrs. De Mendoza
declared angrily.

" Could these matters wait for a moment? " I intervened. " Our immediate task is to try and recover the
necklace. I wish every one to leave this place — except
you, sir, " I added, addressing the manager, " and
myself. "

The manager was a person of determination, and
in a moment or two the corridor was empty. Mr.
Stanfield lingered on the threshold of his room.

" Can I remain? " he enquired. " In a way I am
interested, as my room is so near. "

The manager waved him back.

" I desire to hear what Sir Norman has to say,
alone, " he insisted.

Mr. Stanfield reluctantly withdrew. We first of all
entered the room opposite to us. It was empty and
apparently undisturbed. There was a connecting door
on the left.

" Where does that lead to? " I asked.

The manager unlocked it. It led into a similar room, also empty. The room on the other side was Mr. Stanfield's, also connecting. The outlook of all three was on to some mews.

" These are our cheapest rooms, " my companion explained. " They are generally occupied by servants, or people of an economical turn of mind. "

We withdrew into the first one we had entered.

" Will you lend me that master-key of yours? " I begged.

The manager detached it from his chain and handed it to me.

" If you should be instrumental in recovering the necklace, Sir Norman, " he said, " the hotel authorities would appreciate all possible reticence in the matter. "

I nodded.

" It is hard to keep anything out of the Press, now-adays, " I reminded him, " but so far as I am concerned, you may rely upon my discretion. "

The few days that followed were filled with hysterical and irritating appeals, complaints and enquiries from Mrs. De Mendoza herself, the insurance company and the management. No efforts on our part could keep the affair out of the newspapers, and the disappearance of the necklace became the universal subject of conversation. A hundred amateur detectives suggested solutions of the mystery, and thousands of knowing people were quite sure that they could put their hands on the thief. On the morning of the sixth day after the robbery, I felt that a brief escape was necessary. I pro-

posed to Mr. Stanfield, whom I met in the hall of the
hotel, that we go down to Woking and have a round of
golf, an arrangement to which he agreed with avidity.
We lunched at the club house, and, as on previous oc-
casions we played a careful and hard-fought game. It
was on the eighteenth tee that one of those unexplained
moments of inspiration came to me which serve as the
landmarks of life. We had spoken of that grim tragedy which had interrupted our first game. I thought of
poor Ladbrooke lying there with a bullet hole in his
forehead; Janet, the maid, serene and secretive, with
the strange eyes and unruffled manner. The memory
of these things came back to me as I stood there, with
the wet wind fluttering in the leaves of the trees and
Stanfield filling his pipe by my side, and it seemed as
though my faculties were suddenly prompted by a new
vigour and a new insight. Supposing it had been the
maid who had killed the prying stranger! What was
her motive? Whom was she trying to shield? Could it
be her master? And if her master's name were not
Stanfield, might it not be Pugsley? The two men were
of the same height and build, and the one thing which
Rimmington had always insisted upon was Pugsley's
genius for disguise. ·The pieces of my puzzle fell together like magic, and with them the puzzle of the necklace. I turned back to the tee, and I was suddenly conscious of my companion's intense gaze. His eyes
seemed to be boring their way into the back of my head.
I knew that something in my face had given me away.

" Your honour, " he said tersely.

I topped my drive miserably. My companion's drive

went sailing down the course, and he halved the match in a perfectly played four. We walked together to the club house.

"A whisky and soda?" I suggested.

"I'll change my shoes first," he answered, turning towards the dressing room.

I drank my whisky and soda, exchanged greetings with a few acquaintances, and paid my bill. Then I went to look for Stanfield. I might have spared myself the trouble. He and the taxi had alike disappeared. I had to wait whilst they telephoned for another, and I travelled up to London alone.

The game was played out in quite the grand fashion. On my arrival at the hotel, I found the representative of the insurance company waiting to see me, and I was told that Mrs. De Mendoza was in her room. Accompanied by the manager, we made our way thither. I think that she was well prepared for what was coming, or rather one part of it. She received us a little impatiently.

"I have been waiting to hear from your firm all day," she said, addressing Delchester. "My jewellers who valued the pearls, and my legal adviser have helped to make out my claim. I am anxious to know when I may expect your cheque."

"I am thankful to say, madam, that that will not be necessary," the manager announced, stepping forward. "Here is your necklace."

He handed it to her. She stared at it like a woman transfixed. There were no signs of joy in her face. She seemed, indeed, for the moment stricken with consternation.

" When was it found? " she demanded breathlessly.

" About four o'clock on the morning after the theft, " I told her.

" But where? "

" If you will come with me, " I replied, " I will show you. "

I led the way down the corridor to the exact spot where Annette had been attacked and opened the door of the nearest room. I saw Mrs. De Mendoza start when she saw the heavy bolt which had been fitted to the communicating door.

" I came to the conclusion, " I explained, " that the theft was committed by some one hiding in one of these three rooms, and to the further conclusion that the necklace had been hidden on the spot. "

" How did you guess that? " she enquired.

" Because the thief made a slight blunder, " I answered. " For a single moment, as I stood by Annette's side in the darkness outside, I saw a light flash out through the transom of this room. I must admit, however, " I went on, " that it took me four hours to find the necklace. "

" Where was it then? " she asked curiously.

I turned up the rug. In one of the planks of the wooden floor was a knot. I took a little corkscrew gimlet from my pocket, bored through it and drew it out. Then I made Delchester push his finger through. There was a hook fastened in the underneath side of the floor.

" The necklace was hanging there, " I told him. " I imagine it would have been found later on by some one

making a point of occupying this room. As a matter
of fact, I believe it was booked for the first week in
June. "

" By whom? " Mrs. De Mendoza demanded.

" By Mr. Stanfield, " I replied. " He is paying a
return visit in June, and he appears to prefer this room
to the one he is occupying at present. "

There was a brief silence. Delchester held out his
hand.

" We are very much obliged to you, Sir Norman, " he
declared. " Our insurance, as you know, expired at
mid-day to-day. I need not say that it will not be
renewed. I wish you all good morning. "

He took his leave. The manager appealed to me.

" Sir Norman, " he said, " there is a great deal in
this matter which it is hard to understand. I hope
that you will not consider it a case for the police? "

I turned to Mrs. De Mendoza.

" Do you wish to prosecute? " I asked. " There is
a certain amount of circumstantial evidence which
might be collected."

" Against whom? "

"'Against the gentleman whom we have known as
Mr. Stanfield."

She laughed scornfully.

" That funny little man who sits about in the lounge?
I would as soon believe that you yourself were the thief,
Sir Norman! I have my necklace back, and that is all
I care about, " she concluded.

The manager departed, very much relieved. Mrs.
De Mendoza beckoned me to follow her to her suite.

Arrived in her sitting room, she closed the door. She
had rather the look of a tigress as she turned and
faced me. Never was a woman born of more splendid
courage.

" And the epilogue? " she asked.

" I fear, " I replied, " that the epilogue must be
postponed. It was only to-day, on Woking Golf
Links, that a certain little scene of eighteen months
ago became reconstructed in my mind. I saw a motive-
less crime explained. I realised by whose hand that
bullet might have found its way into Ladbrooke's brain,
and for whose sake. "

" Yet you let him go! " she cried.

" If I had dreamed, " I said slowly, " that it was
possible for him to escape, even for an hour, I would
have wrung the breath from his body first. As it is, I
must admit that he has scored a trick. But you must
remember, or perhaps you have yet to find out, " I went
on, " that the world where such a man can live is a
very small place. "

" And what about me? " she asked. " From the
moment when I heard that you had gone out with him
alone, I could foresee what was coming. Yet I was not
afraid. I waited for you. "

I looked at the necklace and shrugged my shoulders.

" It is hard to leave a hundred thousand pounds, " I
pointed out, " and so far as you realised, the game was
not up. Not a soul in this hotel knew that the necklace was in the manager's safe. Yet you had courage
to remain and see the thing through. I admit that. "

She came a little nearer to me. The green lights in

her eyes were soft. I felt the attraction of her as she meant me to.

"Where I love," she said, "I have courage, and my love has every quality which the devil ever distilled, except constancy. Are you afraid of me, Sir Norman, because I killed a man who —— "

"A confession," I muttered.

She laughed.

"No witnesses," she reminded me. "After all, it was you who once said that murder was the easiest of crimes. What you know and what I know will never take me to the dock. Would you put me there if you could, my enemy?"

I drew a little away. Her breath was almost upon my cheek, her lips had taken to themselves the curve of invitation.

"I would put you there without a moment's hesitation," I retorted. "You killed a man in cold blood to shield a murderer and a criminal. The hand of justice is slow, especially where evidence is scanty, but in the end it grips."

She laughed scornfully.

"You speak in ignorance," she declared. "At least be friends," she went on, "until you can drag me to the gallows. I shot him with my right hand."

She held out her left fingers. I raised them to my lips.

"The kiss of Judas," I warned her.

"You will need more than his cunning," she answered.

CHAPTER III

MICHAEL SAYERS

It had taken months to collect all the necessary information and make the preliminary arrangements, but the moment had arrived at last. At twenty minutes to twelve on a Friday morning, I descended from a rather shabby Ford car exactly opposite Bailey's grocery stores at the corner of Menwood Street, in one of the northern suburbs of Leeds. It is a neighbourhood of six-roomed houses and long, cobbled streets; a neighbourhood teeming with men and women when the great factories close at hand are empty, but at this particular hour of the day, before the children's schools have finished their morning session, and whilst the men and a considerable portion of the women are still in the mills, showing signs of something approaching desertion. There was a handsome grey touring landaulette containing two passengers, a man and a woman, drawn up on the other side of the way, apparently to take advantage of the shade of some tall advertisement boardings whilst the chauffeur filled up

with petrol.   Otherwise, a careful glance up and down
the street convinced me that not a soul was in sight.

I walked along a hot, asphalt path, and turned the
corner into what was known as the Boulevard, almost
unnoticed.   On my left was a stretch of waste ground,
black and stinking with refuse, empty tins and bottles,
abandoned even by the children as an undesirable play-
ground.   On my right were more houses in course of
erection, deserted to-day by reason of an opportune
strike amongst the masons.   The only inhabited edifice
was the one where my business lay.   A brass plate upon
the door indicated that this was a branch of Brown's
Bank, planted out here in this uncomely spot for the
convenience of the huge factories which dominated the
neighbourhood.

With my hand upon the swing door I glanced
around.   My luck was certainly in, for there was still
not even a child to be seen.   Inside, behind the counter,
both the manager and his clerk were busy counting out
bundles of treasury notes.   They looked up enquiringly
as I entered.   Strangers in such a place, I imagine,
were rare.   Such a stranger as I was a rarity which
they were never likely to experience again in this
world.

My plans were cut and dried to the last detail.   I
wasted no time in any silly attempt to hold the place
up, but, brief though the seconds were, it was amazing
how my brain chronicled a host of varying impressions.
I saw the bland smile fade from the manager's lips, I
saw the dawn of suspicion in his eyes, the gleam of
terror followed by the spasm of pain as I shot him

through the right shoulder blade. His assistant had
not the courage of a rabbit. White-faced, gasping for
mercy, he stood there with his hands above his head and
his knees shaking. I am convinced that if I had left
him alone for another five seconds, he would have collapsed hopelessly without any interference on my part.
I was not able to take risks, however, so leaning over I
struck him on the point of the jaw. He fell in a
crumpled heap behind the counter. I then helped myself to seven thousand pounds odd in bank and treasury
notes, and in about a minute and a half after I had
entered the bank, I strolled back again the way I had
come.

At the corner of the street, I looked back. There
were no signs of life about the bank, no one apparently
on his way towards it. There were a few children
playing about the unoccupied houses, and behind the
windows of the cottages in the street where I now was
were women intent upon various domestic duties. One
woman was scolding her child just outside the door.
She glanced at me only in the most perfunctory fashion.
My Panama hat was pulled well over my head, a reasonable precaution with the sun at its greatest power. A
man was bending over the open bonnet of the Ford car
which I had left at the corner. I passed him by without a glance and stepped into the grey touring car
behind. The engine was purring gently, the chauffeur's
fingers were upon the gear handle as I appeared. I
took my place by the side of Janet, unrecognisable
beneath her motor veil, and we glided off northwards.
There were no signs of any disturbance as we shot into

the broad main street. We gathered speed up the Chapeltown Hill and very soon we were racing for Scotland.

Janet passed me a silver flask soon after we had passed out of the suburbs. I shook my head.

"You know that I never take anything until one o'clock," I reminded her. "Why should I drink in the middle of the morning?"

I fancied that I caught through her veil a gleam of that almost worshipping fidelity which had led me to trust this woman as I had trusted no other in my life.

"What a nerve!" she murmured.

"I have no nerves," I rejoined, "neither have I any fear. By this time you ought to realise it."

"All went smoothly?" she asked.

"Absolutely according to programme. A chance customer would have been the only possible disturbance, and the position of the bank rendered that unlikely."

"What happened?"

"I shot the manager through the shoulder blade," I told her. "The heart would probably have been safer, but the blinds of the bank were all drawn to keep out the sun, and my Panama was as good as a mask. His clerk was almost dead from fear before I touched him. I had not to waste a bullet there."

"And how much?" she enquired.

"Only just over seven thousand pounds," I admitted. "It seems a pitiful amount for so much planning and risk. Still, something had to be done."

We were up on a stretch of moorland now, well away from curious eyes. Janet and I were busy for some ten minutes, making three parcels of my stock of notes. Then she looked at the map.

"Arthington should be the next village," she remarked.

I nodded. We descended a steep hill. Halfway up the next we came upon a small motor car, drawn up by the side of the road, the bonnet thrown open, its owner seated in the dust. The latter rose to his feet as we approached. I handed him the black bag which I had been carrying, in which was my Panama hat and one of the packets of notes. He raised his cap nonchalantly.

"According to plan?" he asked.

"According to plan," I replied.

We sped on for another twenty miles, when almost a similar occurrence happened. A man seated by the side of his motor bicycle rose to his feet as we approached. I handed him the second packet.

"All well?" he enquired.

"Perfectly," I assured him.

We were off again in less than ten seconds. Our third stop was at the top of a hill forty miles farther north, after we had partaken of a picnic luncheon in the car. A man was seated motionless in a large touring car headed in our direction. He held out his arm as we approached and glanced at his watch.

"Wonderful!" he murmured. "You are three minutes to the good."

I handed him the third packet. He waved his hand

and started up his engine. Soon we left him, a speck
behind us. I leaned back and lit a cigarette.

"I have now, " I remarked, "only one anxiety. "

"And that? " Janet enquired quickly.

"About the greens at Kinbrae, " I confided. "I met
a man last year who told me that they were apt to get
dried up. "

She smiled.

"We had plenty of rain last month, " she reminded
me. "I thought you were going to speak of our
friend. "

I shook my head.

"Norman Greyes is in Norway, " I told her. "I
am not sure, " I went on, after a moment's hesitation,
"whether I do not sometimes regret it. "

"Why? "

I looked out across the heather-clad moor to where
rolling masses of yellow gorse seemed to melt into the
blue haze. It was a very wonderful day and a very
wonderful country into which we were speeding.

"Norman Greyes has made life inconvenient for us
for several years, " I said. "One of our best men has
had to devote the whole of his time to watching him.
We had been obliged to stay away from places which I
very much wanted to visit. He has that absurd gift —
he always had — of being able to connect a particular
undertaking with a particular person. For that reason
we have had to remain idle until we are practically
paupers. When we have paid the expenses of this
coup, and paid the staff, there will be barely enough
left to keep us until Christmas. If we could get

rid of Norman Greyes, we could seek wider fields."
" Why not? " she asked indifferently. " He is only a
man like the others. "

I pretended to be deep in thought. As a matter of
fact, I was studying Janet. No creature or servant
in this world could render such faithful service as she
has rendered me, yet I am one of those persons gifted
with instincts. I know that she has a strange mind,
a strange, tumultuously passionate nature. I have so
far been the man of her life. If it were not I, I sometimes wonder whether it might not be Norman Greyes.

We were to have one tense few minutes before we
reached our stopping place for the night. We had just
passed through a small town, and our silent chauffeur
was preparing to let out his engine again, when we
were confronted by what was, under the circumstances,
a very sinister sight. Two men on bicycles, approaching us, dismounted and stood in the middle of the road
with outstretched hands. The sun, even in the distance, flashed upon their uniforms. We realised at
once that they were policemen. The chauffeur half-
turned towards me.

" What shall you do? " Janet demanded.

" Do? " I replied. " Why, the natural thing, of
course. All this is provided for. Oliver, " I added,
leaning forward, " those policemen seem to want to
speak to us. Pull up. "

We came to a standstill a yard or two away from
them. The larger of the two men, who wore the uniform
of a sergeant, made a solemn and portentous approach.

"Good afternoon, Sergeant," I said. "I hope that we are not in trouble?"

He looked at me as he might have done at a man whose hands were dripping with the blood of his best friend.

"It's your number plate, sir," he announced. "They telephoned us through from Ripon to stop your car and call your attention to it."

"What is wrong with my number plate?" I asked.

"Why, you've been driving where they've watered the roads freely," the sergeant pointed out, "and it's mudded it up entirely. There's no one can read a number of it."

I felt Janet's fingers clutch mine, and they were as cold as ice. It was not a moment which I myself forgot, less for its significance than for its effect upon my companion. The chauffeur, the police sergeant and I solemnly inspected the number plate, and the former, with a duster from his tool chest, carefully rubbed it clean.

"That will be all right now, Sergeant?" I enquired.

"That will be quite all right, sir," he admitted, taking off his helmet and wiping the perspiration from his forehead. "It's a warm day, this, for they bicycles."

It was my policy not to overdo the matter, and indeed it was not necessary, for the man's eyes glistened as I deposited a couple of half-crowns in his hand.

"I am sorry to have given you this trouble," I said. "We tourists are proverbially thoughtless about our number plates. I hope you will accept this and have a drink with me. "

" We will that, sure, sir, " the Sergeant promised, saluting first me and then Janet. " Come along, Jock, " he added, " we'll pay a little visit to the Widow MacGill on the way back. "

So we drove off again northwards. My chauffeur was an elderly man, who has faced all that the world may hold of evil with me many a time, but his driving for the first few miles was erratic. Janet, I could see, although outwardly she had recovered herself, was on the point of hysterics. I settled myself down in my corner, adjusted my horn-rimmed spectacles, and drew from the pocket of the car a new half-crown book on the principles of golf, written by a late beginner. So we travelled until we reached the inn where we stayed for the night, and late on the afternoon of the following day we arrived at our destination. There was just a bare white house, a lodge, the gate of which was held open by a great, raw-boned gillie, miles of what seemed to be interminable moorland, and below, the sea. I looked around with satisfaction.

" You're Sandy Mac Lane, the caretaker here? " I asked, leaning out of the car.

He made a noise which sounded like " Oo ay! "

" Which way might the golf links be? " I enquired.

He pointed with a long and hairy forefinger.

" The club house is yonder, " he vouchsafed; " a step across the road is the fifteenth tee. "

I sighed with content.

"Come up to the house," I ordered. "After tea I shall play a few holes."

NORMAN GREYES

My friend Rimmington called to see me on the night of my return from Norway. He looked around with an air of dismay at my various travelling paraphernalia.

"So you're really off, then?" he remarked.

"On the contrary, I've just returned," I told him. "It was too late in the season to do any good, and I made a mistake in changing my river. The whole thing was a frost."

Rimmington sighed.

"Well, I'm glad to see you back," he declared, sinking into my easy-chair. "All the same, London in August isn't exactly a Paradise!"

"Tell me about Leeds?" I suggested. "To judge from the newspapers, you seem to be having a lot of trouble about a very simple case."

Rimmington frowned. He was silent for several moments, and, glancing across at him, I noticed that he was pale and apparently out of sorts.

"I think I'm stale," he confessed. "The Chief pretty well hinted the same thing, and worse, when I got back last night. I really dropped round to see whether you could help me."

"If I can, I will with pleasure," I promised him. "You know that."

"You read the bare account of the affair, of course," Rimmington went on. "Two fairly credible witnesses deposed to seeing a man in a grey flannel suit, with a Panama hat pushed over his eyes, drive up in a Ford, leave it outside Bailey's grocery stores, walk down the street and turn into the Boulevard where the bank is situated, exactly at the time that the robbery took place. Three women and two children saw him pass up the street two minutes later, and thirty seconds after that he crossed the street and entered Bailey's grocery stores. The clerk who served him with some marmalade, tea and bacon saw him climb up into the Ford and drive away. The man was known at the shop as Ralph Roberson. There is no doubt that it was his car. Half-an-hour after the robbery, he was arrested at his house — he was cleaning the car at the time — and although he had changed his clothes, the light grey suit which he had recently worn was discovered in his bedroom, and the Panama hat, warm with perspiration, in a cupboard. His excuse for changing his clothes was that he put on older things in which to clean the car, and his account of his morning was that he had driven straight up to Bailey's Stores for some groceries, and straight back again. Two witnesses are ready to swear that they saw him get out of the Ford and go towards the bank; the grocer's clerk, who served him, is absolutely certain that he was in the shop within thirty seconds of the Ford pulling up outside, and that when he left he drove straight away."

"What sort of a man is this Roberson?" I asked.

" A man of bad character, " was the prompt reply.
" He was once a bookmaker, but failed. He has been
in prison for obtaining goods by false pretences, and
there are half-a-dozen summonses for debt out against
him at the present moment. The only little money he
earns, nowadays, seems to be by acting as a bookmaker's tout. He knew the neighbourhood well, and
has once been heard to remark upon the isolated position of the bank. In every respect he is just the man
to have done it, and yet there are all my witnesses
swearing to different things. Furthermore, he had
scarcely a shilling in his pocket, and he confessed that
he was going to try and sell the car that afternoon to
raise a little money. "

" It seems to me, " I admitted, " that you have been
a little premature in framing your case against Mr.
Ralph Roberson. "

" So the magistrates thought, " Rimmington rejoined drily. " We managed to get two remands.
This morning he was discharged. "

" If the grocer's assistant is telling the truth, " I
remarked thoughtfully, " Roberson could not possibly
have committed the robbery. What sort of a young
man is the assistant? "

" Highly respectable and very intelligent, " Rimmington replied. " It would be quite impossible at any
time to shake his evidence. "

" So much for Mr. Ralph Roberson, " I said. " And
now who else is there? "

"That's the difficulty, " Rimmington confessed.
" One doesn't know where to turn. The only other

two people who were about the spot at the same moment were a man and his wife touring up to Scotland in a big Daimler car. They stopped to make some purchases at Bailey's Stores, but neither of them alighted. "

" Any description of the man? " I asked.

"Yes, the grocer's assistant who went out to take the order remembers him. He describes him as a sporting-looking gentleman wearing a brown alpaca dust coat and a grey Homburg hat. Such a person could not possibly have left the car and walked down the street without notice. "

"Any description of the woman? "

Rimmington shook his head.

" To tell you the truth, " he confessed, " I didn't ask for one. There were guns and cartridge magazines and golf clubs on the top of the car. The two were apparently motoring up to some place they had hired in Scotland. "

On the face of it, there seemed no possible connection between these tourists and a local bank robbery. Yet the thought of them lingered obstinately in my mind. A man and a woman, a bank robbery, and the fact that I was supposed to be safe in Norway! I began to take up the pieces of the puzzle once more, and fit them in accordance to my own devices.

" You seem to have done everything possible, Rimmington, " I said at last, " but I think, as my Norway trip has fallen flat, I shall go up to Scotland for a fortnight. Would you like me to call over at Leeds and see if I can pick up anything? "

"Exactly what I hoped you would suggest," he confessed eagerly. "I have brooded over the affair so long that I can think of nothing but the obvious side. The Chief will give you a letter to the Leeds people. Would you like me to come with you?"

I shook my head.

"Better not," I told him. "Better for me to go as a stranger."

That night I travelled down to Leeds.

There was nothing about the neighbourhood which differed materially from Rimmington's description. I paid a visit to the place at exactly the hour the robbery had been committed, walked from the grocery store to the bank, carefully timing myself, and made some trifling purchases inside the shop. The neighbourhood seemed to be thickly built over and populated in patches, but here and there were vacant lots. The land opposite the grocery stores was marked out for building, but operations as yet had not been begun. Later in the day, I tracked Roberson to ground in his favourite public-house. Choosing my opportunity, I addressed him.

"Are you the man whom the police made such idiots of themselves about in this bank robbery?" I asked.

"What the hell's that to do with you?" he answered.

His tone was truculent, but he obviously only needed humouring.

"Just this much," I replied. "I am a journalist representing one of the picture papers. It would be

worth a fiver to you if you would let me do a sketch
of you. "

His manner changed at once.

" You don't want an interview? "

" Not likely, " I assured him, commencing a rough
sketch in a notebook which I had put into my pocket for
that purpose. " I read the case myself. A fool could
see that you had nothing to do with it. "

He stopped drinking and looked at me curiously.

' 'If I were the police, " I went on, " I should want
to know a little more about the two tourists on their
way to Scotland. "

" Then you're as big a fool as the police, " he retorted gruffly. " They hadn't nothing to do with it.
They were filling up with petrol and neither of them
budged from the car. "

I smiled in a superior way and went on sketching.
He watched me with thinly veiled anxiety.

" Toffs they were, " he went on, " on their way up
for a bit of sport. "

" Maybe, " I commented. " They didn't seem in any
hurry about it. "

" What do you mean? "

" I don't see why they stayed at the Queen's two
nights, " I remarked.

" Who said they did? " he demanded. " They stayed
one night, and grumbled at having to do that. "

" How do you know? " I asked, looking up at him.

" I spoke to the chauffeur, " he replied sullenly.
" He told me my oil was leaking. "

I changed the subject, finished my ridiculous sketch, and handed over the five pounds. That night I caught the mail train to Scotland.

It took me less than a week to discover the whereabouts of the man and the woman who I learned were passing under the name of Mr. and Mrs. Harold Grover. On the morning after my arrival at the very remote corner of Scotland where they had taken up their temporary abode, I committed an indiscretion. I donned a knickerbocker suit and set out for a tramp over the moors. I had just clambered up to the top of a little ridge overlooking the sea, when I came face to face with a little party ascending it from the other side. The little party consisted of the person I had known chiefly as Mr. Stanfield, his wife, a villainous-looking gillie, and two dogs. It was a curious moment, full of the suggestions of tragedy, afterwards ridiculous in its conventionality. I saw the flash of the man's gun, and I saw the woman's hand restrain him, heard the single word whispered in his ear. I raised my cap, he followed suit. His gun hung idly under his arm. My hand was inside my breast pocket, clutching something hard.

"What an extraordinary meeting!" Janet exclaimed, with a faint smile. "So you sometimes take holiday also, Sir Norman?"

"Sometimes," I admitted. "I came home unexpectedly from Norway. I was disappointed in my fishing."

"Are you aweer that you're trespassing, mon?" the gillie demanded severely.

" I'm afraid I didn't know it, " I replied. " There were no notices. "

" It doesn't matter, " Janet intervened. " We happen to be walking up a covey of birds this way. "

" I put nothing up, " I assured them.

" They lie verra close hereabouts, " the gillie observed. " We'll take a little further sweep. "

" How long are you staying in these parts, Sir Norman? " Stanfield enquired.

" About a week, if I like the golf, " I answered.

" I've taken the Lodge down there, " he pointed out. " Call and see us before you leave. "

" Won't you come and dine with us to-night? " Janet invited, with a challenge in her eyes.

I hesitated. The invitation appealed to me in one way as much as it repelled me in another. Stanfield watched me as though he were reading my thoughts.

" You need not take salt, " he said grimly.

" I shall be delighted, " I assented. " About eight o'clock, I suppose? "

" Not ' about,' I implore you," Janet answered earnestly. " Sandy shall catch you some trout this afternoon and they must be served to the second. Say a quarter to eight, please. "

" I will be punctual, " I promised.

I spent the afternoon wandering about the moor, inspecting the golf links and speaking on the telephone. Punctually at twenty minutes to eight I passed up the long, neglected drive and presented myself at the front door of the sombre-looking house. The sum-

mons of a harsh bell was answered almost immediately
by an immaculate butler. Janet, from the other end of
the cool, white hall, came forward to meet me. Almost,
simultaneously the gong rang, and a few minutes later
we sat down to dinner in a quaint, octagonal room,
with a dome-shaped ceiling of rough oak. The dinner
was excellently cooked and served by the man-servant
who had admitted me. The champagne was of an excellent brand, and my host, with a twinkle in his eyes,
called my attention to the fact that it was opened in
my presence. As soon as the last course was concluded,
Janet led the way out on to the flagged terrace, where
a table was already arranged with dessert and coffee.
We sat in easy-chairs, gazing over a strip of moorland away to the sea. The sun was behind us now,
and the air deliciously cool.

"You are a brave man, Sir Norman," my hostess
said abruptly.

"Why?" I asked.

"You know — and you alone — that I once killed
a man — although you don't altogether know why,"
she went on softly. "How do you know that I have not
within me the makings of a modern Lucrezia? I have
read quite a good deal about poisons — I may be said
even to have studied the subject — and you have
delivered yourself into my hands." "

"Why should you poison me?" I argued. "I will
do both you and your husband the credit to believe
that you don't bear malice. Revenge is a senseless
sentiment. As regards our last conflict, I probably
prevented your drawing a matter of a hundred thou-

sand pounds from the insurance company for the pretended loss of your necklace, but that was all in the day's work. I was paid to match my wits against yours, and I did it. There is no one particularly anxious to take proceedings against either of you for that little — error of judgment. "

My host leaned forward in his chair. His face was solemn and brooding, his gaze was hard and intent.

" You have things against me dating from before that, " he said.

I nodded.

" But I am in the same position as Scotland Yard, " I reminded him. " For those things I have no case. For those misdemeanours of which I suspect you in the past, I could at the present moment go only so far as to procure a warrant charging you with feloniously wounding a police inspector. For the rest, I suspect but I have no proof. "

" You suspect what? " he asked.

I shook my head.

" There are limits to my candour, " I protested mildly. " You must admit that I am not secretive or unduly aloof, inasmuch as I dine at your table, discuss your peccadilloes and pass on, like an ordinary guest. What I may suspect in the past I keep to myself. I am your enemy and you know it. If it pays you to attempt to murder me, I imagine you will try. "

" Janet would desert me if I did, " he declared, with a grim smile. " She finds these little conferences with you so inspiring. "

She looked at me with that wonderful smile of hers.

She was a little way behind a pillar and her face was hidden from her husband.

"I do not like to hear you say that we are enemies," she murmured. "I would rather think that we are like the soldiers who fight in two opposing armies. We fight because it is our duty. So we are enemies because it is our duty. Even that does not interfere with personal feelings."

"That is true," I admitted carelessly. "I could never absolutely dislike a man who played such good golf as your husband."

"And what about me?" she demanded, with some simulated show of peevishness.

"You drive me to be obvious," I replied. "No one could possibly dislike a person who contributed to the beauty of the world."

She laughed softly.

"Why, you are a courtier, Sir Norman," she declared. "Your compliments and the perfume of those roses and the flavour of the Benedictine are getting into my head. I begin to picture you as the serpent who has crawled into this Utopian Paradise."

"Talking about golf," her husband intervened in a harsh tone, "what about a game, Sir Norman? Will you play me to-morrow morning?"

"With pleasure," I assented.

"At ten o'clock?"

"I will be in the clubhouse," I promised him.

"We go to bed up here," he remarked, "practically with the sun."

I rose to my feet. The hint was unmistakable. I

took my leave, and as I walked down the drive, with the yellow moon shining through the sparse trees, I felt the ghosts of tragedy gathering.

At five minutes to ten on the following morning, I watched Mr. James Stanfield push open his private gate leading on to the links, and stroll across towards the clubhouse. I waved my hand and stepped back into the locker room. Three or four men in tweeds and golfing outfit were waiting there. In five minutes my prospective opponent entered. In five seconds the handcuffs were upon his wrist and one of the three apparent golfers had the matter in hand.

" You are charged, " he said, " with feloniously wounding William Harmell, manager, and John Stokes, clerk, of Brown's Bank in the Menwood Road, Leeds, and with stealing from the premises the sum of seven thousand pounds. I should recommend you to come with us quietly and to reserve for the present anything you may have to say. "

Looking at him as he stood leaning a little against his own locker, I could have sworn that there was no manner of change in the face or expression of my enemy. He ignored the others and looked across at me.

" This is your doing? " he asked.

" Altogether, " I admitted.

" You knew it — last night? "

" It was you who reminded me that I need not take salt, " I replied.

He nodded.

" The trick is to you, " he confessed. " I am ready, gentlemen. "

He walked quietly out to a waiting motor car, with a burly policeman on either side of him, and a very important man from Scotland Yard in the party. Rimmington and I were left behind and presently we essayed a round of golf. All the time my eyes kept straying towards the Lodge. No sign, however, came from there.

" I still, " Rimmington remarked, as he waited for a few minutes on the tenth tee, " don't quite understand how you tumbled to this affair so quickly. "

" It was quite easy when you once admit the possibility of the occupants of the Daimler car being concerned, " I replied. " Of course, Roberson was in it up to the eyes. It was Stanfield who drove up in Roberson's Ford and went direct to the bank. The Daimler car was already there, containing Janet Stanfield and Roberson, wearing a grey Homburg hat and a linen duster. The chauffeur brought into the store a small order which the grocer's assistant packed and took out. The chauffeur was taking advantage of the delay to fill up with petrol. The moment Stanfield descended from the Ford and made his way to the bank, Roberson slipped off his linen duster, produced a Panama hat which he pulled over his eyes, and made his purchases in the shop. He came out just as Stanfield reappeared and drove the Ford away. Stanfield just stepped into the Daimler, put on his linen duster and grey Homburg hat, and off they started. The idea was to confuse, and at first it succeeded. The whole affair was ingenious, from the selection of that particular bank, which is wickedly isolated, to the exact location of the Daimler car, which made any one on the off side almost invisible. "

"It's pretty generous of you to let me take the credit of this, " Rimmington remarked.

" If Stanfield turns out to be Pugsley, and Pugsley the man I believe him to be, " I said, " I shall need no other reward than the joy of having brought him to book. "

" Do you believe him to be Michael Sayers? " Rimmington asked.

" I am absolutely certain of it, " I answered.

We completed our round, lunched and played again. There came no sign from the Lodge. Somehow or other, the silence seemed to me ominous. Towards evening I began to get uneasy. Just as we were sitting down to dinner, I was fetched to the telephone.

" Inspector McCall speaking, " the voice I heard declared. " Are you Sir Norman Greyes? "

" Yes, " I answered.

" Have you heard the news? "

" I have heard no particular news since early this morning, " I replied.

" Stanfield escaped eleven miles from here, " the inspector declared gloomily.

" Escaped? Ridiculous! " I exclaimed.

" He did it, anyhow. He shot both his guards with an automatic pistol fixed in the sole of one foot and worked with the toe of the other. Mr. Gorman from

Scotland Yard is seriously wounded, and one of the others is shot in the leg. Stanfield then threatened the driver until he released him from the handcuffs and took him to within a mile of a railway station. There he tied the man up, drove the car on himself and disappeared. So far we have no news. "

I could make no intelligible reply. I muttered something to the effect that Rimmington and I would come on to the police station the first thing in the morning. Then I walked outside, a little giddy, sick at heart, furious with myself and Fate. I stood looking towards the Lodge until at last I yielded to an irresistible impulse. I hastened across the few yards of heather-grown common, crossed the road, made my way up the straggling avenue and rang the great front-door bell. There was a suggestion of emptiness about its rankling echoes, no sound of any one moving or stirring within. I was inclined to laugh at myself for my pains. I was indeed on the point of turning away when the great door swung silently open. Janet stood there, looking out at me.

I freely admit that I lost my nerve. I lost my poise, and with it all the gifts which enable a man to face an exceptional situation. For this woman showed no signs of any mental disturbance. I had never seen her look more beautiful. She wore a loose white gown, open at the throat and tied with a girdle at the waist. Her hair shone like burnished copper, her eyes were almost fiercely yet softly bright. She moved away from the door.

"Come in," she invited. "I have been expecting you."

Our footsteps awakened strange echoes in the hall. She led the way into the sitting room which opened on to the terrace, and sank back on to the divan, where apparently she had been resting.

"Judas!" she murmured.

"You know, then?" I demanded harshly.

"Everything — even the last little episode. What fools you policemen are!"

"He isn't safe yet," I muttered.

She laughed mockingly.

"I worry no more about him," she declared. "It is not an equal struggle. I worry only about myself."

"Alone — here!" I echoed, dimly conscious of the fact that I had been aware of it all the time.

She nodded.

"Harding, our butler-chauffeur and confederate, has taken the car — where you can guess. Our gillie broke his leg this morning and has gone to hospital. I am not afraid of burglars but I am terrified of mice, and the place is overrun with them. Also, I simply loathe the idea of having to get up and make my own coffee in the morning."

I rose to my feet.

"There are empty rooms at the Dormy House," I told her, "where you could obtain service and be made quite comfortable. I am going back now. Shall I bespeak one for you?"

"You would really have me there," she asked curiously, " under the same roof as your august and respectable self ? "

" Why not ? "

" The wife of a famous criminal, " she reminded me, " the wife of the man whom you have betrayed! You and I share a secret, too, don't we? Would you vouch for my — respectability ? "

I moved a step towards her. Her eyes were filled with a mingled light, a light of allurement and cruelty. Her lips were moist and quivering — was it with anger? A long, bare arm was withdrawn from behind her head. Then a voice fell upon the throbbing silence like a douche of cold water.

" Hands up — like lightning ! "

I obeyed. I recognised the voice of the man in Harding's livery. It was Stanfield who had crept in upon us, unheard.

" A mixture of Lothario and Inspector Bucket ! " he mocked. " Any prayers to say ? "

" If you are going to shoot, let's have it over quickly, " I answered.

The woman slipped from the divan and stood between us.

" Don't be absurd, " she said to the newcomer. " We couldn't afford to part with Sir Norman. Life would be too dull without him. Put him on parole. He is perfectly trustworthy. "

Stanfield lowered his pistol.

" You are right, " he admitted. " Take your choice, Greyes — twelve hours' silence or Eternity. "

" I will be silent for twelve hours, " I promised.

He pointed to the door.

" I cannot have the last few hours I may ever spend with my wife, disturbed, " he said. " Kindly leave us. "

I went without a backward glance. I opened and closed the front door and walked down the straight avenue. In the woods beyond, the owls were hooting. Bats flew through the twilight before me, and a quarter of the yellow moon showed behind the hills. I realised all these things dimly. There was a mist before my eyes, a cloud befogging my brain. For those few moments, Stanfield's escape, the steadiness of his automatic pointed directly at my heart, were vague memories only. I was angry and humiliated. I was filled with a man's hatred of his own weakness.

Rimmington was sitting in the porch, smoking, when I got back. He moved his head towards the Lodge. It was obvious from his dejection that he too had heard from McCall.

" What do you think about taking a look around there? " he suggested.

I think that, if anything, I went beyond the obligations of my parole.

" Quite useless, " I replied tersely. " Let's have a game of billiards and try and forget the damned business. "

CHAPTER IV

THE HONOUR OF MONSIEUR LUTARDE

MICHAEL

It was perhaps the greatest surprise of my life when the trim, benevolent-looking gentleman with the red ribbon in his buttonhole, who was sharing my seat in the Jardins des Invalides, suddenly addressed me by name. For over a year — ever since, in fact, my escape from the English police in Scotland — I had been engaged in the strenuous task of founding and cultivating a new identity. My name was Mr. John D. Harmon. I was a retired dry-goods dealer from Providence, U.S.A., and I spent most of my time at the Grand Hotel, talking with compatriots and playing dominoes and billiards. A trip across the ocean, a few days spent in Providence, and a general knowledge of the structure of American life had been all the actual training necessary. I had a circle of friends willing to vouch for me, whom I could have increased almost ad lib; a *dossier* accepted and pigeonholed by the police; a general appearance which, thanks to my manner of dressing, my horn-rimmed eyeglasses, my short beard and moustache, would have left me unrecognised even under the scrutiny of the great Sir Norman Greyes himself. I had not even heard the sound of one of those names under which I had passed in England for many months. It came upon me, therefore, as a thunderclap when my companion, to all appearance a person of the upper and official classes, whom I had noticed many mornings when strolling in the gardens, deliberately went behind the many aliases of which I had made use at different times and addressed me by my baptismal name.

" A little chilly for April, is it not, Monsieur Michael Sayers? Yet the Spring marches well. You perceive that the chestnut buds are already waxy. "

I turned a little towards him, my right hand stealing towards my pocket. He bore my scrutiny without flinching.

" By what name did you address me, Monsieur? " I asked.

" By your own, " was the courteous reply. " You have borne many others, have you not, Monsieur, yet between us the real one is perhaps best. "

He was of the French police, I decided, and my hand stole a little deeper into my pocket. My mind began to contemplate the chances of successful escape. There were not many people about, and the nearest Metropolitan station was close at hand.

" Permit me to offer you my card, " my companion proceeded, drawing an elegant case from his pocket and handing me a thin strip of ivory pasteboard. I read it carefully. My eyes, however, were watching for any movement on his part:

Monsieur Gaston Lefèvre
Agent de Compagnie d'Assurances
13 *Rue Scribe*

" That, Monsieur, " my companion confessed, " is not my name. "

" Indeed? " I muttered.

" It is an identity, " he continued, " which I have fixed upon the little world in which I spend the greater part of my time, a name under which I have earned a certain reputation, a certain social standing. But it is not my own. I was christened Paul and my surname is Gont. "

"Paul Gont? " I repeated incredulously.

" I am indeed he, Monsieur, " was the convincing reply.

My fingers once more gripped the butt of the weapon from which they had been momentarily withdrawn.

" It was reported, " I said, watching him steadily, " that Paul Gont had joined the secret police of France. "

A flicker of annoyance passed across my companion's face. His expression was no longer so beneficent.

" If that were true, Monsieur, " he rejoined, " I should by now have become their chief. I address you, believe me, as one master craftsman to another. "

" Why do you imagine that my name is Michael Sayers? " I asked cautiously.

He smiled.

"I take a keen interest," he confided, "in the exploits of my — shall I say fellow adventurers? — in other countries. I read with much amusement — not unmingled, believe me, sir, with admiration, of your escape from the police in Scotland, and the arrival of Mr. John D. Harmon from Providence here shortly afterwards also interested me. There is little that goes on in Paris of which I do not hear."

"You have your own secret police?"

"Certainly, Monsieur," he assented, "but they work for me and not for the law."

He lit a cigarette from a handsome gold case which he passed courteously on to me. With his hands upon the carved top of his malacca cane, he gazed benignly around.

"It is indeed a spring morning," he declared. "There is a perfume of lilac in the air. Even the hard faces of the flower sellers are softened by the sunshine. And you observe the little nurse girl over there, my friend, how wistfully she looks around, and how coquettish the little ribbon at her throat? Even we elders —— "

"I should be glad to know," I interrupted, "why you addressed me as Michael Sayers?"

"It was a risk, I imagine," my companion admitted. "You are reputed to be a man who shoots from his pocket with great skill. However, remind yourself that I have trusted you with a secret at least as amazing as your own."

My hand came out from my pocket. The man indeed spoke truthfully. The name of Paul Gont was even better known in the history of crime than the name of Michael Sayers.

"You had some reason for making yourself known to me?" I queried.

He bowed.

"Apart from the pleasure of meeting so distinguished a confrère," he said, "there is a scheme in which I am at present interested, in which it might amuse you to take part. You are probably a little wearied by the idleness which must go with the building up of a new identity."

"Let me hear about it," I begged.

My companion brushed the ash from his trouser leg and rose to his feet.

"Let us walk to my office," he suggested. "We will see whether any fresh business has come in. Afterwards, we will, if you choose, lunch together at some discreet place. How the police of the world would tremble if they saw our heads together over a bottle of wine!"

I could not altogether discard my suspicions, for it seemed incredible that this man was really the daring criminal whom the police of three countries had sought for many years in vain. Nothing in the least disturbing happened, however. We visited a reputable and quietly handsome suite of offices in the Rue Scribe, where my companion conversed for several minutes on various matters of business with his clerks, gave some general instructions and signed his letters. Afterwards we walked across to the Place Gaillon, where my host selected a lunch with the skill of the born gourmet. He refused to allow me an apéritif but ordered the choicest of wine. In the course of our meal he asked me a most surprising question.

" Do you hear frequently from your friend, Sir Norman Greyes? "

" If I heard from him at all, " I replied, " I imagine that the situation would be, to say the least of it, precarious. What do you know about him? "

My companion smiled.

" I had a little affair of the same nature," he confided, " with the sub-Chief of the Police here. Francois Dumesnil, his name was. "

" And where is he now? " I asked.

" He disappeared, " was the considered reply. " A great many people disappear in Paris. It was a battle of wits between us, and I was almost sorry when the end came. Self-preservation, however, makes strenuous demands upon one sometimes. "

" Concerning Norman Greyes? " I persisted.

" Forgive me, I wandered a little from the point. I mentioned Norman Greyes's name because he is in Paris. "

" In Paris? " I exclaimed.

" He arrived by the Calais train last evening. I fancy that later on in the day he may probably stroll into the American Bar at the Grand Hotel. "

The news was in its way terrible, yet I could think of no broken link in the chain of incidents connecting my new life. If Norman Greyes were indeed upon my track, he was possessed of gifts for which I had never given him credit. Either that, or there had been treachery in the one direction where I knew no treachery was possible.

"I take it, " I said slowly, " your suggestion is that Norman Greyes has discovered my whereabouts? "

"I will be perfectly frank, " was my companion's prompt avowal. " I do not know that. I am as anxious to discover the truth as you are. There is a distinct possibility that Norman Greyes has come over here in connection with another affair in which I am indirectly interested. If that should be so, his coming may be, so far as you are concerned, only a coincidence. I have a proposition to make to you. Take a taxicab and drive out to Versailles for the afternoon. On your way back, stop at the Taverne Bertain, near the Armenonville. I will meet you there at seven o'clock. By that time I shall know. I propose a perfectly fair bargain to you. If he is here on your business, I will assist you to escape. If he is interested in the other little matter I spoke of, I shall claim your help. "

"It is a bargain, " I promised.

"So to our chicken, " my companion murmured, eyeing with approval the dish which had been extended towards him.

It was about half-past five that afternoon when I dismissed my taxi and seated myself at one of the small tables under the trees outside the Taverne Bertain. The chairs were set far enough back to avoid the dust, but commanded a pleasant view of the constant stream of passing vehicles. I ordered a glass of tea with a slice of lemon, a packet of Caporal cigarettes, and settled down to one of my favourite tasks — watching my fellow creatures. Every variety of the human race was in evidence, riding in every description of carriage: the sublimely insolent Parisian beauty with her cavalier of the moment, she the last word in elegance and perfumes, he almost apish in his sartorial vanity; the shopkeeper and his family; the prosperous merchant with his richly dressed wife; the man of serious affairs, generally with a comely companion. So they passed on, their momentary quest of fresh air an obvious hiatus in the greater and more strenuous pursuit of what for them meant life. A rabble, I told myself a little contemptuously. Not one of them had realised the supreme joy of existence.

It was as though Fate had suddenly decided to deal my philosophy a mortal blow. The thing which I should have deemed impossible was there before me. In a handsome limousine car, traveling slowly in the trail of other vehicles, appeared my enemy, Norman Greyes — and by his side Janet. He wore a light grey suit and a Homburg hat; his long, lean face seemed as sombre as ever. Janet was talking whilst he listened — talking of something, it seemed, more important than the idle flotsam of the moment. The car passed on. I remained seated in my chair. I do not think that I had turned a hair, yet an icy hand seemed to be gripping my heart. I had a moment's wild and savage desire to throw my glass at a thrush hopping contentedly around me.

A quietly appointed electric brougham turned in at the entrance to the café, and the man who had introduced himself to me as Gaston Lefèvre, descended. He was looking very spick and span, dressed with the utmost care and apparently fresh from the barber's. He approached and seated himself by my side.

" You have self-control, my friend, " he observed, " but perhaps you did not believe your eyes. "

" My eyes are the only things in this world which I do absolutely trust, " I answered coldly.

My companion stroked his grey imperial.

" I will drink absinthe to-day, Francois, " he told the bowing waiter. " See that it is made as I like it. Come, my friend, " he added, " throw away your wishy-washy tea and join me. "

I shook my head.

" Alcohol is not one of the necessities of life with me, " I said. " It stimulates some, I suppose. It merely depresses me. Tell me what you know about the coming of this man Greyes? "

" In the first place, then, " Lefèvre announced pleasantly, as he helped himself to one of my Caporals and lit it, " let me reassure you. Greyes is not in Paris on your account. "

" And his companion? "

" For the moment I am puzzled, " was the frank confession. " I can tell you this, however. Your wife was sent for according to my instructions. I know very little about her, it is true, but I have agents in London who keep me well-informed as to what goes on on your side of the Channel, and, from certain things

I have heard, I came to the conclusion that she was the one person who could bring to a successful issue the little affair which I shall presently propose to you. "

" You seem to be taking things rather for granted, " I reminded him.

" Your coöperation is a certainty, " he replied, with a smile. " There will be half a million francs for you, and you must be getting short of money. Furthermore, by a very pleasing coincidence, the brains of the other side are controlled by your ancient enemy. "

" The scheme is already commended to me, " I admitted. " Nevertheless, expound it. "

My companion glanced around as though to drink in the pleasant spring air and to bask in the warm sunshine. He drew a little sigh of content. All the tables around us were empty.

" I will tell you a curious story, " he proposed.

NORMAN GREYES

I celebrated my return to England and civilisation by a stroll down Bond Street on the morning after my arrival. A light but gusty wind was blowing, fleecy fragments of white clouds were being driven across the blue sky. The occasional sunshine was deliciously warm, the air was full of perfume from the florists' shops and from the flower-sellers' baskets at the corners of the streets. After two years' absence, it was like a new city to me. I met a few acquaintances and exchanged greetings with a couple of friends. Then, at the corner of Conduit Street, I came face to face with Janet Stanfield.

We stopped as though by common consent, and the civilisation by which we were surrounded seemed to fall away. The last time I had thought of her was when I had lain on the edge of a windy precipice in northwestern India, fastened by my belt to the roots of a stunted shrub for safety, with a camp fire throwing strange and lurid lights into the black gulf below, and my little corps of guides in their picturesque costume murmuring low chants after their evening meal. In that eternal silence, the woman's inscrutable face, her cold yet seeking eyes, the constant invitation of her reluctant lips had held and filled my thoughts. Sleep had come only with the pink dawn, and a troubled sleep at that. Now I was face to face with her, unchanged, with the same riddle in her eyes and smiling lips.

" Welcome home, Sir Norman Greyes, " she said.

" Thank you, " I replied. " I only arrived last night. "

She looked at me critically.

" A most becoming shade of brown, " she commented. " And you are thinner, too. Have you been going through hardships? "

" None but those I have sought, " I assured her. " I was in Mesopotamia for eight months, and in India most of the rest of the time. "

" Big-game shooting, the papers said, " she continued. " Tell me, my enemy, was it as interesting as man-hunting? "

" Each has its thrill, " I replied, " but you must remember that I long ago ceased to be a professional hunter of men. "

She smiled.

" So that is why you have let my husband alone? "

" It was not my affair to search for him. That was a matter for the authorities. If my help is sought in solving the mystery of a crime, I am generally prepared to do my best. Otherwise, I do not interfere. You have news of him? "

She laughed bitterly.

" Since he left the Lodge that night, " she replied, " and you kicked your heels over at the Dormy House because of your parole, I have neither seen nor heard of him. "

" Do you mean that? "

She nodded.

" Scotland Yard, " she declared, " has not imagination enough to juggle with facts, but as regards detail its myrmidons are wonderful. I think that I was watched every day up to the end of at least the first year. Wherever my husband may be, he will not approach me until it is safe. "

" And when it is safe? " I ventured.

" I shall go to him, I suppose, " she answered.

I suddenly realised with a little shock that she was plainly, almost shabbily dressed. The undefinable elegance of her still remained, she was still distinct from all other women, but she owed nothing to her clothes. She read my thoughts in most disturbing fashion.

" A terrible neighbourhood, this, to frequent in

one's last year's garments," she observed, smiling. "I was just thinking that I should like a black and white check tailored suit. Would you like to buy me one, Sir Norman? You really ought to, you know. We made terribly little out of that Menwood Street Bank affair, owing to your flash of inspiration."

"I admit the liability," I replied. "Which establishment shall we patronise?"

She shrugged her shoulders.

"At heart, I believe that I am an honest woman," she sighed. "I cannot bear the thought of your paying out notes for the adornment of my person. You shall give me lunch instead. For all that you know, I may be as short of food as I am of clothes. I am certainly very hungry."

We turned towards Regent Street and lunched in a restaurant of bygone fame, half bourgeois, half Bohemian. She would tell me nothing of her manner of life or of her abode, yet somehow or other I fancied, reading between the lines, that life had become something of a struggle for her. She asked me deliberately for my address, but refused me hers. She angled for another invitation, but shook her head when I proffered it. If ever she had been in earnest in her life, she was in earnest when we said good-by.

"These meetings with you," she declared, "stimulate me more than I can tell you, but they leave something behind which I cannot define. I do not think that I will dine with you, Sir Norman — not just yet, at any rate."

She glanced at her watch and hurried off. I had an idea that she was returning to some daily task. I called at my club, talked for an hour or two with some friends, and in due course made my way back to my rooms. I was restless and ridiculously disturbed. It was the most accursed stroke of ill-luck that I should have met with this woman on the very day after my return. Fortunately, distraction awaited me.

" Mr. Rimmington has been waiting for you for some time, sir, " my servant announced. " He is in the sitting room with another gentleman. "

My friend rose eagerly to welcome me as I entered. I shook hands with his companion, who was known to me slightly.

" The Chief asked me to bring Lord Hampden to you, " Rimmington explained. " He came this morning to ask for our help in an affair which is rather outside our province. The Chief thought that you might be of assistance. "

" Let me hear about it, " I begged.

My distinguished visitor plunged at once into the matter.

" The story is simple enough, Sir Norman, " he said, "but serious. You are in touch with French politics? "

" Scarcely, " I answered. " I have been in India for the last eighteen months and only arrived in London last night. "

" French politics to-day, " Lord Hampden explained, " hinge chiefly upon the question of France's attitude towards Germany. There is a party — the patriotic and military party — fiercely determined to

make Germany pay to the uttermost farthing, and to
squeeze the last drop of blood out of her by force of
arms. The opposing party is all for compromises,
encouragement of German trade, and even for a rap-
prochement with Germany. You know, of course, who
is the leader of the patriotic party? "

" Lutarde, I should imagine. "

" Philippe Lutarde, " my visitor assented. " He is
hated by the pro-German party, as I will call them,
first because of his bitter enmity towards Germany,
secondly because of his devotion to England, and
thirdly because of his unfaltering rectitude. An attempt was made upon his life not long ago, and the
French police have been instructed to watch him night
and day. Lately, however, there has been more uneasiness than ever amongst the patriotic party. It is,
I fear, true that the Chief of the Police is of the pro-
German party, and there is, without doubt, a plot brew-
ing at the present moment against Lutarde. It has
been suggested to us that a thoroughly capable secret
service man from this side might be of assistance in
unravelling it. You follow me, I hope, Sir Norman? "

" I think so, " I admitted, " but what is the nature
of the plot? "

" One can only surmise, " Lord Hampden replied.
" We do not believe, however, that it is assassination.
That would only make a martyr of Lutarde and sanctify his cause. We want you to go over to Paris and
consult with a person whose name I will give you. You
will be backed in any steps you may think well to take,
by unquestionable authority. It will be a difficult

commission and in a sense a vague one, but I may say that, in the event of your achieving any success, the Government would consider itself under the deepest debt of gratitude to you. "

" I will do what I can, of course, " I promised. " When do I start? "

" We should like you to catch the eleven o'clock train to-morrow morning, " the Cabinet Minister suggested, rising to his feet. " If you will dine with me at eight o'clock to-night in Carlton Terrace, I will furnish you with every other detail. "

So on the following morning, in less than forty-eight hours after my return to England, I found myself going through the ordinary routine of the continental traveller, registering my luggage, arranging my smaller belongings in the seat which had been reserved for me, and strolling back to the bookstall for a few final purchases. There I came face to face with Janet Stanfield, engaged upon the same task. She was studying a ladies' journal and looked up at the sound of my voice. For the moment her indifference deserted her. She was frankly amazed.

" You? " she exclaimed. " Where are you going? "

" To Paris, " I answered. " And you? "

" We are fellow travellers, " she said slowly. "Why did you not tell me yesterday? "

" In an armed truce, " I pointed out, " the combatants do not usually disclose their future plans. "

She turned a little pale.

" So we are in the lists again, " she murmured.

"I thought you enjoyed the struggle," I reminded her.

"I am a little tired," she admitted.

I performed several small offices for her on the journey, for which I could see that she was thankful. At Calais she had no reserved seat in the crowded train. I did my best to procure one for her, but in vain. I had no choice but to offer her a place in my reserved compartment. She was looking very fragile and tired as she accepted my offer with a grateful smile and sank into a vacant seat.

"You are a wonderful enemy," she confessed. "I am losing all my hatred of you. I will be franker with you than you have been with me, and tell you that when we met yesterday I had no idea of this journey. I am not used to travelling and I hate the sea."

She curled up as gracefully as a cat and went fast asleep. When she opened her eyes, the people were streaming down the corridor in answer to the call for the first dinner.

"Have you eaten anything to-day?" I enquired.

"Nothing, and I am ravenous," she admitted frankly.

I committed the atrocity of dining at half-past five. Afterwards, she once more took a corner seat in my compartment and lit a cigarette. She was a good deal more like her old self.

"Has your husband sent for you?" I asked bluntly.

"The parole has expired," she reminded me.

I nodded.

"Listen," I continued, "I am not out to do the

work of Scotland Yard. I do not know where your husband may be hiding. My journey to Paris has nothing to do with him or his affairs. Yet you must understand this. If chance at any time should put me upon his track, I should follow it up and hand him over to justice. Nothing, " I added, looking her steadily in the eyes, " could alter my determination so far as that is concerned. "

This time she did not take up the challenge. She only sighed and looked out of the window.

" You are very hard, " she murmured.

" I have been a servant of the law, " I reminded her, " and I belong to those who choose to abide by the law. "

" Why, " she asked, " have you never denounced me as the murderess of that man at Woking? "

" Because there has never been a tittle of evidence against you, " I replied. " There are any quantity of known criminals walking about to-day, in the same position. "

" Supposing there were evidence and it came into your hands? " she persisted.

I hesitated, and my hesitation seemed to count to her as a triumph.

" I cannot assume a situation that has not arisen, " I told her stiffly.

I saw her luggage through the Customs, for which, as she knew no French, she was grateful. I offered her a seat in the car which had been sent for me, but she shook her head.

" I am going to the Gare de l'Est, " she said.

" Where you will take a fresh cab and drive to the
address which you do not intend me to hear, " I remarked. " You need not go out of your way. I will
give you another parole. I will make no effort to discover your address, so you can take your taxi and
drive straight there. I shall be at the Hotel Meurice.
If you have an hour to spare, we will drive in the Bois
to-morrow. "

For the next few days I was fully immersed in the
complications of the business which had brought me to
Paris. Rather to my surprise, Janet called to see me
at the hotel and we took our drive in the Bois. It was
easy to realise that, whatever the business which had
brought her to Paris may have been, it was of a disturbing nature. She was nervous and ill-at-ease, looking around all the time as though she were afraid of
being observed. There was a certain hardness, too,
which seemed to have returned to her. Somehow, I
gathered when we parted that she was obsessed by
some new fear, some underlying dread of circumstances
of which, however, she gave me no inkling. It was only
after she had gone and I found myself thinking over our
rather disjointed conversation, that I came to a certain conclusion. I decided that she had received definite and disquieting news of her husband. I could
scarcely believe that he was in Paris. Rimmington had
assured me that he had been located in Central America,
and after all, I decided, the affair was no concern of
mine. Some day or other would come the reckoning
between this man and myself. I frankly confess that I

had not the ghost of an idea that such a day might dawn within the next few hours.

At the end of the third day of my stay, a little conference was held in my salon between Guy Ennison, who had worked in the English Secret Service during the war, and whose headquarters had been in Paris; myself, and Monsieur Destin, an ex-Chief of the Police, now a member of Lutarde's Government. The latter was a short and corpulent little Frenchman, with black moustache and imperial, vivid black eyes, and a most vivacious manner. He spoke English with a marked accent but with great fluency. He opened our conference with a few words of plain speaking.

" Sir Norman Greyes, " he said, grasping my hand, " you are welcome. If you can help us to save our Chief, you are more than welcome. He is in danger — of that I am assured. "

Much of the rest of his speech was irrelevant. The gist of the matter, however, was contained in his concluding sentences.

" They will seek to strike through his one weakness — his sentimentality, his too great good-nature. Philippe Lutarde has always been a lover of women, a kindly and a generous lover. He can resist no appeal to his sympathies, and our French public — you know, perhaps, how strange they are. Whatever our own private lives may be, we tolerate not even indiscretions from our great men. We glorify and sanctify them, we place them on a pedestal, and if they fall we depose them from our hearts. All nations have their peculiar form of hypocrisy. That is ours. Lutarde's daily life is being examined at the present moment, hour by hour. "

" By the police? " I asked.

" No! By the agents of a very dangerous gang of criminals, whose chief we believe to be in league with the other side. "

" Why not give warning to Monsieur Lutarde? "

" That has been done. He is haughty and impetuous. He will brook no interference with his actions. "

" Is his life above reproach? " I asked bluntly.

" Absolutely, " was the confident reply. " He is seventy years of age and a philosopher. He has too much natural dignity to attempt that side of life for which his age renders him unsuitable. At the same time, he is full of sentiment. He likes to dally with the finer emotions. He would inhale the perfume of the roses from his neighbour's garden, but he would never seek to pluck the blossoms. "

" Can I meet him? " I suggested.

" To-day at the British Embassy, " Guy Ennison replied. " We have arranged a little luncheon. He does not know your errand, and he scarcely even realises our anxiety. "

Our conference broke up soon afterwards. At luncheon I found Philippe Lutarde gracious, charming and brilliant. He had the clear skin and bright eyes of a younger man, his snow-white hair was a veritable adornment. His sense of humour was abundant and his laughter infectious. He was a delightful companion, and I easily understood the enthusiastic adherence of his friends. Towards the close of luncheon, Ennison spoke to him quite seriously of the existence of some conspiracy against either his life or his honour. Lutarde only smiled.

" My friend, " he said, " I much appreciate all your efforts on my behalf, but behold, I am seventy years old! A few years more or less of life now are little. As to my honour, that no enemy can besmirch. If I were to surround myself by guards, as you suggest, place myself in a glass house, I should live an artificial life. I know that without me things might for a time be difficult, and relations between our two countries might suffer. In a month or two, however, all that will be changed — we shall have entered upon a new era — and for these few months I choose to take my risk. I will not submit to espionage."

" You are subject to it at present from the other side," Ennison reminded him gently.

" If I find a man attempting it," was the fierce reply, " I will shoot him."

Nevertheless, for the next three days I cast away my name and I resorted to the meaner walks of my profession. I shadowed the great French statesman from the moment when he rose until nightfall. I accompanied him, unseen, on those midnight walks against which his friends had protested so forcibly. I watched him give alms freely, speak kindly words to the distressed, and I watched other things a little more tensely, understanding what lay behind them. There was a young girl, very beautiful, with great dark eyes and an appealing face, who stopped him one night with some pitiful story. She was limping, and she pointed continually to her foot. Lutarde called the *fiacre* which she indicated. She leaned her fingers upon his arm. I was close enough to see the pressure of them, to note the subtlety of her upward glances. He handed her to the cab. I heard her pleading words. She was so lonely. If monsieur would drive with her a little way! But Lutarde shook his head gravely. He paid the taxicab man a fare which surprised him, lifted his hat courteously and walked away. I saw the change in the girl's face as he disappeared. That was just one of his escapes. We had a more exciting few minutes one night when he insisted upon walking home from the Quai d'Orsay. I saw the four dark, silent figures gliding together, two of them in front of him and two behind, and I saw the waiting motor car at the corner of the street. Prudence led me to anticipate their action, whatever it might be. When they heard the spit of bullets against the wall, they took to their heels and ran. To the gendarme who came hurrying up, I had only to show my little badge of authority and he procured for us at once a taxicab. Lutarde, convinced now that his enemies were in earnest, yielded to my first proposition. I was installed in his house as major-domo.

We had three or four days of absolute quietude. Then the moment which we had been expecting arrived. It was about six o'clock in the evening, and I was seated in Monsieur Lutarde's study, copying some letters at a desk and posing as his secretary. A servant brought in a note, which the Minister read hastily and passed to me. It was written on British Foreign Office note paper and signed by a very important personage. The gist of it was contained in these lines:

The bearer can be altogether trusted. He brings you a verbal message of great importance. You will further our mutual interests if you give it your most serious consideration.

"This, at any rate, is genuine," Monsieur Lutarde observed.

"It would appear so," I admitted.

"You can show the bearer in," the Minister ordered, addressing his servant.

It was a mere chance which led me to retire to what Lutarde was pleased to call my spy hole. Notwithstanding my disguise, it was perhaps as well that I did so, for, to my amazement, it was Janet who was presently ushered in. Monsieur Lutarde rose to his feet in some surprise.

"You are the bearer of this letter, Madame?" he queried, touching it with his forefinger.

"In a sense I am not," she replied, taking the chair to which he pointed and leaning a little over his desk. "It is my husband who should have come. He would have waited upon you and brought the letter and message to which this note refers, but he was attacked last night by an old complaint of his — sciatica — and he is absolutely unable to move. He asked me to hasten to you, and to beg that under the circumstances you would do him the honour to come to the hotel. He is ashamed to have to ask you, but the doctor who is with him now absolutely forbids him to stand up. I have here his certificate."

"I will come without delay, Madame," Lutarde promised, waving away the half-sheet of note paper which she had tendered.

"I came in a taxicab — it is waiting," she continued. "You doubtless would prefer your own car?"

"It is no matter," he answered. "At which hotel do you stay?"

"The Hotel Napoleon in the Rue Tranchard," she replied.

The Minister started. I, too, received a shock, for the district was the most notorious in Paris.

"My dear Madame," he protested, "the neighbourhood of the Rue Tranchard is certainly not a fit place for you and——"

"That is what distressed my husband so much in having to ask you to go to him," she interrupted. "It was the particular desire of the person on whose behalf he has come that his presence in Paris should not be known, and my husband deliberately chose this hotel, where he sometimes stayed when engaged in secret service work during the War. He desired me to say that, if you preferred not to risk being seen in such a locality, he would endeavour to procure an ambulance car from the hospital and come here."

"Such a thing would be unheard of," Lutarde protested. "I will come with you, of course."

He touched the bell.

"Show this lady back into the taxicab which is waiting," he instructed the servant. "Afterwards, fetch my coat and hat at once."

Janet passed quite close to me on her way to the door. She was her old self — quiet, impassive, deliberate. There was not the slightest sign of satisfaction in her face that she had so far succeeded in her mission. She was just the anxious wife performing a necessary duty for her husband.

I emerged from my hiding place as soon as she was safely out of the way.

" Well? " my temporary Chief asked, looking across at me.

" The moment has arrived," I answered.

Monsieur Lutarde, who by nature was one of the most unsuspicious men that ever breathed, looked positively aghast.

" You suggest that the woman is an impostor? " he exclaimed.

" She is the wife of a well-known English criminal," I declared. " Her story was plausible but very improbable. What about the letter that she brought? "

Monsieur Lutarde searched his table. I watched him grimly.

" You will not find it," I told him. " I saw her pick it up as she passed."

" What shall we do? " he asked.

" Keep her waiting for a few minutes and then go to the address she gave you but nowhere else," I decided. " I am going to telephone to Ennison and I shall be there before you. If we see this thing through, we may find out who is at the bottom of it. I will see that you run no risk."

"I have no fear," Monsieur Lutarde asserted, frowning.

"I referred only to your reputation," I assured him.

The two drove off together after a brief delay. Ennison, to whom I had telephoned, picked me up almost immediately in his car. We made one more brief call and reached the hotel as the taxicab containing Monsieur Lutarde and his companion was turning into the other end of the long street. Madame, from behind the glass windows of her bureau, eyed us a little suspiciously as we entered. I engaged her in confidential conversation, however, respecting a suite, and she did not even notice the three or four men who had followed us at intervals into the hotel and who disappeared in various directions. Presently I heard the taxicab stop. I made an excuse and we hurried into the *salle à manger*. Janet, followed by Monsieur Lutarde, who, although he had taken off his hat, held it in front of his face, crossed the floor swiftly towards the lift. Madame held out her key, which Janet accepted with a little nod. They passed into the lift and we heard it ascend. I returned to the bureau. I allowed myself to show much interest.

"But surely, Madame," I whispered, "that was Monsieur Lutarde, the great statesman, who entered with the lady?"

Madame smiled at us knowingly.

"In effect it is he," she admitted. "Madame is the

wife of an old client, an American gentleman who left this evening for London."

" A love affair? " I queried under my breath.

Madame shrugged her shoulders. Her glance was eloquent.

" What can one do? " she murmured. " Only I hope that monsieur will never discover. He has a violent temper. Ah! The merciful heavens! It is monsieur himself who returns! Now there has tragedy arrived indeed! "

Into the hotel with his coat tails flying behind him came a man who for long I did not recognize. I myself had stepped back out of sight and I watched the scene. The newcomer acted his part well.

" My key, Madame," he shouted, banging his fist against the counter.

Madame pretended to search for it. She too had been schooled in her part. So had the guests who, with a little crowd of journalists, came closing around.

" But I have it not, Monsieur," the woman faltered. " Madame herself —— "

The newcomer strode towards the lift, which I imagine was wilfully delayed. He shook the gates and pressed the bell furiously. Madame leaned over the counter.

" But what ails Monsieur? " she demanded.

" What ails me? " he replied at the top of his voice, speaking now in broken French, now in English with an American accent. " I tell you that not three minutes ago I saw my wife enter this hotel with a man —

she who saw me off, as she thought, at the Gare du
Nord not an hour ago! A curse upon your lift,
Madame! This is a plot!"

"But, Monsieur —— " Madame faltered.

"Hell!" the outraged husband interrupted angrily.

He turned and ran for the stairs, followed by a little
crowd, amongst whom I easily escaped detection. We
reached the second floor. The man who now, to my
amazement, I realized must be Stanfield, was banging
at the panels of a closed door and shouting.

"It is locked!" he cried. "I knew it! Locked!
Open, Suzanne! You gain nothing by this. I come if
I blow the hotel about your ears!"

The door opened. A few of us were almost pushed
in. Janet, with her face buried in her hands, turned
away. Monsieur Lutarde, not wholly at his ease, stood
there with folded arms.

"Who are you, sir, and what are you doing in my
salon?" Stanfield demanded fiercely.

"I am here at your wife's bidding to receive a
message which she assures me that her husband has
brought from London," Lutarde replied.

"It is a lie!" Stanfield shouted. "I am her husband and I know nothing of you. It is years since my
wife was in London. These are subterfuges. Tell the
truth, woman?"

Janet threw herself on the couch and hid her face.

"He is your lover?" Stanfield insisted.

"I could not help it," Janet sobbed. "You have
been so cruel lately. Why did you come back?"

There was a little murmur amongst the curious crowd in the background. A thin, dark man with *pince-nez*, obviously a journalist, was on the point of stealing away. The time had come for action. I disentangled myself from the group. Stanfield looked into the muzzle of my automatic.

"Hands up, Stanfield!" I ordered. "Close in behind, Ennison. Pass the word down to bolt the doors of the hotel."

I had once come to the conclusion that, no matter how long our duel might continue, I should never see a sign of feeling in my enemy's face. Through his wonderful disguise, however, the real man at this moment leaped out. He stood staring at me, viciously yet with the half-fascinated amazement of one who looks upon a new thing in life. Janet was crouching back upon the couch, shrinking away from me as far as possible, her fingers tearing to pieces some shred of antimacassar. Suddenly she sprang like a cat between her husband and me. He saw his chance and leaped for the door. The crowd of stupefied people opened as though by magic to let him pass. I lowered my pistol and shouted a warning at the top of my voice. There was the sound of a shot below and the trampling of many feet. A grey-haired, well-dressed man with a red ribbon in his buttonhole, whom I afterwards discovered to be the editor of a leading journal, pushed his way through.

"Monsieur," he said to me, "is there any answer to this riddle?"

"You will find it below," I answered shortly. "There

has been a plot to compromise the personal honour of Monsieur Lutarde here, which you have seen frustrated. The injured husband is an English criminal. His wife " — I hesitated — " his accomplice. Monsieur Lutarde has never seen either of them before in his life. You journalists were invited here to witness something different. If I may be allowed to say so,‹ you will do well to give what pledges may be required of you. The hotel at the present moment is in the hands of agents of the French Government."

There was a little murmur.

" Might one enquire your name, sir? " my questioner demanded.

" My name is Norman Greyes," I answered. " I was once an English detective. I am now in the employ of the English Government."

The man bowed low.

" The affair is explained, sir," he said.

The curious crowd of onlookers melted away. Downstairs, behind the locked doors, an inquisition was being held. Monsieur Lutarde came over and shook me by the hand.

" My thanks later, Sir Norman," he began. " Meanwhile —— "

Ennison entered, accompanied by Monsieur Lutarde's private secretary and a personage whom I recognized as a high official of the French Court. There was a great deal of rapid conversation between the four, a mingled outpouring of congratulations and wonder. Then we all moved to-

wards the door. I touched Ennison on the arm.
" What about Stanfield? " I enquired eagerly.
" Escaped for the moment," was the reluctant admission. " He got through the back premises of the hotel, somehow."
" Escaped! " Janet murmured, in enigmatic accents.
They were filing out of the room. I was the last. Janet rose to her feet. She stood there looking at me.
" What happens to me? " she asked.
" There is no charge against you that I am aware of," I replied.
She came a step nearer.
" I am afraid," she muttered. " They will say that it was my fault."
Ennison was already out of the room, leaving the door, however, wide open. The woman and I were alone.
" I am afraid," she repeated, and she came still a step nearer.
Below, the hotel was in a turmoil. I was suddenly sick of the whole business, a sordid piece of chicanery.
" You descend the ladder," I said. " I scarcely believed that you would stoop to an intrigue of this sort."
" We needed the money," she declared hardly. " He had spent everything, and I had only what I earned as a dressmaker. The people who stood behind this affair were generous. It would all have been so easy and so safe if you had not interfered. I begin to think that you are my evil genius, Norman Greyes."

I heard myself called from below. I took a last glance at her. Her beautiful body was drawn to its utmost height. She was breathing quickly, as though with some suppressed emotion. The danger lights were gleaming in her strange-coloured eyes. For a single moment temptation raged within me. Then I remembered.

"If you need money to get you back to England," I said, "you can apply to the British Consul. I will arrange it for you."

"I may not come to you — for it?"

"No!"

I heard Ennison's returning footsteps upon the stairs. I turned away and closed the door behind me.

"Everything O.K.," Ennison declared triumphantly. "Our friends have made quite a coup."

"Any further news of the outraged husband?" I asked.

"I'm afraid he's got clean away," Ennison confessed. "Our people declare that he was helped by the police. Come on, old fellow, my car's waiting and we're going to have an absinthe at the Café de la Paix."

A quarter of an hour later, we sat amongst the most cosmopolitan crowd in the world outside the Café de la Paix, sipping our absinthe and watching the passers-by.

"A very successful evening's work," Ennison declared thoughtfully.

"So far as it goes," I acquiesced. "After all, though, a man with so many enemies can never be held altogether free from danger."

" We have gone to-night further than you think," my companion assured me. " The agents of the French police who were with us extracted confessions from the hotel proprietor and his wife, amongst others, which implicate some very well-known people. I need not explain further to you, I am sure. You can rely upon one thing for certain, however. From this evening Monsieur Lutarde is free from the danger of any attempt upon either his life or his honour."

" In that case," I agreed, " our work has indeed been well done."

We drank our absinthe in great content. Many months afterwards, a curiously insignificant episode of those next few minutes was brought forcibly to my mind. Near us, a very precise and elderly man, carefully dressed, with a red ribbon in his buttonhole and a stiff, official bearing, raised his hat to Ennison as he passed us. My companion returned his salute, and I watched his dignified wandering amongst the chairs until he found one to his liking. The waiter, seeing him approach, bowed low and hurried away without waiting for his spoken order.

" Who was that? " I enquired curiously.

" An insurance agent in the Rue Scribe," Ennison replied. " His name, I think, is Gaston Lefèvre."

" A type," I observed.

" There are many here," my companion assented.

CHAPTER V

JANET

It was about four months after I had been in the service — how I hate the phrase! — of Mrs. Trumperton-Smith, that I decided to rob her. I first went to her because, day by day, I felt the need of money for those luxuries to which I had become accustomed. After my disastrous visit to Paris, no news whatever had come to me from my husband. A slack period had set in at the dressmaking establishment where I had been employed, and I was informed that my services were no longer necessary. I spent a month at a manicurist's and a few weeks at a photographic studio. I left them for the same reason. I have killed a man with my own hand and been a partner in more than one robbery, but the one virtue of my plebeian ancestors has remained — an uncomfortable, sometimes an almost accursed gift. I have never lost my self-respect. The touch of an unloved hand upon my fingers awakens in me at once a passionate repugnance. It was that feeling which was responsible for my one great crime.

Mrs. Trumperton-Smith advertised in the *Morning Post* for a companion-lady's maid. I secured the post on account of my manners and appearance, but I soon found that the duties which I was expected to fill pertained far more to the latter position than the former. My mistress was a lady of ample person and ample means. She lived in excellent style and apparently had plenty of money. She was a widow about forty-five years old, still good-looking in a florid sort of way, and well enough educated from the middle-class point of view. She wasted no time upon pets. Men were her one and everlasting hobby. She was not difficult to please, but in a general way she preferred them young and silly. I do not think that matrimony ever entered into her designs. I gathered later on that she had been ill-treated by two husbands, each of whom, however, had left her a substantial fortune.

We were staying at the Magnificent Hotel at Brighton when the idea which I have mentioned — of robbing my mistress — first took definite shape in my mind. I should have bided my time, I think, but for two reasons. One was that the salary which she paid me was absurdly small and I saw no chance of saving anything, and the other was the very imminent fear of being anticipated. Mrs. Trumperton-Smith was not always so discreet as she should have been in her acquaintances. At the present time she was on exceedingly friendly terms with a Mr. Sidney Bloor, whom I put down, from the moment I first saw him, as an undoubted adventurer. He was young and rather pimply-faced, with weak eyebrows and eyelashes, small, cunning eyes, a vapid expression but an acquisitive mouth. He was always dressed in the height of fashion, and he had acquired the shibboleth of the up-to-date young man of the moment. Mrs. Trumperton-Smith admired and believed in him. I mistrusted and despised him. He made languid attempts to kiss me whenever he found me alone in the sitting room, attempts which I always managed to evade without exaggerated prudery, and without thinking it necessary to refuse the frequent tips which his position as my mistress's declared admirer seemed to render my due. I knew exactly what he was after, though. I had seen his covetous eyes light up when my mistress had more than usually overloaded her portly person with some of the magnificent jewels in which a portion of her large means was invested. I had seen him make mental calculations as to their value with a greedy, almost ferocious light in his unpleasant eyes. There was a particular diamond necklace which seemed to move him more than any other of her possessions. I felt sure that, when he made his attempt, it would be this necklace which he would endeavour to secure.

He found me one evening, some four months after our arrival in Brighton, alone in the sitting room at about the hour when Madame was sometimes pleased to dispense cocktails. A spasmodic attempt at gallantry having been met and repulsed, he lingered to watch me busy repairing a hair ornament which my mistress desired to wear that evening.

"Where is the old bird?" he asked confidentially.

I did not discourage this familiarity as I should have

done, because I was really anxious to make a guess at
his plans.

" Madame is out playing bridge with some friends,"
I told him.

" What little gewgaws are you sending her down in
to-night? " he enquired, with affected carelessness.

" Whatever she chooses to wear," I replied.

" Only last night," he remarked, " she told me that
it was generally you who made the selection."

" She usually does wear what I put out," I assented.
" Which do you admire her in most, Mr. Bloor? "

The young man scratched his chin thoughtfully. All
the amorousness of the barroom lounger was in his tone
and expression as he glanced down at me.

" It doesn't matter to me what she wears," he sighed.
" I know a little girl, though, who would look the real
thing decked out in those diamonds, eh? "

" I expect you have a large acquaintance amongst
my sex," I replied demurely.

" Wasn't thinking of any one farther away than
this room," he assured me. " You're a damn good-
looking girl, you know, Janet."

" Do you think so, Mr. Bloor? " I ventured, without
looking up.

" I do, indeed," he insisted, edging a little nearer
towards me. " I say, go and fetch them just for a
joke and try them on. I'd like to see how they look on
that white throat of yours."

" And have Madame come in and send me away without notice! No, thank you, Mr. Bloor! "

" If you lost your job through me," he declared

magniloquently. " I should take good care to make it up to you."

" Your way of making it up might not appeal to me," I answered.

" You're a cold young woman, Janet," he complained. " My last evening, too."

" Are you going away? "

" Back to the City to-morrow. I'm my own master and all that, of course — take a week or two just when I want it — but one has to pick up a bit of the rhino now and then. We haven't all got Mrs. Trumperton-Smith's money."

" If it is really your last night," I said, " tell me what jewellery you would like the mistress to wear this evening, and I will put it out for her."

He affected to treat the matter with indifference, but it was obviously what he had been leading up to.

" What about the diamond necklace, then? " he suggested. " She's coming to dine at my table, so I ought to have a say. The diamond necklace, earrings and bracelet! What-ho! We shan't need any other illumination! "

" I will do my best," I promised him.

My mistress came bustling in, a moment or two later, and busied herself making the cocktails. I went through into her bedroom to lay out her gown. It was perfectly clear to me now that if I were going to rob Mrs. Trumperton-Smith at all, it had better be done quickly. Mr. Sidney Bloor's choice showed that he had a very fair idea of the value of jewels.

The drinking of cocktails was concluded a little more

quickly than usual, and Mrs. Trumperton-Smith joined
me in the bedroom, full of what passed with her as
geniality. She was always agreeable when things had
been going her way, and she had a certain florid good-
nature which made her popular in the hotel and
amongst her casual acquaintances. It was a quality,
however, which was entirely superficial, and in a general
way I found her disagreeable, selfish and jealous to a
degree. Her whole expression altered as she submitted
herself to my ministrations.

"How long had Mr. Bloor been here?" she asked.

"About five minutes, Madame."

"Another time," she said stiffly, "it would be more
seemly if you brought any work you had to do in here,
whilst he was waiting for me."

"Very good, Madame."

"And what a mess you've made of this aigrette!"
she went on. "I don't think I shall ever wear it again."

"I have arranged it exactly according to your instructions, Madame," I told her.

"Don't answer me, woman," she snapped. "And
be careful with my hair on the left side. You're making me look a perfect fright. Here!"

She withdrew the key of her jewel case from a bracelet, and passed it to me.

"As Madame is wearing black," I said, "I thought
she would prefer the diamonds."

"Bring them along and don't talk so much," was
the curt reply.

I selected the diamond necklace, earrings and bracelet, locked up the case and returned the key. My mis-

tress's expression softened as she looked at herself in the glass.

"I really think," she reflected, with a little sigh, "that black does become me."

"I have heard a great many people say so, Madame," I assured her.

She picked up her gold bag, looked inside to see that I had placed her handkerchief there, and turned away.

"See that the fire is kept up in the sitting room, Janet," she ordered. "Mr. Bloor and I will take our coffee there."

"Very good, Madame," I replied.

I went into the steward's room and had my supper as usual, and I also paid a visit to Mr. Bloor's bedroom and borrowed certain trifles which I proposed to use later on. It was not yet clear to me by what means the young man was scheming to possess himself of the jewels, but I was quite convinced that the attempt itself would be made that night. I happened to know that both he and Mrs. Trumperton-Smith were engaged to play bridge after dinner at a neighbouring hotel, and I was quite sure that it was the jewels she was wearing, rather than those left in her case, upon which he had designs. I contrived to leave open the connecting door between the bedroom and sitting room, and to be in the former when they returned for their coffee. Madame had come in for her cloak and they were on the point of starting out again, when her escort at last gave me the cue for which I had been waiting.

"I say, Mimi," he drawled — he called her "Mimi" although she weighed fourteen stone — "I don't feel comfortable walking along the front with you in those diamonds. Leave them behind, there's a dear. All those women at the Royal wear flashy jewellery. You'll look much more the real thing with none on at all."

"Just as you like, dear," she assented meekly. "Perhaps you're right, especially if we go on to supper afterwards. Here, Janet!"

I hurried out.

"Yes, Madame?"

"Take these off — all of them," she directed, extending her arms and poising her neck. "I am going out and may be late."

I relieved her of the jewels. All the time Mr. Bloor was watching with a gleam in his eyes.

"If you will give me your key, Madame, I will lock them up," I suggested.

I could judge that this was the critical moment for Mr. Bloor. He had gambled correctly, however, upon Mrs. Trumperton-Smith's general indolence.

"Oh, that will do when I get back," she said. "Put them in one of the drawers, Janet."

They went off together. I did exactly as I had been bidden, and afterwards lingered in the sitting room whilst I completed my plans. I had just come to a decision when there was a sharp knock at the door. The manager of the hotel — a Mr. Léon Grant — made his appearance. He looked around the empty sitting room.

"I understood that Mrs. Trumperton-Smith was up here," he said courteously.

"Mrs. Trumperton-Smith went out some little time

ago," I told him. " I think she has gone into the Royal Hotel to play bridge."

He seemed disappointed. He was a thin, rather nervous-looking person, with a very agreeable face and manner, but with lines about his eyes and a general air of over-anxiety. It was rumoured that the hotel was not doing quite so well as some of its rivals, a state of affairs which he felt keenly.

" What time do you expect your mistress back? " he enquired.

" She did not say, sir," I replied. " The last time she went out to play bridge, it was about one o'clock when she returned. Mr. Bloor is with her."

The manager nodded and turned away.

" Can I give her any message, sir? " I added.

He hesitated, closed the door and came back again.

" I should imagine," he said, looking at me attentively, " that you are a trusted servant."

" I was engaged as companion-lady's maid, sir," I told him. " I believe that my mistress has every confidence in me."

He nodded.

" To tell you the truth," he explained, " I am a little worried about your mistress's jewels. There was a small robbery last night at an hotel in the neighbourhood, and I have had an indirect sort of warning from the police that there are thieves about. Mrs. Trumperton-Smith has the reputation of being very careless. I came to ask her if she would allow me to keep her jewels in the hotel safe."

" I should be very glad if you could persuade her to

do so, sir," I assured him. "I suggested it when we arrived, but Madame likes to take them out and look at them when she is alone."

"It is scarcely fair upon any hotel," the manager pointed out, a little querulously. "Will you be so kind as to tell me where she keeps them?"

I showed him the case, although I said nothing of the diamonds in the drawer. He frowned severely.

"It is placing temptation in people's way," he declared.

"The door of the bedroom is always locked," I reminded him, "and you have a night watchman. Then, too, we are on the fourth storey ——"

"My dear young woman," he interrupted irritably, "those things are nothing to an experienced thief. The hotel safe is the only place for such jewellery as Mrs. Trumperton-Smith possesses. I shall wait upon her to-morrow morning and tell her so."

He said good night pleasantly and left me. I went back to my room, undressed, and donned a complete suit of Mr. Bloor's evening clothes, and theatre hat, which I had taken the liberty of borrowing from his room. At the time when I knew that the night watchman's back was turned, I slipped out, descended a few of the stairs which were exactly opposite my door, ascended them again noisily, walked along the corridor, entered Mr. Bloor's room, waited there a moment or two, came out again, and entered the sitting room of our suite. In ten minutes I was back in my bedroom with the diamonds. In an hour's time, Mr. Bloor's clothes were back in his room and the diamonds safely disposed of.

NORMAN GREYES

It was really, in the first place, not owing to any request from my friend Rimmington that I became interested in the Brighton robbery and murder case. Philip Harris, who was a director of the hotel company, wrote me a personal letter, asking me to represent the interests of the hotel in any way I thought fit, and it was on the strength of this appeal that I travelled down to Brighton and took up my temporary residence at the Magnificent Hotel. Within a few minutes of my arrival, the manager himself waited upon me. As was only natural, he was in a state of great distress. Almost before we had shaken hands, he had commenced to unburden himself.

"Forty different people," he told me distractedly, "have given notice to leave the hotel within the next few days. Several have gone already, right in the middle of the season."

I probably seemed a little unsympathetic.

"It was another tragedy I came down to investigate, Mr. Grant," I reminded him.

I think that he perceived the justice of my rebuke, for he apologised at once.

"I am sorry, Sir Norman," he said, "but there are times when one can't help being selfish. Mr. Johnson, the chief of the local police, is here waiting to see you.

Is there anything I can tell you first? You will visit the suite in which the affair happened, of course? "

" Presently," I answered. " Apart from the obvious evidence, have you any personal impressions you would like to confide? "

Mr. Léon Grant hesitated.

" There is just one small matter, Sir Norman," he said, " which worries me a little. Mr. Sidney Bloor is all the time practically under arrest. He has left the hotel and is staying in lodgings on the front, but he is watched night and day."

" There seems to be a moderately clear case against him," I remarked.

" In many respects it would appear convincing," the manager asented. " His antecedents are bad, his attentions to a woman nearly twenty years his senior are difficult to explain on any other basis except that of self-advantage. He escorted her round to the Royal Hotel to play bridge, cut out during the evening, came back to this hotel, and was seen by the fireman, who acts as night watchman, to enter Mrs. Trumperton-Smith's suite. The presumption is, of course, that he stole the jewels then, left the hotel with them in his pocket, and passed them on to a confederate. Mrs. Trumperton-Smith and he returned together early in the morning, between one and two, and he escorted her to her suite. His story is that he stayed there for about five minutes and had a whisky and soda in the sitting room, parted with her on friendly terms and subsequently went to his room, to be awakened at nine o'clock and told by the floor valet that Mrs. Trumperton-Smith had been murdered in the night and her jewellery stolen."

"And what is your comment upon his story?" I enquired.

"Just this," was the earnest reply. "There is no doubt whatever that the young man did return to the hotel alone, but whereas the night watchman swears that he saw him enter Mrs. Trumperton-Smith's suite at half-past ten, the hall porter downstairs, two of the pages and a reception clerk are equally positive that it was exactly midnight when he came in and went upstairs."

"Could he have paid two visits?" I suggested.

"It is exceedingly unlikely, Sir Norman. If he had come in at the time that the night watchman swore that he saw him go into Mrs. Trumperton-Smith's suite, he must have been noticed downstairs."

"This divergence of evidence," I observed, "is interesting, but I scarcely see what it leads to. Perhaps I had better talk to Mr. Johnson for a little time."

The Chief Constable himself paid me the honour of a visit, accompanied by Johnson, who was an exceedingly painstaking and capable officer. They had very little fresh information to give me, excepting certain technical details which certainly told against the young man Bloor.

"You say that none of the jewellery has been recovered?" I enquired.

"None of the jewellery in question, I fear," Johnson admitted. "Mr. Bloor has two very handsome pins in his possession, but he was clever enough to admit at once that these were given him by the deceased."

" Is he short of money? "

" Apparently," was the somewhat dry reply.

" You haven't been able to collect any evidence as to his having spoken to any one outside, on his way back to the Royal? "

" Not at present, I am sorry to say, sir. We are working on that now."

" What about this discrepancy in the alleged time of his visit? "

" That is another of the things we are trying to straighten out. Anyway, the night watchman, who is a very respectable fellow, is prepared to swear that he saw Sidney Bloor reënter the suite, even though his idea of the time seems to be out. Assuming that the theft took place then, though, the motive for the murder becomes obscure."

" And Mr. Bloor's own story? "

" He came a terrible cropper, sir," Johnson declared, a little triumphantly. " He at first stated that he only left the bridge table, when he cut out, to get some fresh air ; that he leaned over the wall of the promenade, looking at the sea, the whole of the time. Afterwards he admitted that he had visited the hotel and gone up for a moment to Mrs. Trumperton-Smith's suite, where he thought he had dropped his cigar case."

" Did he mention any time? " I asked.

" He thought it was about midnight."

" The inquest," I remarked, " has been adjourned."

" Till Thursday week, Sir Norman," the Chief

Constable told me. " The evidence given at the inquest
is at your disposal at any time."

"I have already studied it, thanks," I said. "I
should like, if possible, to have a few words with the
night porter and with the deceased's maid."

The former, whose name was John O'Hara, proved
to be a very respectable, stolid and obstinate man.
Nothing could shake his conviction that he had seen
Sidney Bloor enter Mrs. Trumperton-Smith's suite at
about half-past ten and emerge from it five minutes
later. He admitted that the corridor was badly lit, but
he would not hear a word against his watch. I dismissed
him with the conviction that, so far as he knew it, he
was speaking the truth. Then I sent for the maid.
There was a brief delay, followed by the sound of soft
footsteps outside and the opening and shutting of a
door. I glanced up from the copy of O'Hara's evidence
which I had been studying, and I received, I think, the
greatest shock of my life. With her back pressed to
the closed door, her fingers clinging to the handle, stood
the woman whom I had known as Janet Stanfield!

Neither of us spoke for several moments. Her lips
were parted, but if she gave vent to any exclamation it
was inaudible. Her eyes were fixed upon my face in a
stare of amazement. I could see the rapid rise and fall
of her bosom. It was obvious that no one had mentioned my name — that she had come to me as a
stranger — that her surprise at this meeting was as
great as mine. I rose to my feet, and then, at the
moment of attempted speech, a new horror seemed to
flow in upon my senses. She had been the maid of the

murdered woman! It was, in any case, an ominous coincidence!

Janet came slowly over towards me.

" I did not know that you were here," she said.

" Nor I that you had reëntered domestic service," I replied.

She flinched a little but she answered me quite quietly.

" Poverty is a hard mistress. When you met me in Bond Street some months ago, and I lunched with you, I was engaged at a dressmaker's establishment. Then my husband sent for me to go to Paris. You know very well what happened to us there. I returned to London worse off than when I had left it. I lost my situation. Then I became a manicurist. I stood that for about three weeks. I had nine shillings in my purse when I saw Mrs. Trumperton-Smith's advertisement. I answered it and came here."

" You are better off now? " I ventured.

She was beginning to recover her self-possession.

" Hadn't you better warn me that anything I say may be used as evidence against me? " she asked mockingly.

" I agree. Yet I shall ask you one question, and one only."

" I do not promise to answer it."

" But you will answer it," I insisted, watching her steadily, " and you will tell me the truth. Had you anything to do with Mrs. Trumperton-Smith's death? "

" I had not," she replied unfalteringly.

I sat down with some abruptness. Psychologically

it was impossible for me to explain the feeling of relief which seemed to be lightening my whole being.

" You were not even an accomplice? "

" One question you promised to ask, and one I to answer," she said. " I have finished."

I was thoughtful for a moment. I was thinking of the doctor's evidence at the inquest. The coroner had asked him whether the injuries on the throat of the deceased could have been inflicted by a woman. The reply was there on the depositions before me: " I should think it very unlikely."

" Very well," I said, " I will waive my second question. Instead I will make an appeal to you. I am here to try and discover the person who robbed and murdered your late mistress. Can you help me? "

" If I could, why should I? " she demanded. " We are in opposite camps."

" There will certainly be a reward for the recovery of the jewels."

" I should very much like to earn it," she admitted. " I do not know who stole them."

" Have you any idea," I asked her, " why Mrs. Trumperton-Smith left the hotel for her bridge party that night without any jewellery at all? "

She considered for a moment.

" Mr. Bloor suggested that she should take off her diamonds and leave them at home," she answered.

" And did she? "

" Yes ! "

" You know that Mr. Bloor came back to the suite? "

" I have been told so."

" And you know that the evidence is very conflicting as to what time he paid his visit? "

" Yes, I know that. Why shouldn't he have paid two? "

" It is an idea," I admitted. " Do you think that Sidney Bloor is the man we want? "

" Why should you imagine that I would help you if I could? " she asked coldly.

" From the little I have heard of Mr. Sidney Bloor, I should have looked upon him as a nincompoop," I continued.

" I should not have thought," she agreed, " that he would have had courage enough to wring the neck of a chicken."

I regarded her fixedly.

" Why don't you try to earn the reward? " I asked.

" I am thinking about it," she replied. " If I have any luck, I'll come to you."

She left me then and I went for a stroll along the front. Seated in one of the shelters, a little way towards Hove, was a young man whom I felt sure, from his description, was Sidney Bloor. I looked around and found that one of Rimmington's men was seated on the other side of the shelter. I touched the young man on the arm, and his violent start assured me that I had not made a mistake.

" I believe that you are Mr. Sidney Bloor," I said. " Can I have a few words with you? "

" If you're a journalist," he began surlily ——

" I can assure you that I am not," I replied. " My

name is Norman Greyes. I was once a detective, but at present I do not hold any official position. It is more likely to be to your advantage than not, to spare me a few minutes."

He rose doubtfully to his feet.

"We can't talk here," he objected.

"Let us take a stroll along the sands," I suggested. "We shall be sufficiently alone there."

We walked side by side over the pebbles to the edge of the sea and turned towards Hove. My companion was obviously in a state of nerves. He walked unsteadily. He was out of breath before we had gone fifty yards.

"I have no official connection with this case, Mr. Bloor," I began, "but the hotel company have asked me to make a few enquiries. If you are guilty, the police will probably bring the crime home to you. If you are not —— "

"I am not!" he interrupted passionately.

"If you are not," I repeated, "I am here for your assistance. Remember I am here to discover the truth, not to try and fix the guilt on any particular person. Why don't you tell me the truth?"

He was silent for several moments, probably, I decided, piecing together the story he had made up his mind to tell. He went further, however, than I had expected.

"I have never laid violent hands upon a woman in my life," he declared. "I never would. All the same, I did mean to rob her. I meant to steal her diamonds."

"Why didn't you?"

" They were stolen before I could get at them. I
made her take them off before we went out to bridge.
They were left in a drawer, not even locked up. The
first time I cut out of the rubber, I came back to the
hotel. I went up to her room and searched the
drawer where the jewels had been put. They had gone.
I concluded that some one had either been before me,
or that Mrs. Trumperton-Smith's maid had put them
in a safer place. I went back to the bridge party, came
home with Mrs. Trumperton-Smith about two o'clock,
said good night to her in her sitting room, had a whisky
and soda and went to bed. That's all I know about it,
so help me God! "

We turned around and retraced our steps.

" When you couldn't find the diamonds, why didn't
you take the jewel case? " I asked.

" I should have been seen carrying it," he replied,
" and I had no tools with which to open it. I am not a
professional thief. That night I almost wished I had
been."

" You are aware that the evidence looks rather black
against you? " I pointed out.

" I can't help it," he answered sullenly. " I didn't
do it."

" Have you any theory as to who did? "

" The maid, I should think," he replied. " She was
much too superior for her job — a secretive, unsociable
sort of person. She wasn't there for nothing."

We reached the steps leading to the promenade.

" I am sorry that you made that last suggestion," I
said. " Otherwise, you have done yourself no harm by

your frankness. Your story may possibly be true. If it is, you have nothing to worry about."

I left him on the promenade and saw him stroll across the road to a chemist's shop for a pick-me-up. I went back to the hotel and discovered that my friend Inspector Rimmington from Scotland Yard had already arrived and had taken over formal corduct of the case. He had already had some conversation with the manager, and had interviewed Janet and the night watchman. He was now waiting for Sidney Bloor, whose very unenviable *dossier* he had brought down with him. I glanced it through without any particular interest. Rimmington watched me curiously.

"The young man is a thoroughly bad lot," he observed.

I nodded.

"There's only one thing in his favour. When you talk to him, you will realise that he is absolutely a decadent, a young man without nerve or any manlike quality. Now I don't know whether it has ever occurred to you, Rimmington, but I should imagine that it would take a person with great strength of nerve to hold a woman by the throat and watch her die. Somehow, I don't believe Bloor could have done that."

Rimmington was singularly unconvinced.

"I shall know better when I have talked to him, perhaps," he remarked.

"Don't encourage these local fellows to make an arrest until to-morrow," I advised.

I took the midday train to town, and travelled in the Pullman with Mr. Léon Grant, the manager of the

hotel, who was on his way up to confer once more with
the directors. It was obvious that he had taken the
tragedy very much to heart. He showed me a cable
from Mrs. Trumperton-Smith's son, who was on his
way back from Egypt. It ran as follows:

Greatly shocked. Arrive 17th. Hope police will
discover criminal. Believe jewels principal part
mother's estate. Offer reward immediately for return
any one not connected crime.

" I am suggesting a tenth part of the insured value,"
he announced. " I shall see the solicitors before I
return."

As we drew into Victoria, I offered my companion a
lift. He refused, however, on the ground that he had
a case of wine in the van, which he was taking back to a
wine merchant. I made a few calls, dined at my club,
and travelled back again to Brighton by the late train.
I met Rimmington in the hall of the hotel and we
strolled into the manager's office. Mr. Léon Grant,
looking more tired than ever after his long day in town,
was speaking passionately down the telephone.

" It is absurd," he declared, as we came in. " I spoke
from the number I am asking for, several times this
afternoon. The telephone is in perfect order."

" If you are speaking of Mayfair 1532, Mr. Grant,"
I intervened, " I am afraid the supervisor is correct.
The number is disconnected."

His face, as he looked at us, grew horrible. The
receiver slipped from his fingers and fell to the ground,
dragging the instrument after it.

" What do you mean? " he gasped.

"Simply that Scotland Yard disconnected your flat in town, for fear you should ring up and find out that the case of wine you brought up to London has been opened," I explained. "Rimmington, this is your job."

Rimmington was quick, but not quick enough. Grant's right hand was in the drawer by his side in a moment, and the silver-plated little revolver at his temple. I believe that he was a dead man before the inspector laid hands on him. I held the door whilst Rimmington telephoned for a doctor. He arrived almost at once and his examination lasted barely a few seconds.

"A clean job," he pronounced. "The man must have died immediately."

Rimmington came to my sitting room, later on, and helped himself to a whisky and soda.

"A little secretive this morning, weren't you, Sir Norman?" he observed.

"We wanted the jewels," I pointed out. "Directly the man told me he had a case of wine in the van, I knew that everything was all right."

"When did you get his *dossier?*"

"By the second post this morning," I replied, "and a pretty bad one it was. He has a flat in town under another name; he owes one bookie alone over two thousand pounds; and his domestic arrangements were, to say the least of it, irregular. He was desperately in need of money."

"Even now the reconstruction isn't absolutely simple," my companion mused. "Léon Grant evidently

made his way to Mrs. Trumperton-Smith's rooms after
her return; she woke up whilst he was making off with
the jewel box, and he strangled her. But what about
the two visits from Bloor, earlier in the evening, and
the missing diamonds? I think you said that they
were not in the jewel case which you have recovered?"

"I imagine that the night watchman must have made
a mistake," I told him. "On the other hand, Bloor
may have already disposed of the diamonds. Again,
they may have been mislaid and will be brought in for
the reward."

"What first of all made you think of Grant?" Rimmington asked, a little later, as he was preparing to
take his leave.

"A very slight thing," I answered. "The woman
was strangled, as you know, although the fingermarks
were undistinguishable. There was a scratch upon her
throat, and a few drops of blood, evidently caused by
the finger nail of the murderer. Now Sidney Bloor's
finger nails are bitten almost to the quick. The manager's, on the other hand, were really noticeable. They
were long and brought to a point. The nail on his
right forefinger, however, was broken off short."

"I see," Rimmington replied. "Good night!"

I sat up for some little time, waiting for what I felt
sure was inevitable. It was nearly one o'clock when
there was a soft knock at the door and, in reply to my
invitation, Janet entered. She was still fully dressed,
her manner was as composed as ever. She closed the
door behind her and came over towards me.

"I have found the diamonds," she announced.

" I congratulate you," I replied.

" I have heard all that has happened," she continued. " There will be no trouble about the reward? "

" None whatever," I assured her.

She laid them upon the table — the necklace, the bracelet and the earrings.

" Where did you find them? " I asked.

" In the small silk bag which Mrs. Trumperton-Smith took with her to the bridge party," she replied. " She came back to her room for a moment just before starting, and must have taken them without saying anything to anybody."

" A most ingenious supposition," I murmured.

She looked at me for a moment with the strangest light in her eyes. She had no need of speech. I knew perfectly well of what she was reminding me. I opened the door for her.

" Good night, Janet," I said. " I have stood in the way of your fortunes more than once. This time I am able to remind myself that Mrs. Trumperton-Smith is not my client. The reward will certainly be paid."

CHAPTER VI

THE WINDS OF DEATH

NORMAN GREYES

I know nothing of psychology, or any of the mental or nervous phenomena connected with the study of this abstruse subject. What happened to me during the autumn following my visit to Paris remains in my mind unexplained and inexplicable. I shall just set it down because it becomes a part of the story.

A strong man, in the possession of vigorous health, living an out-of-door life in a quiet country neighbourhood, I suddenly became afraid. I had the strongest conviction that some terrible disaster was hanging over me. Every morning, when I took up my gun for a tramp or stepped into my car for any sort of an excursion, I felt a chill presentiment of evil. It was not that I lost my nerve. I was still shooting and playing golf as well or better than ever. I drove my car and went about the daily pursuits of life with an even pulse. My fears were unanalysable, and it really seemed as though they reached me through the brain rather than the nerves. I felt evil around me and I looked always for an enemy. I woke often in the night and I listened for footsteps, unafraid yet expecting danger, I altered my will and sent it to the lawyer's.

Several matters connected with the letting of my farms I cleared up almost hastily with my agent. I was conscious of only one enemy in the world, and it was practically impossible that he should be in England. Yet I expected death.

I was living at the time at Greyes Manor, the small but very pleasant country house which had come to me with my inheritance. My establishment was moderate, even for a bachelor. There was my housekeeper, Mrs. Foulds, who had been in the service of my uncle, an elderly lady of sixty-four, who had lived at Greyes all her life, was related to half the farmers in the neighbourhood, and was a pleasant, high-principled and altogether estimable person. Adams, her nephew, was my butler and personal servant. There was a boy under him, also of the district, a cook and three maid servants whom I seldom saw. The only other member of my household was Miss Simpson, a secretary engaged for me through a well-known office in London, to whom I dictated, for several hours a day, material for the work on Crime which I had made up my mind to write directly I had relinquished my post at Scotland Yard. She was a woman of about fifty years of age, small, with grey hair parted neatly in the middle, the only sister of a clergyman in Cambridgeshire, an agreeable and unobtrusive person, whom I invited to dine downstairs once a week, but whom I otherwise never saw except when engaged upon our work, or in the distance, taking her daily bicycle ride in the park or the lanes around. Out of doors there was Benjamin Adams, my gamekeeper, the brother of my butler; and

Searle, my chauffeur, who came to me from a place in
Devonshire with excellent references, a simple-minded
and almost over-ingenuous youth. These comprised
the little coterie of persons with whom I was brought
into contact, day by day. Not one of them could
possibly have borne me any ill will, yet I lived amongst
them, waiting for death.

One morning — I remember that it was the first of
November — I set out for a long tramp, accompanied
only by Adams, the keeper, and a couple of dogs. We
were on the boundary of my land, looking for stray
pheasants in a large root field. On my right was a
precipitous gorge which extended for about half a
mile, thickly planted with small fir trees. I was walking, by arrangement, about twenty yards ahead of
Adams, when I was suddenly conscious of a familiar
sensation. There was the zip of a bullet singing
through the air, a report from somewhere in the gorge,
a neat round hole through my felt hat.

" Gawd A'mighty ! " yelled Adams, leaping into the
air. " What be doing? "

I showed him my hat. He stood with his mouth open,
looking at it. There was no further sound from the
gorge except the tumbling of the stream down at the
bottom. It was an absolutely hopeless place to search.

" We'll be getting home, Adams," I said.

" There be some rascal about, for sure," the man
gasped, gazing fearfully towards the gorge.

" As he can see us," I pointed out, " and we certainly
shall never be able to see him, I think we'll make for the
road."

Adams complained sometimes of his rheumatism when I walked him too fast, but on this occasion he was a hundred yards ahead of me when we reached the lane. On our homeward way he was voluble.

" There be James Adams, my nephew," he said, " and William Crocombe, who do farm them lands. They be harmless folk, if ever such were. Some lad, I reckon, have got hold of the roof-scaring rifle."

" Do either of them take in tourists? " I asked.

Adams was doubtful. That afternoon I motored over to make enquiries. Neither of the farmers accepted tourists, neither of them had seen a stranger about the place, and as regards rifles, the only one I could discover had obviously not been discharged for a year. I drove on to the County police station and left a message for the inspector. He came over to see me that evening, solemn, ponderous and unimpressed.

" I suspect some farmer's lad were out after rabbits, sir," was his decision.

I showed him my hat.

" Farmers' lads," I pointed out, " don't as a rule shoot rabbits with a rifle which carries a bullet that size."

He scratched his head. The matter was certainly puzzling, but apparently without absorbing interest to him.

" Them lads be powerful mischievous," he remarked, wagging his head.

I dismissed him after the usual refreshments had been proffered and accepted. A few further enquiries which I myself made in the neighbourhood led to nothing. I took my little two-seater out to call on a friend, a few afternoons afterwards, and found the steering gear come to pieces before I had gone a mile. I was thrown into a ditch but escaped without serious injury. I scarcely needed Searle's assurance to convince me that he knew nothing of the matter, but even in its damaged state it was quite obvious that the pins had been wilfully withdrawn from the pillar. The fact that I was a prisoner in the house for several days from an injury to my knee, and worked at unaccustomed hours, was responsible for my accidental discovery of Miss Simpson's diary. I came into the room unexpectedly and found her writing. It never occurred to me but that she was engaged upon my work, so I looked over her shoulder. She was writing in a diary, completing her entry for the day before:

N.G. worked for two hours, practised golf in park, lunched in, took out two-seater in afternoon. Met with accident but was able to walk home. Said little about his injuries, which were not serious. Accepted invitation shoot Woolhanger Manor next Tuesday at eleven o'clock. Probably return across moor at dusk.

Miss Simpson was suddenly conscious of my presence. She placed her hand over the page.

"This is my private diary, Sir Norman," she asserted.

"So I gathered," I replied. "What is your interest in my doings, Miss Simpson?"

"A personal one," she assured me. "I appeal to you as a gentleman to let me have the volume."

I confess that I was weak. An altercation of any sort, however, ending, without doubt, in a struggle for the possession of the diary with this quiet-looking, elderly lady, was peculiarly repugnant to me. I rang the bell.

"I shall order the car to take you to Barnstaple for the five o'clock train, Miss Simpson," I said.

She rose to her feet, grasping the book firmly.

"What is your complaint against me, Sir Norman?" she asked.

"During this last week," I told her, "two attempts have been made upon my life. I am naturally suspicious of people who keep a close account of my personal movements."

She stood for a moment looking at me through her gold-rimmed spectacles in a dazed, incredulous sort of way. Then she turned and left the room. I never saw her again.

That same afternoon, on my return from the village where I had gone to post a letter with my own hands, I found a grey limousine touring car, covered with mud, outside my front door, and Adams announced that a gentleman was waiting to see me in the study. To my surprise and infinite satisfaction, it was Rimmington.

"I have this moment posted a letter to you," I said, as we shook hands.

"Anything doing down here?" he asked quickly.

"Too much for my liking," I answered. "What will you have — tea or a whisky and soda?"

He accepted the tea and ate buttered toast in large quantities.

" I have come straight through from Basingstoke," he explained. " The Chief rather got the wind up about you."

" Tell me all about it," I begged.

" I wish I could," Rimmington replied, as he accepted a cigar and lit it. " You read the papers, I suppose? "

" Regularly."

" You've seen what a hell of a time they've been having round New York? Eleven undiscovered murders in ten days, and several million dollars stolen. The New York police have been working steadily for some time and made their coup last week. They made half a dozen arrests, but the head of the gang escaped."

" A known person? " I asked.

" Personally," was the confident reply, " I don't think there is the slightest doubt but that he is the man who has passed at different times as Thomas Pugsley, James Stanfield, and originally Michael Sayers. He has vanished from the face of the earth, so far as the New York police have ascertained, but they obtained possession of an uncompleted letter which he must have been typing at the time of the raid. The first page he probably destroyed or took with him. The second page refers to you. Here is a copy."

Rimmington withdrew from his pocketbook a half-sheet of paper and passed it to me. I read it slowly, word for word:

Things here have come to their natural end. The last fortnight has been productive, but there is danger in any further prosecution of our energies. There is only one man who stands in the way of my return to London. You know well of whom I speak. I wait day by day for your news of him, and hope to hear of no more blunders. See that the woman you know of, too, is carefully watched. She may be as loyal as she seems, but there are moments when I have had my doubts. If N.G. can be disposed of ——

"Interesting," I remarked, "very! To whom was the letter addressed? "

" To a firm of leather brokers in Bermondsey," Rimmington replied, " and it was written on the note paper of a firm of hide brokers in New York."

" The letter is from our friend, right enough," I decided. " There have been two attempts upon my life within the last two days, and I have just sent away a secretary who was keeping a careful note of my doings."

We talked for an hour or more and arrived without difficulty at a common understanding. Rimmington undertook to send a good man down from Scotland Yard to make enquiries in the neighbourhood, and he promised also to trace my late secretary's antecedents through the office from which she had come. In the meantime, he begged me to return to London with him. The suggestion was not at first altogether attractive to me.

" I don't like being driven away from my own home," I grumbled. " Besides, there will be nothing for me to do in London at this time of the year."

"Greyes," he said earnestly, "listen to me. You can play golf round London and get on with your book. You are far safer there than you would be in an unprotected neighbourhood like this. But apart from that altogether, we want you up there. This wave of crime in New York has ceased. Paris, too, is quieter. The Chief is profoundly impressed with the belief that it is because operations are being transferred to London. That odd sheet of letter which I have shown you confirms the idea. I am perfectly convinced in my own mind that we are going to be up against it hard within the next few weeks."

"When do you want me to come?" I asked.

"Back with me to-night," he answered promptly. "There is a full moon to-night, and my chauffeur knows every inch of the road. We can leave after dinner and breakfast in London."

"Very well," I agreed. "I will order an early dinner and we can start directly afterwards."

I had told Rimmington of all the material things which had happened to me down at Greyes Manor, but I had not spoken of that curious sense of impending evil which had clouded my days, and the prescience of which had been so remarkably verified. We were scarcely crossing the first stretch of Exmoor, however, when the memory of it came back to me, and with the memory an overpowering return of the feeling itself. I filled a pipe, stretched myself out in a corner of the car, and set myself to fight this grim ogre of fear. It was no easy matter, however. All through the night I was haunted with fancies. The gorse bushes on the

moors seemed like crouching men, the whistle from a
distant railway station a warning of impending danger.
In a small town-village before we arrived at Taunton,
a man stood in the open doorway of his house, looking
out at the night. He scanned us as we passed and
turned away. Through the uncurtained window of his
sitting room, I saw a telephone on his table. At
Wiveliscombe, a man with a motor-bicycle stood silent
as we passed. He leaned forward as though to see
the number of our car. In ten minutes he raced past
us, his powerful engine making the night hideous with
its unsilenced explosions. Across Salisbury Plain, as
we drew near Stonehenge, a cruelly cold wind was blowing. We drank from a flask which I had brought and
wrapped' ourselves up a little closer. At some cross-
roads, high up in the bleakest part, another car was
waiting, its lights out, its appearance sinister. We
passed it, however, at fifty miles an hour, and the man
who was its solitary occupant scarcely looked up at us.
We passed through Amesbury, up the long rise to
Andover, through Basingstoke, and settled down into a
steady fifty miles an hour along wonderful roads. The
moon was paling now, and there were signs of dawn;
right ahead of us was a thin streak of silver in the
clouds, slowly changing to a dull purple. Before we
had realised it, we were in the outskirts of London, our
pace gradually reduced, but still racing through the
somber twilight. At Isleworth, just as we had passed
under the railway arch, I felt the brakes suddenly applied and thrust my head out of the window. We had
come almost to a standstill, stopped by a stalwart

policeman who, notebook in hand, had been talking to the occupant of a touring car drawn up by the side of the road. He came up to the open window.

" Are you gentlemen going through to London? " he enquired.

" We are," I told him. " What can we do for you? "

The words had scarcely left my lips when I knew that we were in a trap. I realized it just in time to save my life. I struck with all my force at the ugly little black revolver which was thrust almost into my face. There was a report, a sharp pain at the top of my shoulder, and the revolver itself slipped from the man's crushed fingers. I was within an ace of having him by the throat, but he just eluded me. The touring car was now passing us slowly, and he leaped into it, leaving his helmet lying in the road. A third man, who seemed to rise up from underneath our car, tore along and jumped in behind, and they shot forward, travelling at a most astonishing pace. Rimmington shouted to our chauffeur down the tube, with the idea of pursuing them. We started forward with a series of horrible bumps, and came almost immediately to a standstill. I sprang out. Both our back tyres had been stabbed through with some sharp instrument. In the distance, the other car had rounded the corner and, with screaming siren, was racing away for London.

JANET

It was towards the middle of October when I heard from my husband for the first time for many months.

For a long time my luck had been atrocious. I lost the greater part of the money paid me for the recovery of Mrs. Trumperton-Smith's diamonds by an investment in a small millinery business which I discovered too late to be already moribund. I had lost post after post for the same maddening reason. My looks had suffered through privation, and my shabby clothes were unbecoming enough, but if I had been Helen of Troy herself I could scarcely have evoked more proposals of the sort which must bring to an end ordinary relations between employer and employée. My good resolutions began to weaken. I had almost made up my mind to appeal for help in quarters which would necessarily have meant the end of my more or less honest life, when one morning a young man who looked like a bank clerk was ushered shamelessly by my landlady into my bed-sitting-room. I was folding up a coat which I was going to take to the pawnbroker. I was not in a very pleasant frame of mind, and I was furious with my landlady.

"What do you want?" I asked coldly. "This is not a room in which I can receive visitors."

"My visit is one of business, Madame," he answered. "Are you Mrs. Janet Stanfield?"

"I am generally known by that name," I replied.

He opened his pocketbook and counted out two hundred pounds in bank notes upon the table. After my first exclamation, I watched him, spellbound.

"With the compliments of the bank manager," he said, as he took up his hat and turned away.

" Who sent the notes? " I called out after him.
" What bank is it from? "

" The bank of faith, hope and charity," he answered,
with a smile. " Good morning! "

He was gone before I could get out another word.
I took up the notes greedily. I had done my best to
live without my husband's help ever since certain news
as to his doings in America had reached me. For some
reason which I did not myself altogether understand, I
had, I thought, cut myself off from any association
with him and his friends. Yet, in my present straits,
my attempt at independence seemed hopeless. The
money was a necessity to me.

I paid my landlady and made her a present of my
dilapidated wardrobe. I possessed the art of knowing
how and where to buy things, and before lunchtime that
day I was installed in a small flat in a residential suite
situated in Albemarle Street, wearing clothes which
were in keeping with my surroundings, and with an
evening dress and cloak in reserve. My neck and throat
and fingers were bare, for I had seen nothing of my
jewellery since our ill-omened adventure in Paris. At
five minutes to one, however, even this condition was
amended. A youth from the hall porter's office put a
package into my hand which had just been left by a
messenger. I opened it and found half-a-dozen familiar
morocco cases. A portion of the jewellery which I had
never thought to see again was in my hands. It was
now clear to me that my husband had either already
returned or was on the point of doing so, and that my
help was needed. Nevertheless, three days went by

without a sign or message from anybody, three days during which I lived after the fashion of a cat, curled up in warmth and luxury, clinging to the feel of my clothes, revelling in the perfumes of my bath, eating good food and drinking wine with slow but careful appreciation. I felt the life revive in me, the blood flow once more through my veins. During those three days, nothing in this world would have driven me back to my poverty. I would have committed almost any crime rather than return to it.

On the fourth day I met Norman Greyes. I was leaving a hairdresser's shop in Curzon Street when he swung round the corner of Clarges Street, carrying a bag of golf clubs and evidently looking for a taxicab. I was within a foot or two of him before he recognized me. I was conscious of a keen and peculiar thrill of pleasure as I saw something flash into his stern, unimpressive face. Enemies though we were, he was glad to see me.

" Good morning, Sir Norman," I said, holding out my hand. " Are there no more criminals left in the world that you take holiday? "

He smiled and put his clubs through the open window of a taxicab which had just drawn up by the side of the kerb.

" I am tired of hunting criminals," he confessed. " Besides, they are turning the tables. They are hunting me."

" Indeed? " I answered. " That sounds as though my husband were coming back."

"There are rumours of it," he admitted. "Are you staying near here?"

"I am living at the Albemarle Court," I told him. "Why not have me watched? If he does come back, I am sure I am one of the first people he would want to visit."

"It is a wonderful idea," he agreed, with a peculiar gleam in his keen grey eyes. "I would rather bribe you, though, to give him up."

"How much?" I asked. "He has treated me very badly lately."

"Dine with me to-night," he suggested, "and we will discuss it."

I am convinced that Norman Greyes is my enemy, as he is Michael's, and that I hate him. Nevertheless, he has a power over me to which I shall never yield but which I cannot explain or analyse. At the thought of dining alone with him, I felt a little shiver run through my body. He stood looking down at me, smiling as he waited for my answer.

"I shall be charmed," I assented boldly.

"At my rooms," he suggested, — "Number 13. About eight o'clock?"

"Why not at a restaurant?" I asked.

"Out of consideration for you," he replied promptly. "You are probably more or less watched, and your movements reported to the organisation of which your husband is the Chief. If you are seen dining alone with me in a public place, they may imagine that you have come over to the enemy."

"You are most thoughtful," I replied, with all the

sarcasm in my tone which I could command. "I will come to your rooms then. "

He nodded quite pleasantly, raised his cap and stepped into the taxicab. I watched him for a moment, hating him because he seemed to be the one person who had the power to ruffle me. He was dressed just as I like to see men dressed, in grey tweed, loose but well-fitting. He wore a soft collar, and the tie of a famous cricket club. His tweed cap was set just at the right angle. He moved with the light ease of an athlete. I hated his shrewd, kindly smile, the clearness of his bronzed complexion, the little humorous lines about his eyes. I went straight back to my rooms and wrote him a few impulsive lines. I wrote to say that I would dine with him at any restaurant he liked, but not in Clarges street, and that he could call for me at eight o'clock.

At half-past three that afternoon, I received the invitation which I had been expecting, and at four o'clock 'I stepped out of a taxicab and entered the offices of a firm of solicitors situated in a quiet square near Lincoln's Inn. An office boy rose up from behind a worm-eaten desk and invited me to seat myself on a hard, wooden chair whilst he disappeared in search of Mr. Younghusband, the principal partner in the firm. The office was decorated by rows of musty files, and a line of bills containing particulars of property sales, the solicitor in each case being the firm of Younghusband, Nicholson and Younghusband. After a few minutes' delay, the boy summoned me and held open a door on the other side of the passage.

" Mr. Younghusband will see you, Madame," he announced.

The door was closed behind me and I shook hands
with a tall, elderly man who rose to welcome me in
somewhat abstracted fashion. He was untidily but
professionally dressed. He wore old-fashioned, steel-
rimmed spectacles, reposing at the present moment
on his forehead. The shape of his collar and the fashion of his tie belonged to a bygone generation. There
were rows of tin boxes extending to the ceiling, a library
of law books, and his table was littered with papers.
He reseated himself as soon as I had accepted his
proffered chair, pushed a thick parchment deed on one
side, crossed his legs and looked at me steadily.

" Mrs. — er — Morrison? " he began, using the
name by which I had been known during the last few
months.

" That is more or less my name, " I admitted. " I
received a telephone message asking me to call this
afternoon. "

" Quite so, quite so, " he murmured, a little vaguely.
" Now let me see, " he went on, looking amongst some
papers. " Your husband appears to have been a
client of the firm for many years, but my memory —
or, here we are, " he broke off, drawing a slip of paper
towards him. " My instructions, cabled from New
York, were to hand you the sum of two hundred
pounds. You received that amount, I believe? "

" I received it and have spent the greater part of it, "
I replied.

His expression became a little less benign.

"Dear me, dear me!" he exclaimed. "That sounds rather extravagant."

"I have been without any means of support for many months," I told him.

He scratched his upper lip thoughtfully.

"Your husband has, I gather, been engaged in operations in New York of a delicate nature. The world of finance has always its secrecies. He appears now, however, to have brought his operations to a close. You are aware, perhaps, that he has landed in England?"

My heart gave a little jump. I could not tell whether the sensation I experienced had more in it of joy or of fear.

"Is he safe?" I asked.

"Safe?" Mr. Younghusband repeated, a little vaguely. "Why not?"

There was a moment's silence. I looked around at the shabby but imposing contents of the office, at the lawyer's mildly puzzled expression. I drank in the whole atmosphere of the place, and I was dumb. Mr. Younghusband suddenly smiled, and tapped with his forefinger upon the table. He was like a man who has seen through a faulty phrase in some legal document.

"I apprehend you," he said. "For a moment I was not altogether able to appreciate the significance of your question. New York is a curious place, and I understand — er — that the financial operations in which your husband has been concerned, although profitable, may have made him enemies. He travelled back to England, indeed, under an assumed name. Let me see, I have it somewhere," he went on, fumbling once more amongst a mass of papers. "I had it in my hand only a few minutes ago. Here we are — Mr. Richard Peters. I am instructed to say, Madame, that your husband would welcome a call from you."

"You have his address?"

For the moment Mr. Younghusband looked vague again. Then, with a little smile of triumph, he turned over the slip of paper which he held in his hand.

"His address," he repeated. "Precisely! I have it here — Number 11, Jackson Street."

"Mayfair?" I enquired.

"Mayfair," he assented. "The address reminds me, Madame," he went on, "that you must be prepared to see your husband — not in the best of health. He is, in fact, in a nursing home."

"Is he seriously ill?" I asked.

"I believe not," was the deliberate reply. "You will have an opportunity of judging for yourself within half an hour. I am to ask you to visit him as soon as you can find it convenient."

I sat quite still. I was trying to get these matters into my mind. The lawyer glanced at his watch and immediately struck the bell in front of him.

"You will forgive me, Madame," he said rising to his feet. "I have a meeting of the Law Society to attend. My compliments to your husband. Tell him to let me know if I can be of further service to him."

The boy was holding open the door. Mr. Younghusband, with a courteous, old-fashioned bow, evidently considered the interview at an end. I went back

to my taxicab, a little bewildered, and drove at once
to Jackson Street. A nurse in starched linen frock
and flowing cap consulted a little slate and led me to a
bedroom in one of the upper storeys.

"Mr. Peters is getting on famously, Madame," she
announced encouragingly. "The doctor hopes to be
able to let him out at the end of the week. Please step
in. You can stay as long as you like. Your wife is
here, Mr. Peters," she went on, ushering me through
the doorway.

She closed the door and I advanced towards the
bedside, only to step back with a little exclamation. I
thought that there must be some mistake. The man
who sat up in bed, watching me, seemed at first sight
a stranger. His hair, which had been dark, was now of
a sandy grey, and he wore a short, stubbly moustache
of the same colour. His cheeks had fallen in, his forehead seemed more prominent, there was an unfamiliar
scar on the left side of his face.

"Michael!" I exclaimed incredulously.

"Capital!" he replied. "You see no resemblance
to Mr. James Stanfield?"

"Not the slightest," I assured him. "The whole
thing is wonderful. But what is the matter with you?"

"Nothing," was the impatient rejoinder. "I have
had to starve myself to get thin. I took the place and
the name of a business acquaintance upon the boat. It
was quite a smart piece of work. I am supposed to be
suffering from a nervous breakdown. Bosh! I haven't
a nerve in my body."

"You left me alone for a long time," I reminded him.

"I was fighting for my life," he answered grimly. "You don't know the inner workings of the game, so I can't explain. I was hemmed in. As soon as I broke away, they were never on to me again. I brought off the coup of my life in New York, but — things went wrong, Janet. You know what that means."

I watched his face whilst I listened to him speak. The man was reëstablishing his strange ascendancy over me, but for the first time I felt the thrill of fear as he spoke.

"You killed some one?" I whispered.

"I had no intention of doing anything of the sort," he answered. "It was Hartley, the banker, himself. He forced me into a fight at close quarters. We exchanged shots. I was wounded. So was he. He was in miserable health, though, and he never recovered. The shock killed him as much as anything. I got away all right, but it means all or nothing for the future."

"If you have enough," I suggested, "why not try the other end of the world?"

His thin lips curled scornfully.

"I have thought of everywhere," he answered, "of Indo-China, the South Sea Islands, New Guinea, the far South American States. They are all hopeless. The eyes follow. There is safety only under the shadow of the arm."

"What about our meeting?" I asked. "I am known."

"It is a problem to be solved," he said slowly.

"There is risk in it, yet the thought of parting with you, Janet, is like a clutching hand laid upon my heart. "

It was the first word of the sort he had ever spoken to me, and again for some reason I shivered.

" What is your need of me now? " I demanded.

" To get rid of Norman Greyes, " he replied.

There was a silence during which I felt that he was studying my face, and although I do not believe that a muscle twitched or that my eyes lost their steady light, still I was thankful for the darkened room. We heard the subdued noises of the house, the distant hum of vehicles, every now and then the sharp honk of a motor horn. In the tops of the trees just outside, some birds were twittering.

" I have figured it all out, " he went on. " I am safe here, safe except from that one man. Even as I am now, he would recognise me. The moment I move, and there are big things to be done here, I shall feel him on my trail. It is his life or mine. "

" Why do you think that I can do this? " I asked.

His lips curled once more in the faintest of mirthless smiles.

" Because, although he does not know it, Norman Greyes feels your attraction. He is too strong a man to succumb, but he can never resist dallying with it because it provides him with something new in life. You suggest to him a sensation which he obtains nowhere else. I know men like books, Janet, and I have seen these things. "

" Do you know women, too? " I ventured.

" Sufficiently, " he answered.

" How do you propose that I should do this? " I asked.

He raised himself a little in the bed.

" Norman Greyes, " he said, " is one of those men whom it is hard to kill. A fool walks to his death. Norman Greyes wears the aura of defiance. They have tried during the last few weeks. One of the finest marksmen in England missed him with a rifle at a hundred yards. He is a reckless motorist, yet he drove a car with safety when the steering-wheel collapsed. Nevertheless, if he had stayed in Devonshire we should have had him. They tell me that he is in London. "

" He is within a few yards of the spot, " I announced, " and I am dining with him to-night. "

For a moment his eyes flashed at me like steel caught in the sunlight.

" I met him at the corner of the street this morning," I explained.

" I ask no questions, " was the cold reply. "I shall know if you are ever faithless. A little present for you, Janet. "

He brought his hand from under the pillow and handed me an exquisitely chased gold box, a curio of strange shape and with small enamel figures inlaid. I exclaimed with delight. He touched the spring. It was filled with white powder on the top of which reposed a tiny powder puff.

" Be careful not to let any of the powder get near

your mouth, " he enjoined. " A pinch upon the food or in the glass is sufficient. Take it. "

I dropped it into the silk bag I was carrying. I was trying to tell myself that I had killed a man before.

" That half-ounce cost me one hundred pounds, " he said. " Men scour the world for it. You can handle the powder freely. There is no danger until it gets into the system. "

" And then? "

" It makes a helpless invalid of the strongest for at least two years. "

NORMAN GREYES

I have come to the conclusion that in future I shall do well to avoid Janet Stanfield. As the cold, mechanical assistant of a master of crime, she interested me. I have even devoted a chapter of my forthcoming book to an analysis of her character. I am beginning to realise now, however, that even the hardest and cruellest woman cannot escape from the tendencies of her sex. In all the duels I have previously had with her, she has carried herself with cold and decorous assurance. There has never been a moment when I have seen the light of any real feeling in her eyes. Last night, however, a different woman dined with 'me. She was more beautiful that I had ever imagined her, by reason of the slight flush that came and went in her cheeks. Her eyes seemed to have increased in size and to flash with a softer brilliance. We sat at a corner table against the wall at Soto's where the room was, as usual, filled with beautiful women. There was no one who attracted so much attention as my companion. There was no one who deserved it.

" You think I am looking well? " she asked, in reply to some observation of mine.

" Wonderfully, " I replied. " Also, if I may be allowed to comment upon it, changed. You look as though you had found some new interest in life. "

She laughed a little bitterly.

" Where should I seek it? " she demanded.

" Perhaps the change is internal, " I suggested. " Perhaps your outlook upon life is changing. Perhaps you have made up your mind to put away the false gods. "

" I have travelled too far along one road, " she answered hardly.

It was at this stage in our conversation that I made up my mind that it were better for me to see this woman no more. Our eyes met, and she suddenly was not hard at all. I seemed to look into her soul, and there were things there which I could not understand. I was thankful that the dancing began just then. It helped us over a curious gulf of silence. Janet danced with little knowledge of the steps but with a wonderful sense of rhythm. I was ashamed of the pleasure it gave me to realise, as we moved away to the music, that this woman of steel had a very soft and human body.

Janet was certainly in a strange and nervous state that evening. We danced for some time without resting. Then she suddenly turned back to the table. I had paused for a moment to speak to some acquaintances. When I rejoined her she was pale, and the hand which was holding her little gold powder box was shaking.

"Has anything happened?" I asked her, a little concerned. "Are you not feeling well? Perhaps the dancing —— "

"I loved it," she interrupted. "I am quite well."

Yet she sat there, tense and speechless. I made up my mind to finish my coffee and go. I had raised the cup to my lips, even, when she suddenly swayed across the table, knocking my arm with her elbow. My coffee was spilt and the tablecloth was ruined. Janet began to laugh. For a moment she seemed to have a fit of breathlessness. Then, as she watched the cloth being changed, she became herself again. She had the air of one who had met a crisis and conquered it.

"I am so sorry for my clumsiness," she said penitently. "Let us dance again whilst they rearrange the table."

This time her feet moved less airily to the music. She seemed heavier in my arms.

"Who gave you that beautiful gold powder box?" I enquired, more for the sake of making conversation than from any actual curiosity.

Something of the old light flashed for a moment in her eyes. Her reply struck me as curious.

"Satan," she acknowledged. "I have made up my mind, however, to send it back."

CHAPTER VII

SEVEN BOXES OF GOLD

MICHAEL

I was at St. Pancras Station to meet Gorty and
Metzger on their arrival in England. I saw the seven
black tin boxes with brass clamps handed out of the
guard's van and placed on the roof of a taxicab. I
knew as though it were foredoomed that the contents
of those boxes would be mine before the week was out.
I felt certain, too, that one at least of the two men
would fight to the death before I obtained possession
of them. They were well worth it, however.

It was a foggy night, and I lingered with perfect
safety on the outskirts of the little throng of people
who had come to greet these two men. They were a
rough lot, on the whole — democrats of the lowest type,
swarthy and unclean. I saw hungry glances directed
towards those black boxes, and I knew that, given
sufficient cunning and address, I should not be the first
by a long way to strike a blow for their acquisition.
But of these others I had no fear. Gorty and Metzger
knew their friends, knew them well enough not to trust
them.

I walked back through the fog to my humble little
flat in Adam Street. Those were gloomy days, even

for me who cared little about the physical comforts of life. I was passing as Mr. Arthur Younghusband, L.L.D., a cousin of the well-known solicitor of Lincoln's Inn, in town to consult works of reference at the British Museum. Day by day I walked to that gloomy mausoleum of dead knowledge, spent an hour or so there, and walked back to my rooms. No one dogged my footsteps. By devious ways I had shaken off all pursuit and suspicion. Yet life was a wearisome thing. I am not a man with many human weaknesses, but I should have welcomed a visit from Janet — a little dinner, perhaps, at the Café Royal, a peep into the world of many-coloured pleasures outside of which my path lay. These things, however, I knew were not for me. Janet was watched, as I knew beyond a doubt, and even if she were not, she had failed me in my last demand. Janet presented a problem presently to be solved.

On the third day after the arrival of Gorty and Metzger, I visited my solicitors, Messrs. Younghusband, Nicholson and Younghusband, at Lincoln's Inn. My reputed cousin accorded me an interview within a few minutes of my arrival. We spoke for a time of my studies and their progress. Then there was a pause. The door was closed, the walls of the room were thick.

" Things progress? " I demanded, leaning across his wide, untidy table.

Mr. Younghusband smiled benevolently. In these moments of direct speech I was accustomed to forget my assumed personality and to speak with all the quick incisiveness that was natural to me. My legal adviser,

however, never altered his manner of reply or deportment.   He was always the same — unctious, legal,
courtly.

"Your affairs are in excellent train," he assured me.
"Of the two people in whom we are interested, one
leaves, as we have surmised, for Manchester to-night,
the other remains alone."

"They have made no arrangement with any bank
yet?"

My companion shook his head.

"They are both, under the circumstances, suspicious," he said.   "Their position, of course, is — er —
peculiar.   They are the custodians of a hundred thousand pounds in gold, with which they hope to establish
a few private credits in this country.   On the other
hand, the country to which they belong owes us something like a hundred times that amount.   They have a
somewhat natural fear that any bank with whom they
might deposit their treasure might be disposed to hand
it over to the Government, or that the Government, by
some legal means, might attach it."

"Therefore," I observed, "it remains in their
rooms?"

"Precisely!   They consider it the lesser risk."

"And Gorty goes to Manchester to-night?"

"That is so," the lawyer murmured.

"So far all seems well," I said.   "The great thing
is that the gold has not been removed and that Metzger
will be alone.   There were other little details."

"Just so!" Mr. Younghusband assented, leaning
back in his chair with his finger tips pressed together.

" So far as regards the setting of the affair, I think you will find it in order. Metzger and Gorty occupy suite Number 89 at the Milan Hotel, which suite consists, as you know, of two bedrooms, a bathroom and a sitting room. The sitting room is on the extreme right-hand side of the suite, and the gold is kept in Metzger's bedroom, which opens from the sitting room. The bathroom is between the two bedrooms. "

" I have had the plan, " I interrupted, a little impatiently.

Mr. Younghusband declined to be hurried. He had the air of giving difficult legal advice on a technical point.

" Suite Number 90, " he continued, " consists of a bedroom, bathroom and sitting room only, and is occupied by Mr. and Mrs. José de Miguel, very rich South Americans. They are leaving to-night by motor car for Southampton to catch the steamer there for Buenos Ayres in the morning. "

" Their luggage is already packed? " I asked.

" Already packed, " Mr. Younghusband agreed. " The porters have commented upon its weight. "

" And Madame? "

" Appears to have fulfilled her task, " was the somewhat hesitating answer.

I detected signs of uneasiness in my companion's speech, and I questioned him about it promptly.

" Have you doubts of the woman? " I asked.

" None whatever, " Mr. Younghusband assured me blandly. " At the same time, she is, without a doubt, the weakest link in the chain. She has temperament enough — Metzger seems to have been an easy victim — but I should have had more confidence in the lady who visited me the other day."

"I can no longer put complete faith in my wife," I replied coldly.

Mr. Younghusband was startled out of his dignified serenity of manner. He leaned across the table.

"What do you mean by that?" he demanded harshly. "Do you know that she has been here, the one place in London you should have kept her away from if you had any doubts?"

"I have no doubts whatever as to her fidelity," I declared. "You know what I mean when I say that, in the parlance of our friends, she has gone soft. It is a pity."

Mr. Younghusband seemed relieved but puzzled.

"A woman who could do what she did on the golf links at Woking," he murmured reminiscently, "must have changed very much if she merits your present criticism."

The subject was not a pleasant one to me. I abandoned it.

"In any case," I reminded him, "she is in touch with Greyes and he knows too much."

"Wonderful capacity for existence, that man," Mr. Younghusband remarked suavely.

I am not a lover of harsh deeds. I seldom go out of my way to kill, or allow my subordinates to do so, if my ends can be obtained otherwise. At that moment, however, I felt a sudden resurgence into my brain of that one bloodthirsty desire of my life.

" As soon as this affair is safely concluded, " I said,
" and we are in funds again, I shall deal with Norman
Greyes myself. "

" It occurs to me that you would be well advised, "
my companion acquiesced. " The person in question
possesses the one gift which might make him dangerous
to us. He has imagination. "

I nodded. I was tracing figures upon the blotting
paper, debating with myself different methods of deal-
ing with Norman Greyes.

" Every channel which might lead to the firm of
Younghusband, Nicholson and Younghusband, " the
lawyer continued meditatively, " seems, so far as human ingenuity could arrange it, permanently blocked,
but a man with imagination who is not afraid to work
on guesswork is always to be feared. "

" It will not be my fault, " I promised, as I took my
leave, " if you have any cause to fear Norman Greyes
after the next month or so. "

That night, in the language of those forgotten war
communiqués, everything happened according to plan.
At a quarter to nine, Metzger, who was writing alone in
his sitting room, heard a soft knocking at the door
which communicated with the adjoining suite. He rose
promptly to his feet, locked the outside door of his
own rooms, and softly withdrew the bolt. He stood
there with an inviting smile upon his ugly face.
Madame di Miguel laid a cautioning finger upon her
somewhat overpainted lips, as she stole over the
threshold.

" There is one hour that my husband will be away, "

she whispered, gliding past him. " You may kiss me. "
Metzger bent towards her. I moved noiselessly, but
I think he would not have heard me if I had worn hob-
nailed boots. The rest was easy, for it was a trick I
knew well. He collapsed with scarcely a gasp. I
tightened the cord a little and the deed was done.

NORMAN GREYES

It was entirely by accident that I had dined that
night in the grillroom of the Milan Hotel with Rimmington. He had asked me for an interview that
afternoon over the telephone, and, being disengaged,
I had suggested a little dinner at my club. We had
arrived there to find the place packed and the best
tables full. Sooner than wait, we had strolled down
to the Milan and at a corner table there enjoyed a
comfortable meal. Rimmington was in the act of disclosing his reason for wishing to see me, when the
manager, who was an old acquaintance of mine, stopped
short on his hurried way through the room and came
across to us.

" I wonder whether you would mind coming upstairs
with me for a moment, Sir Norman, " he begged, " and
you too, Mr. Rimmington. I have just been sent for.
Something seems wrong in one of the suites. "

We rose without hesitation and followed him out of
the room, into the lift and up to the sixth floor. When
we stepped out, several of the servants were gathered
together at the further end of the corridor. The manager embarked upon a word or two of explanation.

"There may be nothing wrong at all," he said. "This is just the position as it has been reported to me. Suite Number 89 was taken some days ago by Metzger and Gorty, the two emissaries from our eastern friends. They brought over some gold, as you know, in tin boxes, and, greatly against my advice they had it stored in their rooms. Gorty went to Manchester last night, leaving Metzger alone. Our telephone operator reported that he refused to answer the telephone about half an hour ago. We sent up to his room and found it bolted on the inside. We rang and knocked without the slightest result. Finally we entered the suite through the adjoining room, which had just been vacated, and found that although the outer door was bolted on the inside, the suite was empty. Further, the tin boxes of gold had gone."

"Interesting," Rimmington murmured, "very!"

The manager led us along the corridor, through an empty bedroom which showed signs of recent vacation, into the suite which had been allotted to Messrs. Metzger and Gorty. It had a habitable air, newspapers and magazines lay about, whisky and soda and a bottle of liqueur stood upon the sideboard. There were no signs of any trouble, or disturbance of any sort. We walked through the sitting room, the two bedrooms and the bathroom, and the floor waiter, who had now joined us, showed where the boxes had been stacked.

"Is there any reason to suppose," I asked, "that this man Metzger has not taken away the gold himself?"

"In that case," the manager pointed out, "some one

would have had to carry the cases downstairs. No one has done so. No one has seen Metzger leave the place. "

" We are to presume, then, " I observed, " that he is still in the hotel? "

" Precisely! "

" You have had him searched for? "

" Half a dozen men have searched every corner of the place, from the bars to the private rooms. Furthermore, no one in the hotel has even caught a glimpse of him. "

I went through the rooms again. When I came to the bedroom adjoining the sitting room, and which the floor waiter told me was Metzger's, I noticed that the wardrobe was locked. Not only that but there was a slight strain being exercised against the lock, bending the panel slightly. For the first time I began to look upon the matter as serious.

" This door must be broken open quickly, " I insisted, " or a spare key found. "

The key from the wardrobe in Gorty's room was tried with success. As it was turned, the door flew open. I was just in time to catch in my arms a crumpled mass of clothes and humanity. With a blackened face and protuberant eyes, his tongue lolling out on one side and a little froth at the corners of his mouth, it was still not difficult to recognise from his pictures the man who had refused to answer the telephone.

" My God! " Rimmington exclaimed. " He's dead! "

" He's very near it, " I replied, loosening the slipknot

of whipcord from around his neck. " Send for a doctor
at once, and, Rimmington, you had better ring up the
Yard and get to work quickly. "

Rimmington at that moment justified my confidence
in him. He wasted no time in exclamations or idle
questions. He pointed to the door of the room through
which we had entered.

" How long ago did those people leave? " he asked,
" and what luggage did they take with them? "

" They left an hour ago, " the floor waiter answered.
" They had two very heavy trunks. "

" The affair appears to solve itself, " Rimmington
muttered, after he had spoken a few hasty words down
the telephone.

The floor waiter, who was an intelligent fellow, followed us into the other room, to which we had withdrawn on the arrival of the doctor.

" There is one thing I ought to tell you, sir, " he
said. " The porters tried to move those trunks several
hours ago, while Mr. Metzger was busy writing in his
room. They were too heavy then — and at that time
the tin cases were still in Mr. Gorty's room. "

" You are sure of that? " Rimmington asked.

" Absolutely, sir. "

Rimmington looked around. I could see that the
same thought had occurred to him as to me. The brief-
est of searches confirmed our suspicions. The wardrobe was filled with lumps of heavy stone.

" There is only one point now remaining to be
solved, " I observed, " and that is, did these two, Mr.

and Mrs. José di Miguel, carry out this little affair entirely alone, or had they accomplices? "

" They had a visitor about an hour before they left, sir, " the floor waiter told us.

Rimmington took out his notebook.

" Description, please, " he begged.

" I scarcely saw the gentleman myself, sir, " the man replied. " He seemed quite ordinary-looking. He wore glasses, and his hair was grey. "

" Well, " Rimmington said, as we descended to the ground floor to meet the men whom he had summoned from Scotland Yard, " we get it in the neck sometimes about our failure. This time, if we don't get hold of Di Miguel and his heavy trunks, I should think we deserve all the censure we get. "

" Nothing in it for me, I'm afraid, " I remarked, as I bade him good night.

" It doesn't look like it, " he admitted. " However, one never knows. "

It was the unexpected which happened. Although Mr. José di Miguel and his wife could have had barely an hour's start, and were handicapped by the possession of two trunks of enormous weight, a week passed without any news of their arrest or of the recovery of any part of the gold. Metzger remained in a state of partial unconsciousness and could give no coherent account of what had happened. Gorty returned from Manchester and behaved like a madman. He spent his time between Downing Street, where he boldly accused the Government of having taken the gold, and Scotland Yard, where he expressed his opinion of the

English police system in terms which made him, to say
the least of it, unpopular there. In the beginning the
whole affair had seemed most simple. Mr. and Mrs. di
Miguel, distributing gratuities in most lavish fashion,
had driven calmly away from the Milan at the appointed hour, and had arrived at Waterloo in ample
time for the train which they had planned to take to
Southampton. When that train arrived at Southampton, however, there was no one in it in the least answer-
ing to their description, neither had any rooms been
taken in the hotel, nor passages booked on the steamer.
Curiously enough, too, none of the porters could remember handling any particularly heavy luggage for
that train, or attending upon any passengers answer-
ing to the description of the two missing people, yet
the man who drove the hotel 'bus to the station — an
old servant and a man of excellent character — gave
unfaltering evidence as to his having driven there, and
having left his two passengers waiting on the pavement
while a porter went for a barrow.

I kept away from Rimmington for some time, for I
thoroughly sympathised with his position. On the
tenth day, however, he came to see me.

"Not so simple as we thought," he remarked, as he
accepted a cigar and an easy-chair.

"Apparently not," I assented. "What about the
'bus driver?"

"He's been with the hotel company for seventeen
years," Rimmington replied, "has a wife and children
and an excellent character. Besides, a score of people
saw the 'bus in the station yard."

"And the man who visited them at the hotel at the last moment?"

"We're offering a hundred pounds reward for his discovery. Here's his description."

I read the typewritten sheet which Rimmington pushed across to me and returned it in silence.

"Suggest anything to you?" my visitor asked.

"The description might apply to thousands," I answered, a little evasively.

Rimmington stared gloomily into the fire.

"It might," he admitted. "Do you know who I think it was?"

"No idea," I answered mendaciously.

"Your friend — Pugsley — Stanfield — or to go behind all his aliases and call him by his rightful name — Michael Sayers."

"Do you really believe that that man is in England?" I asked.

"I do," was the confident reply. "He was chased out of the States, we have granted an extradition warrant against him on the charge of manslaughter, we have watched every steamship at every port, yet I don't mind confessing to you that we have reason to believe that he is in London at the present moment and in touch with his old associates."

"If that is so," I declared, "I should imagine that the person who earns your hundred pounds will be able to solve the mystery of the disappearance of Mr. and Mrs. di Miguel."

Notwithstanding Rimmington's conviction, I started on no mad quest of my enemy. Indeed, I had no in-

spiration as to where to commence my search. Janet
had left Albemarle Court and had not replied to the
various notes which I had written her. I had a vague
idea that there was danger in prosecuting enquiries for
her too closely. I had an idea, too, which was by no
means vague, that I was being watched. There was
always a loiterer of some sort or another in the street
when I entered or left my rooms. I felt surreptitious
eyes upon me often, when I lunched or dined or visited
the theatre. Once I walked home late through Lans-
downe Passage, and heard the patter of rubber-shod
feet behind me. I swung around, and my pursuer,
whoever he was, a burly but agile figure, took refuge in
flight. When I regained the entrance to the passage,
he was nowhere to be seen. There were other and similar
incidents. I had gone unarmed through the time of
trouble in Ireland. I carried a revolver with me now,
and I practised getting at it quickly.

It was about three weeks after the attack upon
Metzger and the disappearance of the gold, when I
received a most unexpected visitor. I heard a shrill,
foreign voice in the hall overriding my servant's ob-
jections, and a moment later, a man entered un-
announced and evidently in a state of some excitement.
He was small and of exceeding unprepossessing appearance. His face was pitted with smallpox, he had
wicked-looking teeth, a stubbly black moustache, a
head of black hair as thick and upright-growing as a
porcupine's. He addressed me at once in broken
English.

"You are Sir Norman Greyes?" he said. "I am

Gorty. I came to this country of cutthroats with
Metzger — with him who lies in the hospital. Will you
listen to me? "

I motioned to Adams to leave us and wheeled round
an easy-chair for my visitor.

"Sit down," I invited. "I am glad to see you,
Mr. Gorty, although I think you are a little hard upon
us over here. "

"What am I to think?" he demanded fiercely. "I
come from a great but a poor Government. With much
trouble we get together the gold with which to buy
materials in this country and open credits. It is you
who are supposed to be more civilised than any other
country. I go to Manchester to speak at a meeting.
I come back and what do I find? My comrade brutally
assaulted, my country's gold stolen! Yes, and that in
the heart of your London — in the centre of your
civilisation! What am I to think of you, then, as a
people, I ask? "

"It was a most unusual crime," I told him, "but
you must remember that you were taking grave risks
in having a large amount of gold like that unguarded
in your room. The police, however, are doing —— "

"The police?" he almost shrieked. "Your police?
They are imbeciles — imbeciles or rascals — I know
not which! And as to having the money unguarded,
how could we help it? There are many banks in London who say we owe them money. What would have
happened if I had deposited my gold there? They
would surely have annexed it. And as it is, do you
believe that it is an ordinary thief who has robbed us?

No! I say no! Or if it is a thief, it is one whom your precious police can lay their hands on when they choose, and when they do so, what will happen? The gold will be claimed by your Government. "

" I am afraid, " I said, " that you are taking a very extreme view of things. However, under the circumstances I cannot blame you for feeling ill-used. Tell me what brings you here? "

" Ten years ago, " he went on, suddenly calmer, " I was in the service of the police of my country. There was an anarchist plot. Three criminals escaped to London. You were at Scotland Yard and I came to see you. You found me those criminals. "

" I remember it perfectly, " I answered, " but you have changed your name. "

" It was necessary, " he admitted. " In my country one changes one's name frequently. But you I remembered. Mr. Rimmington spoke of you. I found your address. I am here. "

" Tell me what to do for you? " I begged.

" Find me my gold, " he demanded. " Find me the man who attacked Metzger. "

" If I could do that, " I told him, " I should have done it long ago. I am only too pleased when I can help the police in their duties. "

He drew his easy-chair a little closer to mine. He eyed my box of cigarettes hungrily. I placed it by his side and handed him a match. He smoked furiously.

" Listen, " he confided, " I have a piece of evidence. I will not take it to the police. I do not trust them. You shall find me my gold. "

"What is your piece of evidence?" I asked.

"The little grey man," he answered, "the man whom they spoke of as visiting the South Americans in the next suite. Ah! those South Americans — I never trusted them! I saw Madame make eyes at Metzger. What need had she of Metzger? A woman like that has lovers enough."

"About the little grey man," I ventured.

"They speak of him in the evidence," Gorty went on eagerly. "He was at the suite that night. I saw him with Madame the South American, two days before. I know where he is to be found now."

"Why the devil haven't you told the police?" I exclaimed. "That is the one man they are looking for."

My visitor narrowly escaped a paroxysm. He swept an ornament from the table by his side without noticing it. He gibbered for a moment like a madman.

"But have I not explained?" he expostulated. "I do not trust the police. Six of those solemn constables would march up in uniform to the place I spoke of, and the little grey man would slip away. I tell you. You must find him and see who he is. You must consider how to act. The assault upon Metzger was bad, but it is the gold I want."

"Very well," I said, "tell me where to find him?"

"Go to the reading room at the British Museum between eleven and one o'clock," Gorty told me. "You will find him there, reading. I myself am a student. Twice I have sat at the next table. He is reading from some rare volumes the History of the Rosicrucians."

"Between eleven and one," I repeated.

" You will go? "

" To-morrow morning, " I promised.

Gorty rose up.

" Listen, Greyes, " he said, " you, Sir Norman Greyes. Will you swear that if you recover my gold it comes to me? "

" I swear it, " I answered.

" Then through that man you will find it, " he declared.

Gorty was right. The moment when, from my place of concealment, I saw him come shuffling into the reading room and take his place nearly opposite to me at the great round table, I knew very well that this was Michael. He carried with him two or three books, a volume of reference and a notebook. He had the appearance of the most devout bibliophile, and indeed, having watched him for some time, I came to the conclusion that he was in earnest about his labours. It was in these little ways that Michael achieved real greatness. Detail was a passion with him. He not only appeared to be deeply interested in the Rosicrucian history. He had actually become so.

I was, without doubt, at fault not to have at once passed on my information to Rimmington and to have had my old adversary arrested on one of the many previous counts against him. It seemed to me, however, that this would bring to an end our chances of recovering the gold, and I could not ignore the fact that I was indebted to Gorty for the information which had delivered Michael into my hands. I therefore maintained a strict watch and waited. For three days and three nights I knew Michael's every movement. He made his own breakfast, lunched at a small restaurant near the Museum, and dined each night at the Monico, where he sometimes played dominoes for an hour afterwards, if able to find an opponent. On the fourth night, however, he departed from his usual practices. The young woman whom I had been employing to watch him came to me in haste.

" Our friend, " she announced, "called at the Monico but took only an apéritif there. He walked across to Romano's and has ordered a table and dinner for two. "

" Whereabouts? " I asked quickly.

" Downstairs in the restaurant, on the right-hand side, " she replied.

I rang up Romano's and engaged one of the tables in the balcony. In a quarter of an hour, I was ensconced there behind the curtain, with Miss Rose Weston, the young woman who had brought me the news of Michael's change of plans, as my companion. She had found time to change into evening clothes, and she played her part exceedingly well. We should have passed anywhere as a very ordinary couple, indulging in a somewhat pronounced dinner flirtation. I kept my eye, however, on the table at which Michael was seated below, and in due course I was rewarded. A very elegant, quietly dressed woman came into the restaurant and sank into the chair opposite. I saw at once that it was Janet.

" What you expected? " my companion asked quickly.

" In a sense, " I admitted. "Remember, when they leave, it is the woman you follow. "

I watched them closely from behind the curtain. There was no more distinguished-looking woman in the room than Janet, or more beautiful. She talked in a low tone to her companion, and her manner was often earnest. Nevertheless, she never smiled. She was different in that respect from every one of the diners by whom she was surrounded. There was not a suggestion about her of festivity. She ate moderately, drank sparingly, and talked. All the time she gave one the impression of a great weariness. Towards the end of the meal, what I had been watching for happened. She opened her hand bag and passed something across the table. It was about the size and shape of an ordinary sporting cartridge, but I felt certain, from the way she handled it, that it was heavy. I knew then that we were on the right track.

" You are satisfied? " my companion asked.

" Perfectly, " I assured her. " I am going to run no further risk of being recognised. I shall pay the bill and go. You will remain. Remember, it is the woman you must watch. Engage as much help as you require. She must be watched unceasingly. "

My companion nodded.

" It will not be difficult, " she said.

I took my departure, and at this stage of my search for the missing gold, I took Rimmington into my confidence. He agreed with me as to the advisability of allowing Michael to remain at large for the present, and so far as he was concerned, he satisfied himself

with placing a strict watch upon the house in Adam
Street where we had located him. I myself retired a
little into the background, although I remained in the
closest touch with Miss Weston. Her information
was always interesting, always suggestive. The whole
scheme gradually unwound itself. Rimmington and I
found a certain delight in fitting the pieces together.
He himself brought some valuable information, which
he laid before me a few nights after the dinner at
Romano's.

"One of the out porters at Waterloo," he announced, "seems to remember a small furniture van
backed up against the pavement, some distance away
from where the majority of the taxicabs were un-
loading."

"He didn't notice the name on it, I suppose?" I
asked.

"No such luck! There's another thing, though.
One of the old hands there told another of my fellows
that he noticed several porters about that night whose
faces were quite unfamiliar to him and whom he has
not seen since. The driver of the 'bus from the Savoy
insists upon it, as you remember, that Madame di
Miguel pushed away the first porter who accosted
them, and was determined to employ two of her own
choosing."

"We have got so far, then," I pointed out, re-
capitulating items of information which had been
brought us. "This pseudo South American and his
wife drove up to Waterloo with three heavy cases.
They were met there by confederates dressed in the

uniform of railway porters, who probably took the
boxes into the station and, choosing their opportunity,
brought them out again and got them into the furniture van. The inference is that the gold is still in
London. To proceed. What have we learned about
Janet. She is staying in a boarding house in the
Cromwell Road, frequented by artists. She spends an
hour or two every day at the South Kensington Museum, studying statuary. It is exactly four days since
she brought a little specimen of some sort of work to
Michael, something that, unless I am mistaken, was
of considerable weight, for I noticed that her
hand bag sagged as she walked up the restaurant.
Further, —— "

The telephone bell rang. I recognised Miss Weston's
voice at the other end. I listened to what she had to
say, and in ten minutes we were in my car and on the
way to Twickenham. We picked up Miss Weston herself in Kensington.

" The woman whom I have been following, " she
announced, " is only a few minutes ahead of us. She
is in a private car, and there is a strange man seated
in front with the chauffeur. "

" It looks well, " Rimmington admitted. " Our
friend has ordered the same table for dinner to-night
at Romano's. "

On our way, I had a moment of uneasiness. A grey
touring car passed us at a great speed and shot down
the Brentford Road, considerably ahead of us. Rimmington spoke for a moment through the tube, and we
pulled up at the district police station.

"We've given Michael rope enough," he decided.
"He may get the alarm at any moment now. I'm
going to have him arrested."

I drew a little breath. It was hard to think that I
should not be present at the end for which I had worked
so zealously, but I realised the risk of letting him remain at large any longer. I waited while Rimmington
entered the police station and spoke to headquarters.
When he returned, he brought with him a couple of
plain-clothes men, one of whom sat in the front and
the other with us.

"There will probably be half a dozen of them,"
"Rimmington pointed out, "and from what I know of
the gang that Michael generally employs, there may be
a little trouble. We'll leave Miss Weston in the car."

We turned off the main road at Twickenham, and
finally stopped before the gates of a large, old-fashioned villa, badly out of repair and apparently empty.
The grounds sloped down to the river and the gates
were padlocked. We climbed over, leaving Miss Weston
behind. She detained us for one moment.

"The house is called 'The Sanctuary,'" she said.
"Goodson, the sculptor in bronze, lived here once."

We hurried off. The place showed every sign of
desertion, but there were marks of recent wheels upon
the avenues, and as we turned the last corner we saw
a thin cloud of smoke curling upwards from a long
range of outbuildings which looked like a sort of annex
to the kitchen. Rimmington quickened his pace. We
all broke into a run. We avoided the front door, with
its flight of stone steps, and went straight for the

building which we now perceived to have been the studio.
The door of a long outhouse stood open. We paused
to look inside. There was a furniture van there, and
inside some clothing of rusty velveteen or corduroy.
The porters' uniforms were accounted for. Entrance
to the studio itself was gained by means of a stout
oak door, obviously barred and bolted. We went round
to the back, crossing a lawn where the grass and weeds
were up to our knees. We failed to discover any other
door, but somehow or other we found our way through a
smashed window into the great room with its dome-
shaped ceiling. I think, even as we entered, we realised
that we were too late. The place was empty. A small
forge was burning; there were several strange-looking
vessels lying about the floor, the coffers, covered only
by a piece of matting which Rimmington kicked aside,
were ranged against the wall. There was not a sound
to be heard, but the place smelt of tobacco smoke, and
indeed there was a faint cloud of blue smoke still hanging about the roof.

"We've lost them!" Rimmington muttered.

I thought of Gorty as I thrust by hand down
amongst the gold pieces.

"We have the gold, though," I reminded him.

"And Michael, I trust," was the fervent rejoinder.

We searched the house, which was empty and deso-
late. Then we sent to the local police station and arranged for the gold to be removed. Afterwards, we
called on the house agent. He made a little grimace
when we mentioned The Sanctuary.

"Thought I'd let it to a lady sculptor," he declared.

" She paid for the house for a month, to see whether she could work there — wanted to do her own casting or something. "

" She paid you for the month, I hope? " Rimmington enquired.

" Oh, she paid that all right, " the agent replied. " I wish these old places were all pulled down. They're more trouble than they're worth. "

" Did the lady bring you any references? " I asked.

" I didn't ask for any, " the house agent replied frankly. " I was only too glad to get any one even to talk about the property. Besides, she put the money down. "

" Nevertheless, " Rimmington said quietly, " as a person who has had some experience in these matters — I am Inspector Rimmington of Scotland Yard — I should advise you to be a little careful how you deal with these large, old-fashioned houses. In the present case, you may be interested to know that the little forge in the studio at The Sanctuary has been used for the purpose of melting down Russian gold. "

" God help us! " the agent cried. " What, the Gorty and Metzger gold? "

" Precisely, " Rimmington acquiesced. " They've only got rid of a little of it, as it happens, but, to judge from the preparations, they were going more extensively into it in a day or two. "

We drove back to London, and I followed my friend into his private room with a rare thrill of excitement. I saw his face grow white and stern as he listened to the report of the man who rose to meet him. Then he turned to me.

" The rooms in Adam Street are empty, " he said. " Stanfield has not visited the British Museum to-day. We've lost him again! I ought to have known better, " he added bitterly, " than to have let him remain at liberty for a single moment. "

" And the woman? " I asked, a little nervously.

Rimmington shook his head.

" We don't want her, " he said. " She's just the decoy who may some day whistle her mate to his cell. It's a knock for us, Greyes. Neither Di Miguel nor his wife nor Michael Sayers! "

" But we have the gold, " I reminded him once more.

" Damn the gold! " Rimmington retorted profanely.

But Gorty thought otherwise. So, when he recovered consciousness, did Metzger.

CHAPTER VIII

THE UNFAMILIAR TRIANGLE

JANET

This, as near as I can remember, is a copy of the letter I received that wonderful third day of March:

137 *Golden Square,*
London, W.C.

Dear Madam,
We beg to inform you that, under the will of the late William Soale, gardener, of Mayford, Surrey, you are entitled to a legacy of £250, free of duty.

As the estate is so small, and the assets are chiefly in War Loan, we are in a position to pay you that sum at once, if you will favour us with a call, or your instructions.

Faithfully,
Haskell & Hames.

No one could possibly realise what that money meant for me. I had been working for months at a small dressmaker's in Kensington, earning barely enough to keep myself, slinking to work in the morning and slinking home at night, terrified alike of Michael, the man whom I had once loved, and of Norman Greyes, the man who, without the slightest effort on his part, had attained such a strange and com-

manding influence over my thoughts and life. And
now for a time, at least, I was free. With two hundred
and fifty pounds, I could escape from London and hide.
None of the obvious places appealed to me in any way.
After a great deal of consideration, I took a first-
class passage to Marseilles, in the name of Janet
Soale, on the slowest P. & O. boat I could find.

I spent a moderate sum in replenishing my wardrobe,
sewed a hundred-pound note into my bodice, and started
on my adventure. The first few days were wonderful.
I found all that I craved for in my new surroundings —
freedom from the sordid necessities of daily work, and
an indescribable sense of exhilaration, born of the huge
spaces, the roaring wind and the sting of the spray.
As soon as the sun began to shine through the grey
clouds of the English Channel, I felt something stirring
in my heart — a sort of passionate content which crept
through my whole being as the skies grew clearer
through the Bay of Biscay and the sun went down in
a clear glory of amber and gold. There was so much
that was beautiful in life of which I knew nothing —
and I was so anxious to learn.

I had made no effort to secure any special place in
the dining saloon. Consequently, the seat apportioned
to me was in a somewhat remote corner, and my companions of that negative type who seem born to promenade the decks of steamers, point out perfectly obvious
porpoises and passing ships to their fellow passengers,
and apparently disappear at the end of the voyage
from the face of the earth. It was what suited me best.
Day by day I breathed in an atmosphere of repose.

Then the natural thing happened. My interest in life began to revive. I was young and strong. The sunshine, the salt air, the complete change did their work. I made some slight change in my toilette one night and arranged my hair differently. Half a dozen people made an excuse to come and talk to me that night on deck. I had as many offers of an escort to view the sights when we landed at Gibraltar on the following day. Men, however, made no appeal to me. I preferred to join a small party, mostly composed of people who sat at my table.

We wandered about the place in the usual disjointed fashion, striving to assume the tourist's intelligent interest in the jumble of Spanish remains, modern fortifications, burnous-clad Moors and preternaturally withered Spaniards. We gaped at the shop-windows and bought the usual variety of useless articles. It was here for the first time that I felt a momentary impulse of sadness. Picture postcards were of no use to me. There was not a soul in the world who was interested in my comings or goings. With me acquaintance seemed to spell tragedy.

Finally, we wandered into the hotel for tea, served in a lounge which one of my travelled companions described as the very Mecca of spurious Orientalism. The room had a glass roof but no windows. It was adorned with artificial flowers rearing their heads from brass pots, marble-topped tables and plush furniture. None of these things impressed me at the time, for a very adequate reason. I was steeped in amazement at something I saw in the face of the woman who had been its solitary occupant before our coming. She was moderately young, quietly but expensively dressed, of small but graceful figure and with large dark eyes. It was none of these personal characteristics, however, which compelled and riveted my attention. It was the fact that from her corner in the darkened room she was glaring at me with an expression of intent and deliberate malignity. To the best of my belief I had never seen her before, yet it was a clear and unmistakable fact that in this hotel room at Gibraltar I had suddenly come into contact with a woman who hated me.

We somehow or other found places at a table. My immediate neighbour was an elderly American gentleman who had once or twice spoken to me on the voyage, but who seemed to spend most of his time seeking for ex-business associates. He had, he told me, been a manufacturer of boots and shoes in a place called Lynn. His name was Frank Popple.

"Say, are you acquainted with the lady in the corner?" he asked curiously.

I shook my head.

"I have never seen her before," I assured him.

"Is that so?" he replied incredulously. "I guess she isn't partial to strangers, then. Didn't you notice her looking kind of fierce?"

"I thought that she had probably mistaken me for some one else," I said.

Mr. Popple appeared to find the surmise possible.

"Fiery-tempered lot, these foreigners," he remarked.

I received a further shock about an hour later, when
I found the same woman ensconced in a corner of the
tender which was to take us back to the steamer, surrounded by two much-belabelled steamer trunks, a
dressing case, hat box, and other feminine impedimenta.
She scowled at me sullenly when we came on board, and,
acting entirely on impulse, I walked straight across
to her.

" Have I offended you in any way? " I enquired.
" It seems to me that we are strangers? "

She looked at me steadfastly. Her face, which nor-
mally must have been soft and pretty, had become hard
and cold. Her eyes still told their tale of hatred.

" You are Janet Stanfield, are you not? " she asked.

" That is certainly my name, " I admitted, more
puzzled than ever. " How do you know it? "

She looked at me in doubting silence. The sun was
pouring down upon us. The strange, foreign odour of
the place, pungent but fascinating to me in its novelty,
was in my nostrils. On the quay, a ruffianly-looking
Spaniard, with olive cheeks, jet-black hair and flashing
eyes, was singing a sweet but sensuous melody. In the
background, one heard from across the harbour the
sad chant of the Lascars as they bent over their toil
on the deck of an outgoing steamer. All these things
became mingled with my impressions of the moment.

" I have seen your picture, " she said gloomily.

" Where? "

" In New York. He carried it with him. "

She turned deliberately away, as though determined
not to enter into any further conversation. I found

her unsociability to some extent a relief, but when I stepped on board again my blessed peace of mind was gone. I relapsed into my former frame of mind and endeavoured to keep away from every one. Mr. Popple, however, refused to accept my plain hints. He dragged his chair over to my corner on deck.

"Mrs. Louisa K. Martin, that lady's name," he informed me, " comes from way out west, beyond Milwaukee. She is getting out at Marseilles."

"I had forgotten all about her," I replied mendaciously.

Mr. Popple scratched his chin thoughtfully. He was a large man, clean-shaven, with a ponderous jaw but kindly eyes, with little creases at the side. He seemed a little hurt at my lack of confidence.

"I'd give her a wide berth if I were you," he advised. "Travelling about as much as I do, I've got kind of used to taking stock of people's expressions, and the way she looked at you was real mean."

I declined to continue the conversation and announced my intention of going to bed. As I entered the music room on the way to my cabin, there was a curious cessation of conversation. Mrs. Louisa K. Martin, who was seated in an easy-chair, very becomingly dressed in black, with a long rope of pearls around her neck, looked at me with steady insolence. I walked straight up to her chair. I knew that she had been saying things about me and I was furious.

"Are you meeting my husband at Marseilles, Mrs. Martin?" I asked her.

I was sorry for the question directly the words had

left my lips — sorry for her, too, in a way. She turned deathly pale, and if looks could have killed I should have been a dead woman. She made no answer at all. I waited for a moment and then passed on to my stateroom.

It must have been about ten o'clock that night when I heard a soft tapping at my door. I guessed at once who it was, and I guessed rightly. It was Mrs. Louisa Martin, wrapped in a dressing gown and with slippers on her feet. She closed the door carefully and she put her fingers to her lips.

" We must be careful, " she whispered. " You were mad to speak of Michael openly. "

" Of my husband? "

She laughed contemptuously.

" He married me years before you, " she replied, " and another before either of us. "

I turned away from her that she should not see the hate in my face. Some conviction of this sort had been growing upon me of late.

" When two women love the same man, " Louisa Martin continued, " they should forget everything when he is in danger. I don't see love in your face, " she went on. " Then why are you here? "

" I see no reason why I should discuss that or any other subject with you, " I answered, " but as a matter of fact I had no idea that Michael was in Marseilles. "

I thought that she would have struck me. The fire of unbelief blazed in her eyes.

" What are you doing on this steamer, then? " she demanded.

" I came for a holiday trip, " I told her.

She leaned a little towards me. In the unshaded light of the cabin her face seemed wan, almost aged.

"Listen, " she said, " this is a matter of life or death for Michael. You heard through some one of his being in Marseilles. Tell me through whom? "

" I swear that I had no idea he was there, " I repeated.

" You fool! " she exclaimed. " Can't you see that you are probably followed — that the police are making use of you? "

" You are in the same position yourself, " I reminded her.

" Indeed I am not, " she assured me earnestly. " I was born in Marseilles. I have travelled there repeatedly. I know every corner and stone of the place. It was I who taught Michael that it was the finest hiding place in the world for the educated criminal. It was I who took him where he is now. "

Our conversation was suddenly interrupted in a very unexpected fashion. My stewardess entered, with a thin blue strip in her hand.

" Wireless for you, Mrs. Soale, " she announced, addressing me by the name under which I had booked my passage.

" For me? " I repeated incredulously. " There must be some mistake. Nobody knows that I am on board. "

" It's Mrs. Soale, right enough, " the stewardess assured me. " There's no one else of that name amongst the passengers. "

I tore open the envelope. My companion watched me

with glittering eyes. She could scarcely wait until the stewardess had departed.

"You liar!" she hissed. "You see what you have done! You have laid a trail for the police to follow from London to Marseilles."

She poured out abuse. I heard nothing. My whole attention was fixed upon those few words, staring at me from the telegraph form:

Dombey 31st March Genesis Louise

I felt her wrist suddenly grip mine. She read the message over my shoulder.

"Get the code," she whispered hoarsely. "Quick!"

"What code?" I demanded. "I don't know what you're talking about."

I suppose she must have been convinced at last, for she dropped my wrist and hurried to the door.

"Wait here," she ordered, snatching the message from my hand.

There was a heavy swell that day, and I was glad to sit down upon my bunk. She returned in a very few moments. Her cheeks were flushed. She handed me back the message. Underneath it she had pencilled the interpretation:

Danger 97 it must be dealt with promptly Louisa.

I looked at it and shook my head.

"I suppose I am a fool," I admitted, "but I can't understand a word."

"You are a fool," she agreed. "No wonder Michael

never trusted you with a code! It means that some one dangerous must be travelling in stateroom Number 97, who must be dealt with promptly by me — Louisa — my name. Do you understand now? "

" But how could Michael know that I was on the steamer, and why should he have sent this message to me instead of to you? " I demanded.

" The Chief of Police at Marseilles has a copy of every passenger list of steamers leaving London and calling at Marseilles, forwarded overland, " she replied. " Michael has a friend in the Bureau. It is possible that I am being watched. He knew quite well that I should find you out, and that I should be of more use than you were likely to be. Now to discover who is travelling in stateroom Number 97. "

She called to the steward, who was passing outside. He unhooked the door and looked in.

" Steward, can you tell me the name of the gentleman in Number 97? " she enquired.

He shook his head.

" That's the other side of the ship, Madame. "

She held out a treasury note.

" Please find out, " she begged.

He was back again in less than a minute.

" Mr. Popple, Madame — an American gentleman, " he announced.

Even as he spoke, we heard a familiar and resonant voice outside.

" I put his plant down at a hundred and fifty thousand dollars, and I cleaned up the deal. Some push down our way, sir! "

Mr. Popple passed on. The woman whose name was Louisa stood looking at me.

" From the first I suspected him, " she whispered. He must be Bill Lund, from Chicago. This commercial traveller business is his stunt. "

" What are you going to do? " I asked.

She smiled in a peculiar fashion.

" Obey Michael, " she answered softly.

The next morning, Mr. Popple came over and talked to me again. He had shown me from the first a considerable amount of attention, but his conversation had always been of the most ordinary kind. This morning, however, in the midst of a discussion on ladies' footwear, he broke off and addressed me in different fashion.

" So you're making friends with the woman who looked as though she wanted to bite your head off at Gibraltar, " he remarked.

" I shouldn't have said so, " I replied cautiously.

" She was in your stateroom last night, wasn't she? " he queried.

" For a moment or two, " I admitted. " Why not? "

He watched the smoke from his cigar thoughtfully.

" I guess you've common sense enough to take a word of advice, " he said. " Here it is. Keep out of it. "

" Keep out of what? " I demanded.

He shrugged his shoulders.

" That's a fine shoal of porpoises, " he observed, looking over the side of the ship. " I don't know as I've ever seen a finer in these waters. "

" In other words, " I ventured, smiling ——

" Incident closed, " he declared. " Maybe I've opened my mouth too wide, as it is. "

But as a matter of fact he had not. The last few days had seen a wonderful change in me. I scarcely knew myself, scarcely realised the new thoughts with which I lived, the slow falling away of the spurious fancies which life with Michael had fostered. These few days, freed from the constant environment of the city, with its sordid tasks and obligations, solitude in the great spaces, with the sea and the wind and the stars, had been like a tonic to my soul. In plain words, my association with Michael had become loathsome to me. I was filled with a passionate desire to start life again as an honest woman.

So, although I knew now for certain that Mr. Popple was a detective, I said no word of this to Louisa, even though, during the next few hours, I witnessed an amazing development of their acquaintance. They sat together for several hours, and Louisa's beautiful eyes seemed every moment to become more eloquent. Without a doubt, she had made up her mind to captivate him, and to all appearance she was succeeding. I was walking up and down the deck with the doctor, and we heard scraps of their conversation as we passed — an assignation for the morrow evening at Marseilles, proposed boldly enough by Mr. Popple, and assented to by a timorous but eloquent flash of the eyes by Louisa. After dinner they took their coffee out on deck. Their heads were even closer together, their voices dropped. People, as they passed, began to smile. It was obvious that an affair was in progress. I was surprised, therefore, to hear Mr. Popple suddenly address the doctor, who had joined me again for a few minutes.

" Just one moment, Doc. "

We stopped at once. Mr. Popple seemed to rise with difficulty to his feet.

" Guess I am sick, Doc. Just step round to my stateroom with me for a moment. "

Mr. Popple, suddenly very pale, swayed on his feet and clutched at the doctor's arm. I expected every moment to see him collapse. We all turned to Louisa. She shook her head, apparently as bewildered as the rest of us.

" We had just finished our coffee, " she explained, " when Mr. Popple, who had been talking a great deal, became silent. He spoke of a pain in his head and I thought he seemed queer. Then he called out to the doctor. That is all I know about it. "

By degrees the others melted away. I sank into Mr. Popple's vacant chair. As soon as we were alone, Mrs. Louisa Martin looked at me covertly. There was a flash of triumph in her half-closed eyes.

" So! " she murmured. " I do not think that Mr. Popple will follow me about Marseilles. "

" Do you mean that you have poisoned him? " I gasped.

She looked at me with a queer little smile.

" Some, " she said, " prefer to shoot. I choose the way of safety. "

Then I knew that Michael had told her everything.

In that moment, all that I had ever felt of love for him turned to hate.

We entered the harbour at Marseilles late on the following morning and drifted down on our way to the dock. The sun was shining, and the heat, now that we had left the breezes of the open sea, was almost unbearable. It was a morning of acute sensations. I remember everything — the pungent odours of the harbour, the smell of fresh tar, of a cargo of dried onions, a passing whiff of fragrance from the baskets of the flower women on the quay. We stood leaning over the side, waiting, prepared to land, but waiting for the gendarmes at the further end of the gangway, to give the word. Suddenly I felt a little thrill pass through my whole body. Notwithstanding the hot sunshine, I was so cold that I felt myself shivering. Leaning with his back to one of the wooden pillars was a man with tanned, almost swarthy skin, lean-faced, with a hungry, wolf-like droop of his thin lips. He was shabbily dressed, even for a labourer, with brown overall, ragged blue trousers, boots devoid of laces and a soiled tweed cap. It was more than a disguise — it was a metamorphosis — yet I knew Michael, and although he never glanced again in my direction, I knew that he had recognised me. I did then what was, under the circumstances, a foolish action. I made my way to where Louisa was standing and I touched her on the arm.

" Look there," I said, directing her attention cautiously towards the lounging figure.

She looked at him for a moment without interest. Then suddenly the change came into her face. Her lips

were a little parted, the colour was drained from her
cheeks, her eyes were filled with the anticipation of evil
things. She clutched at my arm.

" There is danger," she muttered. " He has been
obliged to fly. Alas! our week at the Villa exists no
longer."

A moment afterwards there was a movement towards
the gangway. I followed the others off the ship, and
waited until a magnificent-looking functionary, smell-
ing of garlic, had made mystic signs with a piece of
chalk upon my modest trunk. The porter shouldered
it and turned to me for instructions.

" A carriage to the Hotel Splendide, " I directed.

I was on the point of entering it when I felt a touch
upon my arm.

" He insists upon seeing you," she whispered, in a
low tone. " Where are you going? "

" To the Hotel Splendide," I told her, with a sinking
heart.

" I shall fetch you to-night at six o'clock."

" Why does Michael want to see me? " I asked reluctantly.

" One does not ask Michael questions," she answered,
with a sneer. " You should have found that out by this
time."

I felt as though an ugly cloud were looming over this
wonderful holiday of mine, and I spent a restless and
unsatisfactory afternoon. At six o'clock, Louisa
fetched me in a small fiacre, and we drove slowly and
with horrible jolts into one of the foulest seafaring
slums one could imagine. I knew nothing at the time,

but I discovered afterwards that it was a region of evil repute throughout not only Marseilles but throughout Europe, a region of myriad pungent odours, a tawdry medley of cafés, flaunting women, and rollicking groups of drink-inflamed men. I began to feel fear.

"Where are we going?" I demanded.

"To the only place where Michael can hide in safety," Louisa replied. "Even the police of Marseilles would scarcely dare to seek him here."

"It is not fit for us," I muttered, with my eyes fixed upon the streets.

Louisa sneered.

"It is clear that you were never the woman for Michael," she rejoined.

We stopped at last at the end of a dark and narrow street, a place so squalid and unsavoury that I hesitated to leave the vehicle. Louisa, however, elbowed me out and half pushed, half conducted me along an entry, with a high wall on either side, a slimy place with the swish of waves distinctly audible. At the extreme end, she pushed open a door on the left-hand side. We found ourselves in a café of the poorest class, with sanded floors and iron tables. A woman, fat and with a hideous face, stood behind the bar, and whenever I desire to think of something horrible, I think of the stealthy, vicious faces of the men who first glared and then leered at us as we crossed the threshold.

Louisa went straight to the woman behind the bar and whispered in her ear. The woman, who had at least three or four chins, nodded ponderously and smiled, showing a row of yellow, discoloured teeth. She

glanced cautiously around the place, as though to make
sure that no stranger was amongst her clientele. Then,
with a fat, beringed finger, she beckoned us behind the
counter, and led us down some steps, along a passage,
into a sombre and fearsome-looking apartment, tawd-
rily furnished, with a cracked gilt mirror upon the
mantelpiece, walls reeking with damp, and some violet
plush chairs of incredible shabbiness. In the corner
was a bed, and upon it Michael was seated, still in his
disguise of a French ouvrier, but with a new look upon
his face — the hunted, desperate look of a man at bay.
What I read in his eyes as the woman, with an evil
chuckle, left us, made my blood run cold. I had the
feeling that I was trapped.

"You devil!" he said to me slowly and menacingly.
" It is you who have brought your damned lover policeman here!"

" It is false," I replied. " I came to Marseilles for
a holiday only."

" A holiday!" Michael repeated bitterly.

" A holiday!" the woman almost shrieked. " Hear
her! But listen," she added, with a terrible smile.
" There is time yet to show you how Michael and I
deal with informers!"

NORMAN GREYES

During the third week of March, after a somewhat
restless few months of travel in Egypt and Algeria, I
reached Monte Carlo to find a telegram from my friend

Rimmington, begging me to come at once to Marseilles.
I realised that there could be but one reason for such
a request, and in less than twelve hours I found myself
with Rimmington and Monsieur Demayel, the Chief of
the Marseilles Police, ransacking the contents of a
small villa in the suburbs of Marseilles, which had
lately been the scene of one of those crimes for which
the place was fast gaining an unenviable notoriety.

I had had no conversation with Rimmington, and I
had no idea why my help had been sought in this case,
which appeared to have no special characteristics. The
late inhabitant of the villa, a man of over seventy years
of age, had been found twenty-four hours before, suffering from severe wounds about the head and in a state
of collapse. He was lying in a neighbouring hospital
and was unlikely to recover. This much, however, was
clear. He had been robbed of a large sum of money,
the possession of which he had foolishly bragged about
in a neighbouring café, and there seemed to be but
little doubt that the theft had been committed by a
band of ill-doers who for the last few months had been
the terror of the neighbourhood. We went through
the usual routine of examining the means by which
entrance had been forced into the house and hearing
the evidence of the local gendarmerie. Afterwards we
drove, in silence, to the Police Headquarters, and it
was in Monsieur Demayel's private room there that
Rimmington at last explained what had been puzzling
me so much.

"You know, of course, Greyes," he began, "what
my having sent for you means?"

" Michael, I hope? "

Rimmington nodded.   I could tell by the gleam in his rather cold grey eyes that he believed the end to be near at last.

" We traced him to Paris, " he said, " and afterwards here.   Almost immediately, as Monsieur Demayel will tell you, there was not only an increase in the number of crimes in the district, but there were evidences of a master mind behind them all.   Crime here had become brain-controlled.   Monsieur Demayel told me, an hour or so ago, that thefts to the value of over eleven million francs had been committed within the last two months."

" And the connecting link? " I questioned.

" Eight days ago," Rimmington said, watching me closely, " Janet Soale sailed from Tilbury for Marseilles.   The woman who was Michael's companion in New York, who goes by the name of Louisa Martin, after travelling from America to Havre, joined the same steamer at Gibraltar, having evidently chosen a circuitous route to avoid suspicion.   Those two women are both on their way to Marseilles — they are due to arrive, in fact, to-night — and will be closely watched.   Furthermore, I think that Monsieur Demayel can show you something of interest."

Monsieur Demayel placed a leather-bound volume before me and pointed to an entry.

" This," he explained, " is a small collection of *dossiers* which have never been verified."

I read the few lines quickly:

Henri Guy, French-Colonial, bachelor, 5 ft. 6 inches, morose, grey hair and beard, physical appearance described elsewhere, address Villa Violette, Bandol. Has large correspondence, subscribes to English Newspapers, amongst which "Golf Illustrated." Has small car and has been seen on Hyères Golf Links.

" And finally? " I asked.

" The person in question," M. Demayel continued, " is reported to have changed at the Casino at Bandol last evening one of the *mille* notes stolen from the house we visited this afternoon."

I glanced at my watch.

" How far is it to Bandol? " I enquired.

" Forty-seven kilometres," the Chief of the Police replied, " and we should have been there by now but my friend Mr. Rimmington here insisted upon waiting for you."

I asked only one question on the way.

" You spoke of Janet Soale as coming out on the boat," I said to Rimmington. " That was her name before she married Michael."

Rimmington nodded.

" For some reason or other she has renewed it. It is possible that she has discovered something about Michael which I have suspected for some time."

I controlled my voice as well as I could. I did not wish even Rimmington to know how much this meant to me.

" What do you mean? " I asked.

" I believe," he replied, " that Michael was married many years ago to this woman, Louisa Martin. Janet

Soale may have got to know of this. She may be coming out to try and discover the truth. It is certain that for many months she has not been in communication with Michael."

The Chief of the Police gazed thoughtfully out of the window.

"It is a curious circumstance," he remarked, " in the lives of most of the great criminals of modern days, that their end has been brought about by their exciting the jealousy of women. Here are two at the present moment on their way to Marseilles to visit the man whom you call Michael. Louisa Martin has been followed from New York by a United States detective who has been hunting Michael for years, and it was Janet Soale's visit to Marseilles which changed suspicion into conviction with our friend Rimmington here. My predecessor used always to say, 'Give the man rope. Follow the woman.'"

We reached Bandol just before dusk and found the Villa Violette on the outskirts of the town; a secluded little house, built amongst some rocks on the extreme edge of the bay. We left the car in the road and took the path which led to the front door. Our summons was at once answered by a stout, good-humoured-looking French woman, who shook her head regretfully when we enquired for Monsieur Guy.

"Monsieur is out in his automobile," she told us. "He may return at any moment or perhaps not at all to-night. It is most unfortunate. The gentlemen will leave a message?"

"We will come in and wait for a little time," Demayel suggested.

The woman did not remove her portly form from the threshold.

"That, alas, Monsieur, is impossible!" she declared. "My master receives few visitors and he would not suffer any one in the house."

Monsieur Demayel touched her on the shoulder. He was looking curiously into her face.

"Madame," he said, "I am Chef de la Sûreté of Marseilles, and I go where I choose. Furthermore, it seems that your face is familiar to me."

She shrunk away. There was a malign look suddenly in her dark eyes.

"Chef de la Sûreté!" she muttered. "But who has done wrong here?"

We searched the sitting room and dining room of Monsieur Henri Guy and we found nothing that might not have belonged to a French Colonial who had made a small fortune in sugar. But in his bedroom, covered over with a sheet and hidden behind a cupboard, I found a prize indeed. I found the golf clubs which Stanfield had used when he had played against me at Woking. I drew from the bag the putter which had sealed my defeat and, even in that moment of triumph, I felt a little thrill of pleasure when I realised its perfect balance.

"Our search is over," I pronounced.

"Our search is not over," Rimmington reminded me, "until we have found the man."

We were there altogether for half an hour, during

which time we searched the place closely. The small garage was empty and Rimmington pointed out the six or eight empty tins which had evidently just been used.

"Filled up for a journey," he remarked. "I don't think that we shall see anything of our man to-day."

We announced our intended departure. The housekeeper, who now seemed certain of her master's immediate return, did her best to persuade us to linger. Monsieur Demayel cut her short.

"Madame," he said, "you will be so good as to consider yourself under surveillance. I shall leave a gendarme in the house with you. To-morrow you will be examined. In the meantime, make no attempt to communicate with anybody."

The woman was no longer the smooth-tongued, respectable domestic. She burst into a torrent of furious complaints and abuse, relapsing into a French argot which was absolutely incomprehensible to me. Monsieur Demayel listened to her thoughtfully. Then he turned to the gendarme who had accompanied us from Marseilles on the front seat of the car, and whom he was leaving behind.

"Do not let this woman out of your sight," he ordered. "She is of the Maritime Quartier, where I suspect her master is in hiding by now."

The gendarme saluted and laid his hand upon the housekeeper's shoulder. Suddenly she burst into a fit of laughter and pointed up the avenue.

"It is monsieur who returns," she announced. "Now, what will you say to him — you who have ransacked his rooms and upset his house! Chief of the Police, indeed! La la!"

We stood by the front door and I for my part was amazed. An elderly gentleman of highly respectable appearance drove up in a small Citroven car and lifted his soft black felt hat to us courteously.

"Good evening, gentlemen," he said. "You are paying me a visit?"

"You are Monsieur Guy?" Demayel enquired.

"That is certainly my name," was the prompt reply.

"And this is your house?"

"I rent it subject to your pleasure, gentlemen."

He descended from the car and looked from one to the other of us enquiringly. I knew better than any other what a past master Michael was in the art of disguises, but I knew very well that this was not he. Rimmington's eyes met mine. We were both agreed.

"My name is Demayel," the Chief announced. "I am the Chef de la Sûreté in Marseilles. You will be so good as to answer me a few questions."

"Chef de la Sûreté!" the newcomer repeated, and if his amazement were feigned, it was very well feigned indeed.

"But certainly! You have lived here for how long?"

"For ten months, Monsieur."

"You changed a *mille* note at the Casino yesterday?"

"I certainly did."

"From where did you obtain it?"

"From my desk, Monsieur. It has lain there for weeks."

I ventured to ask a question on my own account.

"This is your only car?"

"But naturally," was the prompt response. "There is no room in my garage for more than one."

I excused myself for a moment and returned with the bag of golf clubs.

"These are perhaps yours?" I asked him.

He shook his head.

"They were left by a former tenant," he replied. "I know nothing of their use."

I turned into the garage and wheeled out one of the rubber tyres which were ranged against the wall.

"If you have no other car," I asked him, "how is it that all the tyres in your garage are like this one — two sizes larger than those on the Citroven you were driving?"

He hesitated and turned his head. He knew then that it was the end. The gendarme was returning with a fat little man, who wore no coat and waistcoat and reeked of garlic.

"This man keeps the café at the corner," the former announced. "He knows his neighbour Guy well."

"Is this Monsieur Guy?" Demayel asked.

The innkeeper was more than emphatic; he was vehement.

"Upon my soul, no!" he declared. "Monsieur Guy I know well. This gentleman is a stranger. Monsieur Guy left this morning in his car for Paris, one heard."

Demayel turned to the pseudo Monsieur Guy.

" Well? "

The man shrugged his shoulders.

" I have done what I was paid for," he said sullenly. " I am at your disposal, gentlemen."

" Close the place up," Demayel directed the gendarme, " and take this woman and the man to Marseilles. Nothing more will happen here. As for us," he went on, turning to Rimmington and myself, " we must now await the arrival of the steamer in Marseilles to-night. One of the two women, if not both, will lead us to the man we seek."

We dined that night, Rimmington and I, in a remote corner of a great bustling restaurant, receiving more than our due share of attention owing to the fact that Monsieur Demayel had himself telephoned and ordered the table. The latter had promised to join us for coffee, but, before we reached that stage of our repast, we were surprised to see him coming hastily towards us, followed by a tall, bearded man of military bearing. Demayel was a man of imperturbable expression, yet it was obvious that he brought news.

" Messieurs," he said, as he sat for a moment at our table, " a grave thing has happened. Let me explain briefly. The young man who has acted as my secretary for five years has absconded. It is proved that he has been in league with a great criminal organisation ever since he has held his post. It is he, without a doubt, who warned the man whom you call Michael. Worse than that, his report to me that the *Carlyon* would not reach dock until to-night, was a lie. She arrived this morning and landed her passengers this afternoon.

My plans for having those two women watched have been rendered abortive."

A surge of nameless fears suddenly rose up in my heart. I pictured Janet in danger. I did not believe that she had come to Marseilles to rejoin Michael. I half rose to my feet but Demayel waved me back.

"Listen," he continued. "This much we know at present. The English woman went first to the Hotel Splendide. At six o'clock this evening she was called for by the other woman and they drove off alone. They were shadowed, fortunately, by Lund, the American detective who followed Louisa Martin over, and who reports that his life was attempted last night. This woman Martin, it seems, has an evil reputation. She has been in prison twice in her younger days in Paris, and she was tried for murder seven years ago. She is desperately cruel but of desperate courage. Lund reports that there is ill blood between the two women. He is convinced that the English woman, Janet Soale, as she called herself on the steamer, has been decoyed into some place to meet Michael."

"How far did he follow them?" I asked. "Where is he now?"

"He followed them into the worst quarter of Marseilles," Demayel replied, "but, as soon as he discovered their destination, he had the good sense to return for aid. They are in the one quarter of the city which I have not yet succeeded in clearing. We have hesitated many times when on the point of attempting a coup here. To-night the attempt shall be made."

"Let us start!" I exclaimed eagerly.

We moved towards the door.

"I deeply regret," Demayel announced, "that this is an adventure on which I cannot accompany you. If I were to show myself in the Quartier, I should not only endanger your lives but I should of an absolute certainty forfeit my own. Monsieur Santel here," he added, turning to his companion, "will take command of the expedition. Lund is in one of the cars outside. A sufficient force of gendarmes have already penetrated secretly into the Quartier. It remains only for me to wish you good fortune."

In the car which we found waiting for us, we passed from the broad thoroughfares of the city to a region of increasing squalor and ugliness, along boulevards whose cobbled stones were littered with refuse, where the men and women who sat at their windows became more and more repulsive. The gaiety of the city was succeeded by a sombre silence. There was no music in the cafés, no laughter from the lips of the women. One seemed to read in those hungry, unwashed and painted faces one common characteristic — greed. Furtive eyes followed our automobile lustfully because it meant wealth. Once or twice men half rose from their places, as though to follow us. It was difficult to imagine that this was a street in a civilised city.

"One sees little of the law down here," I remarked.

Our guide shrugged his shoulders.

"The castaways of the world are to be found always in a great port," he said. "We leave them alone when we can. This place is their safety valve. When we are forced to come, we come as we have to-night — in hundreds."

I realised what he meant when we descended, a few minutes later. At every corner of the little network of streets through which we pushed our way, some apparent lounger whispered a word in Santel's ear. When, at last, we reached the end of a gloomy street, which terminated with the great iron gates of a ship-yard, our guide turned and spoke to us.

"Follow me," he directed, "and be discreet. Remember a blow of the fists will send a hundred of these rats to their holes — but always look behind. "

We descended some small stone steps, passed along a narrow passage, and entered a café, the most dilapi-dated and filthy which I have ever been in. There were a dozen men seated around, drinking, two or three asleep or drunk, one who covered up his face. A woman lolled across the counter and looked at us, a woman whose untidy clothing seemed to be falling away from her repulsive body. She had a heavy moustache upon her upper lip and narrow jet-black eyes.

"In the name of the police, Madame," Santel whis-pered in her ear.

"At your service," she replied.

"We want none of your usual jailbirds," Santel con-tined. " Stand on one side, please."

The woman's face was hideous but she shrugged her shoulders.

"There is nothing," she muttered. "One has been here, perhaps, but he has gone."

We passed behind that counter, through a door, into

a noisome house, wrapped in utter darkness. Four
other men seemed to have crept up to us like shadows
and we all had electric torches. Some of the rooms had
been used for sleeping; some, apparently, for a filthy
carouse. All were empty. At a certain point in the
descent of some stone steps, we paused. Three of the
men felt about for some time. Then an unsuspected
door slowly swung open, a door which seemed to lead
into a chasm, black and impenetrable. The man who
had slipped past Santel and become our guide stretched
up his hand and pulled down a long thin ladder. He
let it down until it touched the ground. One by one we
descended into what seemed to be a great cellar. At
the farther end was a chink of light from the room
beyond, and a sound which for the moment made a
madman of me — the sound of a woman crying. I
stumbled across the uneven floor but Santel caught hold
of my arm.

"Be careful," he muttered. "If our man is there
and sees you, he will shoot. Let the others surround
him. We have a plan."

I scarcely heard him, but I held my breath and kept
silence while some one attempted to find means of in-
gress. We were there, seven of us, mad with the desire
for this man's capture, yet, for the first few moments
the stone walls seemed to mock us. Lund was running
his fingers round the chinks of what seemed to be the
door, but could find no handle. Then, suddenly, I
heard Michael's voice. Cold and measured as ever, it
seemed to me, though he must have known that he was
in desperate straits.

"For the last time, Janet, the truth?" he said. "What has become of the money which was handed over to you — the price of the jewels — and why have you followed me to Marseilles?"

There was a moment's silence. It was terrible to hear how weak Janet's voice was.

"No one has given me any money," she replied. "I have earned my own living since we parted."

There was a peal of mocking laughter and I know that the other woman must have been standing over her.

"Liar!" Louisa exclaimed. "Tell us why you came to Marseilles, and why Rimmington, the English detective, has followed. Tell us who called your new lover, Norman Greyes, from Monte Carlo?"

"I know nothing of any of those things," was the weak reply. "My uncle left me two hundred and fifty pounds — Soale, the gardener, who once worked for you, Michael. I came to Marseilles for a rest and a holiday."

Again there was a peal of derisive laughter from Louisa Martin, followed by the soft ringing of an electric bell and a fierce oath from Michael. There was a moment's silence, the scurrying of feet, the flinging back of what sounded like a door. Michael's voice, when he spoke, had changed. Fear at last seemed to have entered into him.

"You have had your chance, Janet," he said. "I shall leave you to Louisa."

Janet's pitiful voice was roused almost to a shriek.

"Don't leave me alone with her, Michael!" she implored. "She terrifies me!"

A fortunate madness seized me. I flung my whole weight against the door and we fell into the place in a heap. The impression of those few moments will never fade from my memory. Janet, her feet and arms tied with cord, white and numb with fear, was lying on the ground; Louisa Martin, with the face of a Fury, and eyes filled with hate, was leaning over her. Michael, with unrecognizable face but unforgettable eyes, was already halfway through a trap-door. He raised his arm simultaneously with mine. Our pistols spoke together and the sound of their report was followed almost immediately by the crashing of the trap-door. I felt a sharp pain in my shoulder, and for a moment I think I went mad. I was cutting the cords which bound Janet's hands and feet, talking to her foolishly, trying to keep back the faintness which threatened me. Then the mist came and the room rocked. The last thing I remembered was Louisa Martin's laugh.

My first visitor in the hospital, six weeks later, was Monsieur Demayel. He adopted a tone of apology.

"That man's escape, Sir Norman," he confessed, "was a most deplorable incident."

"How did he get away?" I enquired.

"He descended through the trap-door from the room in which you found him," Monsieur Demayel explained, "by means of a rope ladder to a narrow inlet of the harbour, which at full tide is directly underneath. He secured the trap-door behind him by means of a bolt, got into a petrol launch and apparently made his way across the bay. The launch was discovered next day upon the beach, and there is a theory that he was washed overboard by a heavy sea. At any rate, he has not been seen or heard of since."

" Louisa Martin? " I asked.

" Safe for seven years," was the grim reply.

" And — the English woman? "

Monsieur Demayel glanced suspiciously at the bowl of flowers by my bedside.

" She remained in Marseilles for some time. I do not know her present whereabouts."

As soon as my visitor had gone, I sent for the nurse.

" From whom did these flowers come? " I enquired.

She smiled as a Frenchwoman does who scents a romance.

" Until you were out of danger," she told me, " a very beautiful English lady called every day. A week ago she returned to England, but she left with the Sister an order on a florist for roses every day for a fortnight."

" She left no note or message? "

" Nothing."

" When can I leave for England? " I demanded.

The nurse looked at me reproachfully.

" In a fortnight, if you behave," she answered. " Perhaps never, if you work yourself into a fever."

" Nurse," I asked, " have you ever been in love? "

" It is not a fit question from a patient to his nurse," she replied, with a pleasant little gleam in her eyes and a quiver at the corners of her lips.

" I need sympathy," I explained, " but if you will not talk to me, I shall go to sleep."

" The more you sleep," she declared, " the sooner you will be able to go to England."

So I slept.

CHAPTER IX

MICHAEL

For many months after my somewhat ingenious escape from the café of Madame Ponadour in the Maritime Quartier of Marseilles, I lived the life of a dog in the Forêt du Dom, on the far side of Hyères. There were three of us woodmen in the hut — Pierre, Jacques and myself. My two unchosen companions, after twenty years of the same monotonous labour, had grown very much like the trees whose branches we lopped off and whose trunks we hauled down the road to the mountainous stack whence they were fetched by motor-lorry from Nice. These two men, so far as I was able to discover, possessed no virtues. They cheated at cards — we had one filthy pack which had lasted them for a year before I came — they drank to excess, when they could afford the wine or the fiery brandy of the country, and I am convinced that they would have murdered any one for a few francs, if they could have been sure of evading detection. Their complexions were, as mine soon became, almost black. They were clods of the earth, men ageless and passionless except when the wine was in their blood, from whom I hid at the same time and with equal discretion my thoughts and my purse.

Solitude more complete than that which I shared with these two men I have never imagined. I grew to hate the very things which had, at first, appealed to me — the fresh, pungent smell of the newly hewn trees, the scent of the earth before and after vineyard time, the freshly turned red soil, cloven by the plough, the sun-baked furrows, scarred with fissures and cracks through which the odours of wine itself seemed to steal. Then there was the smell of the eucalyptus trees and the perfume from the cherry orchards before their blossoms were dashed by the warm, June rain, the moaning of the wind through the pine tops overhead, the creaking of the branches, the night scent of the bursting sap. These things dwelt in my blood for a while as I sat sometimes at dawn and listened to the drowsy song of the birds at their first awakening, and watched the long shafts of green and amber light pierce the clouds eastward, as though to prepare the way for the coming sun. My joy of these things, however, was short-lived. Their appeal was for others, not for such as me. I grew to look upon my queer fancy for them as a phase of weakness, a sign of the marching of the years. For I was under no misapprehension concerning myself and my position in the world. Sometimes, whilst the others slept, I read the newspapers, which we obtained with difficulty from the neighbouring village; read of myself as the most notorious criminal at large; read of all the world-famed detectives of London, Paris and New York, who had sworn to effect my capture; read of my crimes, my daring, my cunning; read of all these things outside my shanty on the hillside — and smiled. Given a certain amount of resignation and patience, and I knew very well that I was safe as long as I chose. There, however, was the trouble. Corduroy trousers and a woodman's smock were not to my fancy as articles of dress. Nor did I care about dark bread and soup, apples and sour wine, as a means of keeping body and soul together. There was money for me in London, plenty of it. I knew that to reach that money I should, before long, come out into the open and challenge once more the world of my enemies.

One day a chance incident set me thinking. We had paused for a second to fill our pipes with filthy tobacco, barely a dozen yards round one of the hairpin corners of the forest road, leaving our wagons, as usual, in the middle of the thoroughfare. Suddenly a car swung round the corner, travelling too fast for the driver to apply his brakes with safety. With great skill he passed us, grazing the long trunks of the lopped trees and escaping the precipice by a matter of inches. The chauffeur drove on, turning round for a moment, however, to shake his fist and shout abuse at us. I waved my hand in friendly fashion, for the incident had given me an idea. That night I saw that Pierre and Jacques drank more than their usual share of the sour wine, and afterwards I propounded my scheme.

" Comrades," I said, " it is a dog's life we lead."

They growled assent. They seldom spoke coherent words.

" To-day," I continued, " an idea came to me. If

our wagons had been an inch or two nearer the outside corner of the road, or the man in the automobile a shade less skilful, he could not possibly have escaped. His automobile would have been smashed and he would have gone over the edge of the precipice."

They made strange noises in their throats and continued to listen.

"It is a dog's life, this," I repeated. "What we need, to make things endurable, is money — money, so that you two can go down to the café at the foot of the hill and drink brandy with the daughters of the village, they who leave you now so unkindly alone because you have nothing to spend upon them."

Their pipes were out of their mouths now and they were listening intently. ·

"A man like that one to-day would have money — a pocketbook. Whilst he was unconscious, look you, we would take it. One of us would bring it up here, here where there are a hundred hiding places, in the ground, the trees, the cracks of the earth. A pocketbook which is lost, is lost. What do you say, comrades?"

There was no doubt about how the scheme appealed to them. Jacques was showing all the fangs of his yellow teeth in one tremendous smile. Pierre's round, black eyes were lit with a covetous gleam.

"It would be an equal share between the three?" he urged.

"Between the three," I agreed. "Leave the details to me."

We went to our work the next morning with a new zest. All the time that we were at work in the forest,

lopping the branches from the fallen trees and piling
them on to the wagons, we were thinking of what fortune might have in store for us on our homeward crawl.
When, at last, the time came to start, my two companions seemed more like human beings than at any
time I had known them. They marched stolidly but
hopefully on by the side of the horses. I, having the
better eyesight, watched the winding road, down in the
valleys below and up on the hillside. We crawled round
each corner, loitering at the psychological spot always
with the same evil hope in our hearts. The affair, however, was not so easy. Sometimes we were seen from
above or below; sometimes drivers were too careful.
On the fourth day, however, success rewarded our
perseverance. A small automobile which I had spotted
from a distance came round the corner where we were,
so to speak, anchored, driven with that full measure of
recklessness which only a Frenchman, anxious to save
his engine, can obtain. There was a wild cry from the
driver, a crash into our wagon, and over went the automobile and man down the side of the precipice. It was
an agreeable sight.

It was I who clambered down to where our victim
was lying and drew a pleasing-looking black pocketbook from the inside of his coat. Afterwards I felt his
heart and discovered that he was alive. I ordered
Pierre to move the wagons over to our own side of the
road and we secreted the pocketbook amongst the
timber we were carrying. Then we waited for events
and, although I really cared not in the least whether
the man lived or died, I found myself, to my surprise,

bathing his head and loosening his clothing. Presently, a public touring car from Cannes, on its way to Hyères, arrived. The accident was explained, room was made for the injured man, and a liberal *pourboire* given us, collected amongst the passengers. Afterwards we made our way home and, later on, when we had lit our evening fire, we opened the pocketbook. There were nine hundred francs there, and I shall never forget the evil faces of my two companions, in the light of the dancing flames, as they leaned over and watched me count the notes. I divided the money into three portions but I spoke to them as a master.

"Listen, Jacques, and you, Pierre," I said. "I am a man of justice, but, although I am one of you, I have travelled beyond these forests and I know the world. If you take this money with you to the village to-night you will be drunk, the truth will be known and we shall all go to prison. I will swear to you the woodcutters' oath, the oath across the flames, that your share shall be saved. But go to the village to-night with, twenty francs each, the *pourboire* given us by the Englishmen, and let me keep the rest for you, or hide it for yourselves."

They had just sufficient wit to realise that I was their superior in intelligence and that my advice was good. So we growled an oath in the strange dialect of those parts and I gripped their gnarled and knotted hands, which reminded me always of the roots of the trees we felled. Afterwards, I went down to the village with them, had one drink for good fellowship's sake, and returned to the shanty and solitude, with a bottle of the best brandy and some tobacco. I drank moderately, as I have always done in life, but the brandy was good to my palate and the tobacco better. I lay at my ease on the outskirts of the clearing, with my back to a sweet-smelling pine tree and my face towards the valley, and I watched the shadows droop over the hills, their slopes become blurred and their summits like a fine-drawn line of ink against the violet background. Here and there a light sprang out from a lonely farmhouse, later a' yellow star gleamed over my head through the motionless branches of the trees and an owl fluttered up from the hollow with a mournful cry. I sipped my brandy and smoked and thought. Dimly though the beauty of my surroundings appealed to me, they filled me with only a negative joy. Still, life at the best could bring me nothing but a kind of passionless content. I thought of the great cities with their thronged thoroughfares, their mighty roar of turbulent life, the crowded parks, the theatres, the Opera, with its wonderful music which I had always loved, the voices and laughter and presence of beautiful women. I would win my way back to these yet. Beauty such as that by which I was surrounded on that still evening was the kind which reaches only through the soul, and its appeal to my æsthetic sense, although disturbing, was wholly unsatisfying. What I craved for was the joy of the cities, the throb of life around me, beauty and comfort from the material point of view, the proper clothes to wear, the proper food and wine to drink.

Our next adventure, engineered in similar fashion to the last, brought us a matter of a couple of thousand francs. This time, however, there was trouble, for the driver's neck was broken as he pitched head foremost from the seat of the car, and his wife, who was only slightly injured, gave vigorous evidence as to the position of our wagon and the disappearance of her husband's pocketbook after we had dragged his body up from a ledge of the precipice. A gendarme from the neighbouring village visited us that same night and made a careful search through our belongings. There was nothing to be found, however, and by preserving a stolid silence and leaving all speech to me, my companions escaped suspicion just as I did. Afterwards, however, I spoke to them seriously.

" Comrades," I pointed out, " this game is too good to last. For a time we must go warily. Afterwards we will seek one more adventure, which we must select with great care, for it will be my last. If it is successful, I shall leave you. Afterwards, you two had better bury your savings in the ground and abandon the game, for it needs brains to be made successful, and you two have not the brains of a rabbit between you."

They knew that I was right and they held their peace. After that we let many cars go by. It was a month later, indeed, before we made our last coup, and it ended in very different fashion from what I had anticipated. From my look-out place on a stretch of the road above the wagons, I saw a grey touring car, piled with luggage and golf clubs, approaching from the direction of Cannes. There was a girl in front, seated by the driver, and an elderly gentleman behind. I called down to the others.

"Comrades, this is our chance," I announced. "Move the wagons on around the corner and be prepared for what may happen."

What did happen was not in the least what I had expected. A certain phase of it remains entirely inexplicable to me, even to this day. From where I lay, crouching amongst the scrub, I could see that something was wrong with the car, or with the manner in which it was being driven. The chauffeur was rocking in his seat and the car was swaying from side to side; it seemed at one time, indeed, as though it would go over the precipice without any intervention on our part. But it was the girl's face from which I could not remove my eyes, the girl's face which produced such an amazing impression upon me. She must have fully realized the danger she was in, but she showed not the slightest signs of fear. I heard her speak to the chauffeur, trying to bring him to his senses, but it was obvious that he was either in a fit or had completely lost his nerve. Then she leaned over and tried to put on the foot brake, succeeding so far, in fact, as to momentarily check the progress of the car. The chauffeur, suddenly seizing his opportunity, jumped from his seat and rolled over in the dust. The girl's foot apparently slipped from the brake and the car once more gathered speed. She clutched at the wheel but it was obvious that she had never driven. Somehow or other she got round the corner but, at the next — the wagons! I saw her eyes, as the car came bumping down the hill, heard the wild shouting and exclamations of the old gentleman behind, and there came to me one of those extraordinary moments, which I make no attempt to explain, moments when action is decided purely by impulse, and by an impulse irreducible to law. We had made the most careful plans to wreck this automobile. I risked my life to save it. I half slid, half scrambled down the slope into the road, drew in my breath, poised myself for a great effort and, at the psychological moment, leaped for the front splashboard. More or less I succeeded. I found myself sprawling across the seat but my left hand was upon the wheel. The girl yielded it as though with instant understanding and slid away to make room for me. In a matter of seconds I had the wheel in both hands, half kneeling, half sitting. We were within two inches of the precipice after my jump and we just touched the farther side of the road with my grab at the wheel. After that it was easy. I righted the car without much difficulty, applied the brake, gently but with increasing force, took the corner with only a moderate skid and brought the car to a standstill within a few feet of the wagon. When the girl saw it, the first look of fear crept into her face. She looked at me with shining eyes.

"You were just in time," she said. "That was a wonderful jump."

"What was the matter with your chauffeur?" I asked.

"Our own chauffeur was taken ill and this was a boy we engaged in Cannes," she answered. "He was not equal to driving the car. He lost his nerve at the top of the hill."

The old gentleman was in the road by this time and gripping my hand.

" My good fellow," he exclaimed, " you have done a great day's work for yourself! For God's sake say that you understand English."

" I have hewn wood in Devonshire," I told him. " I speak English or French, which you will. "

He was recovering himself now, and I could see that he was a very pompous person, the very prototype of the travelling Englishman of wealth, who believes in himself.

" My name," he announced, " is Lord Kindersley. You will never regret this day's work."

I made some attempt to descend but he held me in my place.

" You must drive us to the next town," he insisted, " to Hyères or Toulon. I will reward you handsomely, but we cannot be left here, and I will not let that wretched youth touch the car again."

" Where are you going to? " I enquired.

" England," the girl answered, " to Boulogne."

" I will drive you to Boulogne," I said, " if you will give me that young man's livery and papers, and recompense my comrades there for my absence. They will have to engage another woodman."

The elderly gentleman was spluttering out notes. It seemed as though he could not get rid of them fast enough.

" It is agreed," he declared eagerly. " We shall not quarrel about terms, I promise you! "

A dusty figure came staggering down the hill, a youth sobered by fright but evidently recovering from a debauch. I wasted few words upon him, but I took him round the bend of the road, stripped him of his clothes and left him mine. Then I mounted the driving seat of the car and tested the gears. Pierre and Jacques were gazing with amazement at the little bundle of hundred-franc notes which the English milord had thrust into their hands.

" Farewell, comrades," I said, waving my hand to them. " Some day I may come back, but I think not. Good luck to you both! "

They returned my farewell in wooden fashion. I let in my clutch and glided down the hill. So we started on the way to Boulogne.

During the whole of our four days' journey, the girl, who sat by my side all the time, remained as though wrapped in her thoughts and spoke to me only after long intervals. All the time, though, I was conscious of her presence, and I think that she was conscious of mine.

" How is it that you, a woodman, can drive a motor car? " was her first question.

" I have not always been a woodman," I answered.

" Why did you want that boy's papers? " she asked.

" Because I wished to reach England and I might find it difficult to get a passport of my own," I admitted.

She abandoned the subject a little reluctantly. I

knew very well that she was longing to ask me further questions but I gave her no encouragement. On the following day, after a prolonged silence, she again adopted an interrogative tone. This time I found it less easy to answer her.

" Why did you risk your life for us? " she asked, with curious abruptness, towards the close of a long day's run.

" Because I admired the way you were facing what seemed to be certain death," I told her. " The worst of us are liable to an impulse like that."

" Is it true," she went on, " that some of the wood-men of the Forêt du Dom frequently rob travellers who have met with motor accidents? "

" Quite true," I admitted. " They have even been known to contribute to the accidents. I have done it myself."

She shivered.

" I wish you would not tell me those things," she said reproachfully.

" It is the truth," I assured her. " We rather thought of wrecking your car, but I watched you coming down the hill and afterwards I only thought of saving you."

She laughed a little nervously, but, for the moment, she avoided meeting my eye.

" You are a strange person," she declared. " Why were you masquerading as a woodman? "

" Because I have wrecked other things besides motor cars," I answered. " I was hiding from the police. This is a great opportunity for me to break away."

She sighed.

"I am sorry," she confessed. "All the same, I hope that you succeed."

After that she tried once or twice to get me to talk about myself. She even suggested possible excuses for my imaginary misdemeanours. About myself and my doings, however, I maintained a grim silence. In the end she ceased altogether from conversation.

At Boulogne I was entrusted with the car, which I drove to London and delivered according to instructions at the garage of the house in South Audley Street. There I received a message that the young lady, whom·I had avoided seeing at Folkestone, wished to speak to me the moment I arrived. I was shown into a little sitting room in the great house and she came to me almost at once. The first glimpse I had of her, as she crossed the threshold, gave me almost a shock. This fashionably dressed young woman, notwithstanding her sweet, almost appealing smile, was a strangely different person from the girl with the wind-blown hair and scornful lips whom I had seen hastening on her way to death.

"My uncle wished me to give you this," she said, handing me an envelope, "and I wondered ——" she raised her eyes to mine — "whether you would care to have a little memento of me?"

She gave me a picture of herself in a tortoise-shell frame, and I put it into my pocket with the envelope. She made room for me to sit by her side on the sofa, but I affected not to notice her gesture of invitation.

I had suddenly become conscious of a most amazing and unexpected sensation.

" I shall never forget that evening," she continued softly. " It was a wonderful jump, wasn't it? "

I was the victim of new impulses, bewildering and incomprehensible. They led me in the strangest direction. I wanted to explain to her exactly who I was, to make her realise that I was an outcast for all time. Yet, when I made my effort, I felt that my words were pitiably weak.

" I think, Miss Kindersley," I said, " that you had better forget as much of the whole affair as you can. Remember that I deliberately planned to wreck your car as I had done others. It was only a fancy which made me change my mind. Believe me, I am not a creditable acquaintance."

" But you might be," she persisted. " Won't you try? "

I shook my head.

" It is too late," I told her. " I am a hunted man to-day and shall be to the end. There is no country in the world where I could find safety or even rest for a little time. And what is coming to me I have earned."

In these chronicles of my life there is just one vice, the vice of cowardice, to which I have never had to plead guilty. Just at this juncture, however, the sight of her small white hand stealing out towards me, the little quiver of her proud lips, perhaps a faint waft of that perfume of which I had been dimly conscious on those four days when she had set by my side, some one of these things or all of them together gripped at my

heart, filled me with a vague terror of myself, so that
I did the only thing which seemed possible — I hurried
out of the room and out of the house.

Mr. Younghusband's face was a picture when I
visited him the next morning at his offices in Lincoln's
Inn. I was still in my chauffeur's livery, which, with
its peaked hat, afforded an excellent disguise, but he
recognised my voice at once and he shook in his chair.

" Surely," he faltered, " this is most unwise? "

" My friend," I answered, seating myself at the other
side of the table, " it may be unwise but it is necessary.
I found a perfectly safe means of getting into England,
and now that I am here I want money."

He drew his cheque book from the drawer but I
brushed it on one side.

" I will have a thousand pounds in Bank of England
notes," I told him, " and a draft on the Bank of England for the same amount. Send your clerk out for it,
then we can talk."

He obeyed me, struggling hard to retain his composure. I watched him with a smile.

" They say that you are a brave man when I am
away," I remarked, " that you never show the least
sign of losing your nerve."

" There is no one over here so rash as you," the
lawyer replied promptly. " There is no one else who
plays for such big stakes or runs such risks. The
others I can deal with. They take my advice, they
adopt caution as their motto. When you are in London, I never have a moment free from anxiety."

I shrugged my shoulders.

" I shall not trouble you much longer," I promised. " There is another matter to be cleared up, though. In Marseilles I was told that Janet Soale had drawn a large sum of money from you."

" It is utterly false," the lawyer replied. " She has not even applied for a penny."

I knew the truth then, of course. Louisa was never one to brook a rival. I felt a momentary compunction when I thought of Janet's terror in the café at Marseilles. After all, although we had ceased to care for one another, she had been faithful to me after her fashion.

" We heard that you were drowned at Marseilles," my companion remarked.

" It was a narrow escape," I admitted. " Rimmington and Greyes were both over there, and they got on my track through Janet and Louisa. I had luck that night and I needed it."

Mr. Younghusband moved uneasily in his chair.

" You were mad to come to London, " he declared.

" A species of desperation," I answered calmly. " If you had eaten nothing but black bread and soup and drunk nothing but sour wine for several months, you would be inclined to run a little risk yourself for the sake of a dinner at the Café Royal. "

" Why don't you retire? " the lawyer suggested, leaning across the table. " You have sufficient money and you are fond of the country. Why not make full use of your wonderful genius for disguise, choose some quiet spot and run no more risks? "

" The matter is worth considering," I admitted.
" There are a few little affairs to straighten out first,
though."

Mr. Younghusband looked at me curiously, then he
laid his forefinger upon the copy of the *Times* which he
had been studying when I entered the office.

" You are interested in to-morrow's event, I suppose? "

" What event? " I enquired.

The lawyer shrugged his shoulders. I could see quite
well that he did not believe in my ignorance.

" The marriage of your old friend, Norman Greyes."

I stared across the table incredulously.

" I have, indeed, been living out of the world," I
observed. " Whom is he marrying? "

Mr. Younghusband coughed. He was watching me
closely and he was almost embarrassed.

" Do you mean to tell me that you do not know? "
he demanded.

" Of course I don't," I replied, a little irritably.
" You seem to forget where I have been for the last
four months."

" Norman Greyes is marrying the lady whom I have
met as Mrs. Stanfield. She calls herself now Mrs.
Janet Soale."

That was, undoubtedly, one of the shocks of my life.
Janet and I were parted. I had deceived her as I had
done many other women, and, in her day, she had
served me well and faithfully. I had no ill-feeling
against her, especially now that I realised she had left
my money untouched. More than ever, however, I

meant to kill Norman Greyes. I held out my hand for
the *Times* and read the little announcement.

"Good!" I said. "I shall attend the reception
which I see is being given after the ceremony. It will
be interesting to see Norman Greyes's taste in pearls.
I see that he is having his collection strung as a wedding present for his wife."

"If you do, you're a madman," the lawyer declared
angrily.

"Madmen for luck," I replied.

JANET

It was exactly two months after I had left Marseilles when Norman Greyes walked into my little sitting
room in Smith Street, Westminster, where I was busy
typing a play for the Agency which occasionally sent
me work. He was gaunt and thin, and it was obvious
that he had not wholly recovered his strength, but he
showed every sign of his old promptitude and decision
of character. Before I had got over my surprise at his
coming, I felt his arms around me and every atom of
strength leaving my body. The most wonderful moment of my life had arrived!

"When will you marry me, Janet?" he asked, a
little later on, when he had set me back in my chair and
seated himself by my side.

"Marry you?" I gasped. "How can you talk of
such things!"

"Simply because they have to be talked about before
they can be undertaken," he replied. "I look upon you

as Michael's widow, but you have never cared for him as you are going to care for me."

"But you don't even know if Michael is dead," I protested, my heart beating fast, every fibre of my body quivering at the thoughts evoked by his words. Norman held my hand tightly.

"We are very sensible people, you and I," he said, "and we are going to look stark facts in the face. It doesn't matter in the least legally whether Michael is dead or not. He had at least two other wives alive in America when he married you."

I leaned towards him. Somehow or other, what would have seemed in my saner moments a sheer impossibility, seemed, at that moment, a perfectly natural and reasonable thing. Then, suddenly the old horror rose up in my mind.

"You forget," I told him, "you forget that I too —— "

He placed his hand gently over my lips.

"Janet," he interrupted, "nothing that either of us could do, no penance we could undertake, would bring Ladbrooke back to life. His widow has her pension — I have seen to that. For the rest, you must forget as I have forgotten."

"I killed him, Norman," I faltered.

"I have killed men myself in my day," he replied, "and I shall probably kill Michael, if he is still alive, before our accounts are finally settled. That affair does not concern us any longer. You acted on a momentary impulse. You were protecting the man whom you fancied, at that time, you cared for."

"I was doing more than that," I told him. "I was avenging myself. I was a stupid girl in those days — but I had ideas. No man had ever kised me upon the lips. He took me unawares. If I had had the weapon in my hand then, I should have killed him without any other thought."

I saw a look almost of content in the face of the man I loved.

"I always guessed that there was something of the sort, " he said. "The immediate question is, when are you going to marry me? "

I suppose I was weak, but all women are weak when the man they care for pleads. I had been through years of misery, and the time came when I was simply incapable of any further resistance. I became entirely passive, I did exactly as I was told, and marvellously happy I was in doing it. Just as I was, in my shabby clothes, we went out to a restaurant in Soho and dined. It was a queer little place, overcrowded and not too well ventilated, but to me it was like a room in a palace. All the time we made plans, or rather he made plans and I listened. My long struggle was at an end. We were to be married almost at once, to travel for a time in Italy, Egypt — all the places I had longed to visit — and afterwards to settle down in the country and forget. It was not until after Norman had left me in my rooms, and the joy of the evening was merged into memories, that I felt that chill sense of apprehension which I did not altogether lose until long afterwards. A sudden fear of Michael set me shivering. I could not believe that he was dead. I felt, somehow, that he would come back and stand between me and my new happiness. The fear became almost a paroxysm. I locked the door of my room and lay awake most of the night, terrified of the sound of a passing footstep, terrified when a taxicab stopped anywhere near, fearful even of the darkness of the room, out of the shadows of which I fancied that I could see Michael's cold, ageless face, with his strange smile and grey-green eyes, behind which lurked that curious sense of power. The night passed, but even during those wonderful days that followed the fear remained. It came back even at the moment of my supreme happiness, some weeks later, when I passed down the aisle of the church with Norman — his wife! I suddenly felt convinced that Michael was in the church. It was a terrible moment, although a brief one. I faltered, and Norman looked down at me anxiously. Then I laughed and pretended to gather up my train. It was nothing, I told him — just a shiver.

The rest, for some time, was just a dream. There were crowds of people at the house in Southwell Gardens where Norman's sister was giving a reception for us. Everybody was wonderfully nice to me, and I made new friends at every moment. Just as I was warned that it was time for me to go and change into my travelling gown, an uncle of Norman's, a Mr. Harold Greyes, asked me to show him the pearl necklace which had been Norman's present to me. I took him at once into the little room where the wedding gifts were set out. There was a small gathering of guests there, nearly all of whom were known to me. At the far end of the room, seated in a chair and apparently taking little interest in the proceedings, was the detective who had come from Scotland Yard to watch over the jewellery.

" I know that you have only a moment to spare," Mr. Greyes said to me. " I will just look at the pearls and be off. I am curious to see if Norman is really a judge."

I pointed to where the necklace was lying in its case. I myself was talking to one or two people who had finished their inspection. My companion glanced downwards, frowned, adjusted his eyeglass, dropped it and turned to me with a little smile.

" Quite a reasonable precaution, " he observed, " but was it necessary with a detective in the room? "

" I don't understand, " I told him, a little bewildered.

" The substitution of the necklace, " he explained. " Of course, these are very fair imitations but I wanted to see the real thing. "

I leaned down and felt a sudden thrill of apprehension. The necklace which was twined around its setting of ivory satin was one which I had never seen before. It was certainly not the one which I had taken in my fingers and showed to some friends of Norman's, less than half an hour ago.

I called to the detective.

" My pearl necklace has been taken within the last half an hour, " I exclaimed. " This is an imitation one which has been substituted! "

The detective first closed the door and then came back into the room. We both of us looked around.

Besides myself and my companion, Mr. Harold Greyes, there were present a very charming girl called Beatrice Kindersley, a great friend of Norman's, an elderly lady, Mrs. Phillipson, and a slim, soldierly-looking man who was a complete stranger to me but who, on account of his sunburnt complexion, I put down as an Anglo-Indian.

"Dear me," the latter exclaimed, "this is very distressing! A great many people have passed in and out during the last half-hour."

"It is only within the last three minutes," the detective said, "that I have moved to the further end of the room. May I ask, Lady Greyes, if every one here is known to you?"

"Miss Kindersley, certainly," I replied, "and Mrs. Phillipson. I don't think I have met you, have I?" I added, turning to the man.

He looked at me with a rather peculiar smile and I noticed for the first time that he was wearing rimless spectacles. He had a particularly high forehead and thick, grey-black hair brushed smoothly back. I cannot say that he actually reminded me of any one, yet something in his appearance filled me with a vague sense of uneasiness.

"I fear that I have not yet had that honour, Lady Greyes," he acknowledged quietly. "Your husband, however, is an old friend. My name is Escombe, — Colonel James Escombe of the Indian Army."

"If you are unknown to Lady Greyes, I must ask you to remain until Sir Norman arrives," the detective said.

"With the utmost pleasure," Colonel Escombe replied. "I have already had the privilege of renewing my acquaintance with him."

Beatrice Kindersley, who had been standing looking on, suddenly began to laugh. Her eyes shone and her apparently genuine amusement, after the tenseness of the last few moments, was a very pleasant interlude.

"Poor Colonel Escombe!" she exclaimed, passing her arm through his. "Why, he is one of Dad's oldest friends. He hates weddings and functions of all sorts, but I persuaded him to come here with me because he had met Sir Norman in India once. Please, Lady Greyes, may I take him away? We promised to call for Dad at his Club, and we are half an hour late already."

The detective was obviously disappointed. I murmured something conventional and shook hands with them both.

"I may be permitted, although a comparative stranger," Colonel Escombe said, as he bent over my fingers, "to wish you all the happiness which I am sure you deserve."

They passed out, without any undue haste, laughing and talking to each other. The detective hurried away on the track of some fresh enquiry. I moved back, urged by some irresistible impulse, to the case where the imitation pearl necklace was lying. For the first time I noticed a little label attached to it. I turned it over and read two words, written in a familiar handwriting, — "Michael's Gift."

Suddenly Norman came hurrying in, already

changed into a grey tweed travelling suit. He thrust
his arm through mine and swung me towards the
door.

" Janet dear, " he said, " you have exactly a quarter
of an hour, "

" One question, please, " I begged. " Did you ever
know a Colonel Escombe in the Indian Army? "

" Never in my life, " he answered.

I saw the detective hurrying towards us and I
clutched Norman's arm. I think that he must have
guessed from my face that something had happened.

" Norman, " I whispered, " supposing the necklace —— "

" Well, dear? "

" Supposing it was stolen? "

His grasp on my arm tightened.

" I shouldn't care a hang, sweetheart, " he whispered,
" so long as we catch that train in half an hour and
I have you all to myself for the rest of my life. "

MICHAEL

The greatest genius in the world cannot foresee all
contingencies. It has always been my practice to leave
something to fate. How on earth I was going to get
out of the house in Southwell Gardens, if the theft of
the necklace were discovered before I could get away
by natural means, I had been quite unable to make up
my mind. Fate, however, decided it for me. I left with
flying colours, rescued by the girl with the steadfast

eyes, whose lips had mocked at danger on the precipices of the Forêt du Dom.

" Where to? " she asked, as we took our places in her automobile.

" To the British Museum Tube, if you can take me so far, " I answered.

She gave the order to the chauffeur through the speaking tube.

Then she leaned back in her place. Her expression puzzled me. She was as pale as she had been on the day when she had faced death, but there was none of the exaltation in her face.

" You are disturbed? " I ventured.

" I am unhappy, " she answered.

" You regret your intervention? "

She shook her head.

" It is not that. You stole the pearls. "

" Of course I did, " I admitted.

" You are a thief! "

" I never pretended otherwise. "

Her eyes filled with tears.

" I will give you that credit," she confessed bravely. " Can I — would it be possible for me to buy the pearls from you? "

" For what purpose? " I enquired.

" To return to Lady Greyes, of course. Don't you see that I am partly responsible for their loss? "

" My dear young lady," I said earnestly, " the pearls are yours, with pleasure. I took them because the dramatic side of the theft appealed to me. Norman Greyes and I are old enemies. He has hunted me as only man can hunt man. His wife is an old acquaintance. It flattered my vanity to attend his reception unrecognised and to help myself to his wife's pearls. Allow me. "

I took off my silk hat and laid it upon the opposite seat. Then I passed my hand slowly from my forehead back over my hair, pressed the top of my skull and handed her the necklace. She had been on the point of tears a moment before. She looked at me now, her eyes wide open with wonder.

" I appreciate your surprise, " I told her. " As a matter of fact, this false top to my head is one of the most ingenious things my friends in Paris ever made for me. If Norman Greyes succeeds and I fail, you will probably see it one day in the Museum at Scotland Yard ."

The car pulled up outside the Tube Station. The girl held out her hand. She looked at me, and something of the feeling came into my heart which had driven me, a fugitive, from her house.

" I think that you are a very terrible but a very wonderful person, " she said. " Anyhow, I like to think that I have paid a part of my debt. "

The madness had me in its grip. I lifted her fingers to my lips. I laughed in my soul because she made no effort to withdraw them.

" The whole of it is paid, " I told her, as I turned away.

CHAPTER X

MICHAEL TELLS THE WHOLE STORY

It has always been my custom, as a notorious and much-sought-after criminal, to give special care to the building up of a new identity. It is my success in the various impersonations I have attempted which has enabled me for many years to completely puzzle that highly astute body of men leagued together under the auspices of Scotland.

After my brief but successful career as Colonel Escombe, of the Indian Army, I determined upon a complete change of characterisation and circumstances. I established myself in modest rooms at the back of Russell Square, took a small office at the top of a block of buildings in Holborn, had cards and stationery printed and a brass plate engraved, and made a fresh appearance in the Metropolis of my fancy as Mr. Sidney Buckross, jobbing stationer. I cannot say that my operations made very much impression upon the trade which I had adopted. I transferred a thousand pounds to my credit at a well-known London bank, wrote myself several letters a day, which I opened and replied to at my office, sallied out with a small

black bag, soon after ten, and, with the exception of a
leisurely hour for my midday meal, spent the rest of
my time in the safe seclusion of the British Museum.

I reëstablished a new hobby. In the intervals of
idleness which the spasmodic activities of my profession
had entailed, I had always been fascinated by the subject of ciphers. I knew perfectly well, for instance,
that half the advertisements in the Personal Column
of the *Times*, contained, to the person for whose eyes
they were intended, a meaning utterly different from
their obvious one. For example, one afternoon, after
having wasted a score of sheets of paper and an im-
mense amount of ingenuity, I was able at last to find
the real message conveyed under this absurd medley
of words:

> " Charles. What you require may be found in
> 1749. Laughing Eyes bids you have courage.
> Bring James. "

With only one word of the cipher at first clear to
me, I looked upon it as something of a triumph when
I was able to extract from this rubbish the following
message:

> " Lady in green, man dinner jacket and white
> tie. Frascati's 8 o'clock Monday. Will bring
> documents. Have currency. "

The announcement interested me. If these documents were worth money to the person to whom this
invitation was addressed, they were probably worth
money to me. I decided, without a moment's hesitation,
that I would meet the lady in green and the gentleman

in a dinner coat and white tie on Monday at Frascati's,
notwithstanding the shock to my sartorial instincts
which the costume of the latter was likely to inflict.   My
only trouble was not to clash with the person for whom
the advertisement was really intended.   At this I could
only make an attempt.   I inserted the following advertisement in the Personal Column of the *Times* on
the following morning:

> " Frascati's 7 not 8. "

The upshot I was compelled to leave to fate.

At ten minutes to seven on Monday evening I arrived at the restaurant indicated.   I ordered a table
for three and the best dinner the place could offer.
The moment I stepped back into the reception room I
recognised, beyond a shadow of doubt, my prospective
guests.   The man was a powerful-looking fellow, with
large, clumsy limbs, a mass of untidy hair, a bushy-
brown moustache streaked with grey, a somewhat
coarse complexion and bulbous eyes.   He wore, grace-
lessly, the costume which the advertisement had indicated.   The woman in green had somewhat overdone
her colour scheme.   There was a green plush band in
her hair and she wore an evening gown of the same
colour, cut very low and distinguished by a general air
of tawdriness.   She was, or rather had been, good-
looking in a bold, flamboyant sort of way and she had
still a profusion of yellow hair.   They both stared at
me when they saw me looking around and, with a little
inward shiver, I took the plunge.   I went boldly up to
them and shook hands.

"I have ordered dinner," I announced. "Will you let me show you the way?"

They accepted the situation without demur, and viewed the gold-topped bottle in the ice pail and the other arrangements for their entertainment with considerable satisfaction.

"I must say you're not quite the sort of chap we expected to find, is he, Lizzie?" the man remarked, as he seated himself heavily and performed wonderful operations with his napkin. "I thought all your lot were water drinkers."

I smiled.

"We are often misunderstood," I ventured.

We settled down and took stock of one another. The woman looked approvingly at my black tie and pearl studs. I have made it a rule never to be without a supply of the right sort of clothes.

"I'm sure, if I may say so, it's much more agreeable to do business with a gentleman," she remarked, with a sidelong glance at me. "Makes one feel so much more at home."

"Cocktails, too!" her companion exclaimed cheerfully, as the wine waiter approached with a silver tray. "You're doing us proud and no mistake."

I bowed and drank their healths. A cordial but cryptic silence seemed to me to be my best rôle. I had always the fear, however, of the other man arriving before the business part of our meeting had been broached. So as soon as the effects of the wine had begun to show themselves in some degree, I ordered another bottle and leaned confidentially forward.

"You have brought the documents with you?" I asked.

"You don't think we are out to make an April fool of a gentleman like you!" the lady replied, with a languishing glance. "But I would like you to understand this, Mr. — Mr. — "

"Martin," I suggested.

"Mr. Martin," she went on — "I would never have rounded on Ted if he had kept straight. He and I didn't get on, and that's the long and short of it. He was all right so far as the drink was concerned, and I never see him look at another woman in his life. All the same, Mr. Martin, for a woman of my temperament he was no fitting sort of a husband."

I felt a moment's sympathy for Ted. The lady, however, had more to say.

"When first he started those proceedings for divorce," she went on, dropping her voice a little and adopting a more intimate manner, "I was knocked altogether silly like. You know that, Jim, wasn't I?" she added, appealing to her male companion.

"Same here," he growled. "I'd have broken his blooming 'ead if I'd thought he was having us watched."

"And it's a broken head he'll get, the way he's going on, if he's not careful," the woman continued truculently. "Talk about making him a Cabinet Minister, indeed, and me left without a penny just because he got his divorce! I'll show him!"

"To revert for a moment to the documents," I ventured.

The lady touched a soiled, shabby hand bag, opened it and gazed inside for a moment.

"They're here, all right," she announced in a tone of satisfaction. "Mixed up with my powder and rouge and what not. You shall have them presently, Mr. Martin."

"That is, if you are prepared to part," the man intervened. "Cash down and no humbug about it."

"Part? Of course he's prepared to part!" the woman declared sharply. "Wouldn't be here if he weren't. That's right, isn't it, Mr. Martin?"

"Naturally," I agreed. "I have brought a considerable amount of money with me, quite as much as I can afford to part with, and the only question left for me to decide is whether the documents are worth it."

"You talk as if you were doing this little job on your own," she remarked, looking at me curiously.

"I have to be as careful as though I were," I replied. "I am sure you can understand that."

Her escort laughed coarsely.

"I guess you'll see there's some pickings left for yourself," he observed. "You know what I heard your boss say at Liverpool once."

"That will do, Jim," the woman interrupted impatiently. "Remember we are here for business."

I returned to the subject of our meeting.

"I think," I suggested, "the time has arrived when you might allow me to glance through those documents."

The woman looked across the table at her companion. He nodded assent.

" No harm in that, so far as I can see, " he observed.
" There's all in them as I promised, and a trifle more.
Enough to cook Ted's goose, and his swell friend's. "

The woman opened her handbag and produced a
dozen pages of type-written manuscript, soiled and a
little tattered.

" Just cast your eye over that first, " she invited.
" That's an exact copy of the speech which Ted prepared for the mass meeting in Liverpool in March. "

" In Liverpool, " I repeated, hoping for some elu-
cidation.

" The meeting that was called to decide upon the
Shipping Strike, " she explained, a little impatiently.

I glanced through the type-written pages. They
seemed to consist of a vehement appeal to the dockers,
bonders and Union of Seamen to inaugurate on the
following day the greatest strike in history, promising
them the support of the miners and railwaymen, and
predicting the complete defeat of the Government
within six weeks. The speech concluded with a pero-
ration, full of extreme revolutionary sentiments, and on
a blank page at the end, under the heading of " ap-
proved of ", were the signatures of a dozen of the best
known men in the Labour world.

" This speech — " I began tentatively, for the matter
was not yet clear to me.

" Was never delivered, of course, " the man interrupted. " You know all about that. Ted went down
to Liverpool as mild as a lamb. He stood up there on
the platform and told them that the present moment
was inopportune for a strike. Not only that, but the

next day he bamboozled them into accepting the employers' terms. "

" Satisfactory so far as it goes, " I observed, didactically but with caution. " And now ——— "

" Here, " the woman interrupted triumphantly, " is Lord Kindersley's letter, delivered to Ted that afternoon in Liverpool. "

I read the letter, dated from South Audley Street, and its opening phrases were illuminative. I knew now that Ted was Mr. Edward Rendall, the present leader of the Labour Party in the House of Commons.

> My dear Mr. Rendall, it began,
> This letter, which I am despatching by aeroplane messenger, will reach you, I trust, before you address the Meeting this evening. The matter with which it is concerned cannot be dealt with by the Federation of Shipowners, but, confirming our recent conversations, Sir Philip Richardson and I are willing, between us, to advance to-morrow Bank notes to the value of fifty thousand pounds, to be paid to the funds of your cause or to be made use of in any way you think fit, provided the strike threatened for to-morrow does not take place.
> Faithfully yours,
> Geoffrey Kindersley.
> P.S.—In your own interests, as well as ours, I suggest that you immediately destroy this letter. "

Things were now becoming quite clear to me. I even began to wonder if I had brought enough money.

" As a matter of curiosity, " I asked, " why did your

husband not take Lord Kindersley's advice and destroy
this letter? "

The woman laughed unpleasantly. There was
mingled cunning and self-satisfaction in her expression.

" He told me to, " she replied. " As a matter of
fact, he thought he saw me tear it up. It was just at
the time that I was beginning to have my suspicions
of Master Ted, so I tore up a circular instead and
put this by for a bit. "

· " A pretty clever stroke of work, too, " the man
opposite murmured, with an approving grin. " You
put a rod in pickle for Ted that day, Lizzie. "

" And serve him right, too, " the lady remarked,
glancing in her mirror and making some trifling re-
arrangement of her coiffure.

There was a brief silence. The man drew his chair a
little closer to the table and addressed me with a
businesslike air.

" Now, Mr. Martin, or whatever your name is, let's
finish this job up, " he proposed. " You've got a copy
of the speech that Ted Rendall promised his pals to
deliver at Liverpool, typed at Mrs. Simons' office,
Number 23, Dale Street. You've got the original
letter from Lord Kindersley, proving up to the hilt
why he didn't deliver it, and, " he went on, striking the
table with his fist, " I am now going to tell you that
that fifty thousand pounds was handed over to Ted at
the National Liberal Club the following evening at six
o'clock and was paid in by him, to his own credit, to
five different banks on the following morning. The

names of the banks are there, in pencil, on the back of Lord Kindersley's letter. "

" And when I asked him for a hundred a year to keep me respectable, " the woman declared, with an angry colour rising to her cheeks, " he sent my letter back through his lawyers, without a word. "

I leaned back in my chair and felt my way a little further.

" If we make a deal and you part with these documents to me, " I said, " what use do you expect me to make of them? "

" Any use you choose, so long as you pay enough, " the woman answered bluntly.

" We know pretty well whom you're acting for, " the man put in, with a knowing grin. " I guess it won't be long before Charlie Payton handles these documents, if we come to terms. "

" You have no conditions to make? " I asked.

" None! " the woman snapped. " I've finished with Ted. He's a cur. You can publish the whole lot in the *Daily Mail*, if you like, for all I care. "

" Then there remains only the question of price, " I concluded.

The flush of wine and the momentary expansiveness of good feeding seemed to pass from the faces of my two guests. A natural and anxious cupidity took its place. They feared to ask too little, they were terrified lest they might scare me away by asking too much.

" They'd be worth a pretty penny to Ted, " the woman muttered.

" You don't want to sell them to him, " I pointed out.

"I don't and that's a fact," she admitted. "Look here, Mr. Martin, they're yours for a thousand pounds."

A thousand pounds was precisely the sum I had brought with me. Without remark, I counted out the notes and pocketed the documents. The man and woman seemed very surprised at this uneventful finish to the proceedings. The latter tucked away the notes in her hand bag, whilst I paid the bill. When I rose to take leave of them, I could see, standing in the doorway and looking at us with a puzzled expression, a middle-aged man, whom I decided at once was the individual whom I had impersonated.

"The business is over, and, I trust, pleasantly," I said. "Will you forgive me if I take my leave. There are others who are anxious to hear from me."

The woman clutched her bag with her left hand and extended her right.

"Well, I'm sure you've been quite a gentleman, Mr. — Mr. — let me see, what was the name?"

"Well, it doesn't matter, does it," I replied, "especially as it was only assumed for the evening? Good night and good luck to you both," I added, as I made my escape.

There was a fine rain falling outside but I walked steadily on, obsessed with the sudden desire for fresh air. The atmosphere of the place I had left, the character of my companions, the sordid ignominy of the transaction which I had just concluded had filled me with disgust. Then I began to laugh softly to myself. It was a queer anomaly, this, that I, the notorious criminal, for whom the police of the world were always searching, should feel distaste at so ordinary an ill-deed. I had robbed, and struck ruthlessly enough, in my time, at whomever might stand in my way, but, as a matter of fact, blackmailing was the one malpractice which had never happened to come my way. In any case, as I reminded myself, the ignominious part of the affair was over. Its continuation was likely to appeal more both to my sense of humour and my natural instinct for cruelty. Over a late whisky and soda that night in my room, I began to build my plans. It seemed to me that the career of Mr. Edward Rendall, M.P., and the reputation of Lord Kindersley were equally in my hands. It was surely not possible that the two combined would not produce a reasonable profit upon my outlay of a thousand pounds. As I sat and smoked, another idea occurred to me and, before I retired to rest, I wrote a long letter of instructions to Mr. Young-husband.

I remained at my office in Holborn on the following morning until I heard from Mr. Younghusband upon the telephone. As usual he was most formal, addressing me as though I were one of his ordinary and respected clients. It was obvious, however, that he was perturbed.

" I have carried out your instructions to the letter, Mr. — er — Buckross, " he announced, " but the magnitude of the operation which you have ventured upon has, I confess, rather staggered me. "

" Let me know exactly what you have done, " I said.

" I have sold, " he continued, " on your account,

through various firms of stockbrokers, twenty-five thousand ordinary shares in the Kindersley Shipping Company at six pounds each. Fortunately, there is no
immediate prospect of a rise in shares of this description and I was able to arrange to leave cover amounting
to only ten shillings a share, namely, twelve thousand,
five hundred pounds. "

" Very good, " I assented. " What is the price just
now? "

" The shares have dropped a trifle, naturally, " the
lawyer replied, " owing to your operations. The stock-
broker, however, at whose office I now am, advises me to
disregard that fact. He thinks that they will probably
recover during the day. "

" Just so! When is settlement day? "

" On the fourth. Apropos of that, the various
brokers with whom I have had dealings on your behalf
desire to know whether you would wish to close your
transactions or any portion of them during the next
few days, if a profit of, say, a quarter a share is
shown. "

" Not on any account, " I insisted. " The transaction must remain exactly as it is until I give the word. "

I rang off, filled my bag, as usual, with stationery
samples and took the tube to Bond Street, where I
walked to South Audley Street. Upon arrival at my
destination, I was informed, by an imposing-looking
butler that Lord Kindersley was at home but it was
scarcely likely that he would receive me unless I had
an appointment. I risked the butler's being human,
and bought my way as far as the waiting room. Once

arrived there, I managed to impress an untidy and
bespectacled secretary with the idea that it might be
worth Lord Kindersley's while to spare me a few minutes of his time. In the end, I was ushered into the
great man's sanctum.

"What can I do for you — Mr. Buckross?" he
enquired, glancing at my card.

I was anxious to test my new identity and I stood
full in the light. It was obvious, however, that Lord
Kindersley had not an idea that we had ever met before.
He did not connect the slightly nervous business man
who now addressed him with the woodman-chauffeur
who had brought him safely from the Forêt du Dom to
England.

"I have come to see you on a very serious matter,
Lord Kindersley," I said, "and I am anxious that
there should be no misunderstanding. I do not wish
for a penny of your money. I am here, in fact, to save
you from the loss of a great deal of it. My visit, nevertheless, has a very serious side."

He looked at me steadily from under his bushy eyebrows.

"Go on," he invited curtly.

"Last March," I continued, "you averted the
threatened shipping strike and saved yourself the loss
of at least one of your millions by bribing a well-known
Labour leader to declare for peace instead of war.
You and one other great shipowner were alone concerned in this matter. That other man, I gather, is
dead."

Lord Kindersley was looking at me with a queer look

in his eyes. I realised suddenly how heavily pouched they were underneath, how unwholesome the power of his face. His voice, when he answered me, was unsteady.

"What on earth are you talking about?"

I took the two documents from my pocket and moved a little nearer to him.

"Here," I said, "is Rendall's proposed speech, counselling the strike and signed by the leaders of the various Unions. Here, also is your letter to Rendall, making him the offer of fifty thousand pounds to with-hold it, which sum was paid to him the next evening at the National Liberal Club."

All the initial affability and condescension had gone from Lord Kindersley's manner. He looked like a man on the verge of a collapse.

"My God!" he muttered. "Rendall swore that he had destroyed my letter!"

"He instructed his wife to do so. She retained it for her own purposes. A few months ago her husband divorced her. This is her revenge. She has sold the copy of the speech and the letter to me. I know, also, the other facts in connection with the case."

Lord Kindersley took out his handkerchief and mopped his forehead. Already he began to see his way.

"I will buy those documents from you," he proposed.

"Your lordship," I replied, "I am not a black-mailer."

"You shall receive the money quite safely," he went on eagerly. "I should not dream of communicating with the police. I shall look upon it as an equitable business transaction. Name your price. I am not a mean man. "

" Neither, as I remarked before, am I a blackmailer, " I persisted. " My use for these letters is predestined. They go to the Press. "

Lord Kindersley sprang to his feet.

" What good will that do you? " he demanded hoarsely.

" Not very much financially perhaps, " I acknowledged. " On the other hand, I know one newspaper, I think, which would pay me a large sum for them. "

He brushed the idea on one side.

" Listen, " he said, impressively, " no newspaper would deal with you as liberally as I am prepared to. Those documents must not be published. If it were generally known that I had bribed Rendall to hold up that speech, the Unions would declare war against me to-morrow. Not a man would stay in my employ. Besides, it would bring discredit upon my Party. It would ruin me politically as well as actually. Come now, Mr. Buckross, you look like a business man. Let's talk business. I'll write you a cheque for ten thousand pounds this morning. "

" Your lordship, " I replied, " if I dealt with you in the way you suggest, it would amount to a criminal offence. My conscience forbids it. I can deal with the Press fairly and openly. Your political ruin I cannot help. Your financial ruin I may help you to modify. I offer you four days' grace, during which time you had better get rid of as many of your shares in the Kindersley Shipping Company as you can. "

" You promise to do nothing for four days? " Lord
Kindersley exclaimed eagerly.

" I promise. "

He leaned back in his chair and mopped his forehead.

" Well, that's a respite, at any rate, " he said. " Now
Mr. Buckross, you and I have got to understand one
another on this deal. "

" We shall never get any nearer understanding one
another than we are at present, " I assured him.

" Rubbish! " he answered. " What I want you to
do is to get that blackmailing idea out of your head.
You have something to sell and I want to buy it. It's
a commercial transaction, pure and simple, and the end
and aim of all commercial transactions is to obtain the
best price possible for what you have to sell. I mentioned ten thousand pounds. It seemed to me a comfortable little sum but I can afford more, if necessary.
Look here, stay and have lunch with me, and we'll discuss the matter over a cigar and a glass of wine. "

" I should be taking your lunch under false pretences, " I replied, rising and buttoning my coat.
" You shall have the four days' grace which I have
promised. "

He followed me to the door, entreating me for my
address. So convinced was he that I would change my
mind that he sent his secretary out into the street after
me. In the end I made my escape by promising to see
him again on the evening of the third day. I made the
promise in my one moment of weakness. It occurred
to me that it would give me pleasure if, by any chance,
I should see, for a moment, the girl whose courage was

of so fine a quality that she neither feared a hideous death on the verge of a precipice nor disgrace in a London drawing-room.

I took my usual leisurely lunch and afterwards made my way to the uninspiring neighbourhood of Streatham. " The Towers, " which I had discovered from a book of reference to be Mr. Edward Rendall's address, was a hopelessly vulgar edifice of grey stone, approached by what is generally described as a short carriage drive. An untidy-looking servant admitted me, after some delay, and escorted me across a linoleum-covered hall, odoriferous of a hot meal, to a small study at the back of the house, filled with shoddy furniture and hung with imitation prints. The popular M.P., as was his boast, was not in the least difficult of access. He came into the room within a few minutes, a pipe in his mouth, and giving evidence of all the easy good-nature which befitted his position.

" Don't know who you are, Mr. Buckross, " he said, noticing with some surprise that I had not availed myself of the opportunity of shaking hands with him, " but sit down, and welcome. What can I do for you? "

" I have brought you bad news, Mr. Rendall, " I announced.

" The devil you have! " he answered, removing his pipe from his teeth and staring at me. " Who are you, anyway? I don't seem to recognise your name. "

" That really doesn't matter, " I replied. " You can call me a journalist, if you like. It's as near the truth as anything about myself that I'm likely to tell you. Something very disagreeable is going to happen to you

on the fourth day from now, and, as I am partly responsible for it, I have come out here to give you a word
of warning. "

" You're getting at me, " he protested uneasily.

" Not in the least, " I assured him. " The facts to
which I allude are these. I have in my possession a
copy of the speech which you ought to have made at
Liverpool last March and didn't, and also the original
letter from Lord Kindersley, offering you fifty thousand
pounds to hold it up. I also know that you received
that money on the following evening at the National
Liberal Club, and I know what banks you entrusted
it to. "

Rendall was, I believe, at heart, just as much of a
coward as Kindersley, but he showed it in a different
fashion.

" You d — d, lying blackmailer ! " he shouted.
"How dare you come here with such a story ! Get out
of the house or I'll throw you down the steps."

" I have fulfilled my mission, " I told him. " I shall
be very glad indeed to go. "

" Stop ! " he shouted, as I turned towards the door.
" How did you come by this cock-and-bull story? "

" How should I have come by it at all unless it were
the truth? " I answered. " The whole world will know
the facts soon enough. I obtained the papers from
your wife. "

" That's a lie, then, " he declared truculently, " for
I saw her destroy the letter."

I smiled. The man, after all, was poor sport.

" She deceived you, " I replied. " You saw her destroy a circular. She kept the letter. Perhaps she had her reasons. I bought it from her and another man at Frascati's restaurant last night. "

Conviction seized upon Mr. Edward Rendall and, with conviction, fear.

" Look here, " he proposed, " let's sit down and talk this over. I'll tell the girl to bring in cigars and a drop of whisky. "

" I have not the least idea of accepting any hospitality from you, " I assured him. " The documents are going to the Press in four days' time. I came here to give you that much notice. "

His eyes narrowed a little.

" How do I know that the whole thing isn't a kid? " he said suspiciously. " Have you got them with you? "

" I have, " I told him.

He attempted nothing in the way of subtlety. He relied, I suppose, upon his six feet and his brawny shoulders. He came at me like a bull, head down and fists swinging. It was a very ridiculous encounter.

Next morning there were sensational paragraphs in most of the financial papers. Shipping shares all reacted slightly in sympathy, but the slump in Kindersley's was a thing no one could account for. They had fallen from six to five within twenty-four hours, and as soon as I reached my offices in Holborn, I received frantic messages from Mr. Younghusband, imploring me to close with a profit of over twenty thousand pounds. There was nothing whatever wrong with the shares, he assured me, and they were bound to rally. I listened to all he had to say, gave him positive instructions not to disturb my operations in any way and, disregarding his piteous protests, rang off and made my way to the great newspaper offices, where my business of the morning lay.

It took me an hour to get as far as the assistant editor. He was a lean man, with horn rimmed spectacles and an inevitable sequence of cigarettes. He told me frankly that I had as much chance of seeing the editor as the Pope. So I told him my story and showed him the documents. He went out of the room for a moment and returned with the editor. They both looked at me curiously.

"Who are you, Mr. Buckross?" the editor asked.

"A speculator," I answered. "I bought those papers from Rendall's divorced wife. She has a spite against him."

"How can one be sure that they are genuine?"

"Any one who studies them must know that they are," I replied. "If you want confirmation, I told Lord Kindersley yesterday of their existence and forthcoming publication and advised him to sell as many of his shares as possible. Your financial column will tell you the rest of the story."

The two men whispered together for some time. Then the editor, who was a grey-haired, clean-shaven man, with a mouth like a rat trap and a voice like a military martinet, drew up an easy chair and seated himself by my side.

"What do you want us to do with these documents, Mr. Buckross?" he asked.

" I want you to give me a very large sum of money for them and then publish them, " I replied.

" You know that there will be the devil of a row? "

" That will be your lookout. Their genuineness will be your justification. "

The editor looked thoughtfully out of the window. His face was as hard as granite but he had very grey, human eyes.

" We should have no compunction about bringing the thunders down upon Rendall, " he said, " but with Lord Kindersley it is a little different. He is a considerable and reputable figure in Society. "

" He might survive the disclosures, " I suggested. " After all, there was a certain amount of justification for his conduct. He averted a national disaster, even if the means he used were immoral. "

" A case can be built up for him, certainly, " the editor remarked musingly. " What is your price for these documents? "

" Ten thousand pounds, and they must not be used before Thursday, " I replied.

" Why not before Thursday? "

" I have given Lord Kindersley so much grace. "

" You will leave the documents in our hands? " the editor proposed.

I considered the matter. I could think of nothing likely to alter my plans, but I was conscious of a curious aversion to taking the irrevocable step.

" You shall have them, " I agreed, " if you will give me a letter acknowledging that they are my property, and promising to return them to me without publication, should I desire it, on Wednesday afternoon. "

" What about the money? " the editor asked. " Do you want anything on account? "

" You are prepared to give me the ten thousand pounds? "

He shrugged his shoulders.

" We never bargain, " he said. " There is no standard value for such goods as you offer. The question is whether you want anything in advance? "

" No, thank you, " I answered. " I'll have the whole amount on Wednesday afternoon, or the documents back again. I think that it will be the money. "

" I trust so, " my two editorial friends replied, in fervent unison.

On Wednesday morning the Kindersley Shipping Company shares stood at three and three quarters, and a brief notice in the *Times* announced that his lordship was confined to his house in South Audley Street, suffering from a severe nervous breakdown. Some idiotic impulse prompted me, after I had paid my brief visit to my office, to take a stroll in that direction. A doctor's carriage was waiting outside Kindersley House, and, as I passed on the other side of the way, the front door opened and the doctor himself stood on the threshold. The thought of Lord Kindersley's sufferings had, up to the present, inspired in me no other feeling than one of mild amusement. By the side of the doctor, however, Beatrice Kindersley was standing. I knew then that the end of my career must be close at hand. I was weakening. My nerve had gone. The instincts of childhood were returning to me. The morbid curiosity which had brought me to the house had been gratified with a vengeance. I had received a psychological stroke. The girl's drawn and tear-stained face had disturbed the callousness which I had deemed impregnable. A new scheme was forcing its way into my mind. There was only one redeeming point about it all — I walked for the next few hours in peril of my life.

At half-past two that afternoon, Beatrice Kindersley hastened into the little morning room on the ground floor of Kindersley House to receive an unexpected visitor. Her lips parted in amazement when she saw who it was. I held up my finger.

"Colonel Escombe," I reminded her.

"You!" she exclaimed.

I knew that there was not a flaw in my make-up or deportment. I was the Colonel Escombe who had attended Norman Greyes's wedding, and, in connection with whose presence there had been some slight question concerning a pearl necklace.

"What do you want?" she asked breathlessly.

"To help you," I answered. "I saw you this morning and you seemed in trouble."

She smiled at me gratefully but a moment later her face was clouded with anxiety.

"It is dear of you," she said, "but you must go away at once. You are running a terrible risk. Sir Norman Greyes is in the house. He is with my uncle now."

"What is he doing here?" I demanded.

"My uncle sent for him to see if he could help. There is some serious trouble. I don't know what it is but my uncle says that it means ruin."

At the thought of the near presence of my old enemy, my whole being seemed to stiffen. Yet, alas! the weakness remained.

"Listen," I said, "what does your distress mean? Has your uncle always been good to you? Is it for his sake that you are unhappy?"

"Entirely," she answered without hesitation. "I know that a great many people call him hard and unscrupulous. To me he has been the dearest person in the world. It makes my heart ache to see him suffer."

I glanced at my watch.

"Listen," I said, "give me five minutes to get clear away. When I am gone, give him this message. Tell him that Buckross has changed his mind and that he will hear from him before five o'clock."

"What have you to do with all this?" she asked, wonderingly.

"Never mind," I answered. "Be sure to give me five minutes, and don't deliver my message before Norman Greyes."

She walked with me to the door, but when I would have opened it she checked me. Already her step was lighter. She took my hands in hers and I felt her soft breath upon my face.

"I am going to thank you," she whispered.

It was an absurd interlude.

Both the editor and the assistant editor did everything, short of going down on their knees, to induce me to change my mind. They offered me practically a fortune. They hinted, even, that honours might be obtained for me. They tried to appeal to my patriotism, to every known quality, not one of which I possessed. In the end I obtained the documents, addressed them to Miss Beatrice Kindersley, bought a great bunch of fragrant yellow roses, hired a messenger to go with me in the taxicab, and saw them delivered at Kindersley House.

That night I spent in my room, taking stock of myself. On the credit side, my deal in Kindersley's had brought me a profit of something like thirty thousand pounds, likely to be considerably added to as I had bought again at four. Further, I had abstained from becoming a blackmailer and I had knocked Mr. Edward Rendall down. On the other hand, I might easily have made a hundred thousand pounds — and I had behaved like a fool.

Perhaps the most disquieting feature of it all was that I was satisfied with the deal.

CHAPTER XI

NORMAN GREYES

It was towards the close of a dinner party at Kindersley Court, in Devonshire, where Janet and I were spending a fortnight, that our host suddenly directed the conversation to me.

"One has heard a great deal of your successes, Greyes, especially during your last few years at Scotland Yard. What do you count your greatest failure?"

"My inability to bring to justice the greatest criminal in Europe," I replied, after a moment's hesitation. "I had him on my book for three years, but when I retired, he was still very much at large. We have been up against one another continually. Sometimes he has had the better of it, sometimes I. But the fact remains that, though there have been at least a dozen misdemeanours which might have been brought home to him, he has slipped out of our hands every time we have formulated even a nominal charge."

"Has he ever been in prison?" some one asked.

"Never," I replied. "Not only that, but he has

never even been apprehended, never even brought before a magistrate. "

" What is his name? " Lord Kindersley asked, with some interest.

I smiled.

" A name with him, I suspect, is an affair of the moment. I have known him under a dozen different pseudonyms, but his real name is, I believe, Michael. He did me the honour to attend my wedding reception as Colonel Escombe. "

I happened to meet the glance of Beatrice Kindersley as I looked across the table. She drew herself up for a moment and I fancied that there was a steely glint in her very beautiful eyes.

" I met a Colonel Escombe there, whom I thought charming, " she said coldly.

" It was probably our friend, " I assured her. " He is quite the most accomplished scoundrel in Europe. "

" Sometimes, " she remarked, " I think it would be interesting to hear how the goats talk of the sheep. I expect they would be able to find faults in the lives of the most perfect of us law-abiders. "

" But tell us more about this man Michael? " Lord Kindersley intervened. " I remember, seven or eight years ago, hearing something about the duel between you fellows at Scotland Yard and a wonderfully led criminal gang. Where is the fellow now ?"

" The answer to that question, " I told him, " would bring you in about five thousand pounds in rewards and possibly a bullet through your heart as an informer. "

" You really couldn't lay your hand upon him at the present moment if you wanted to? "

I shook my head.

" I shouldn't have the faintest idea where to look for him. If he comes into the limelight again, my friend Rimmington at Scotland Yard will certainly send for me. "

" And you would join in the hunt? " our host persisted.

" I am not sure, " I admitted.

" You would do nothing of the sort, " Janet intervened, looking across at me. " That is a promise. "

I smiled back at her reassuringly. Prosperity and peace of mind had agreed with Janet. The dignity of wifehood sat well upon her. Her complexion seemed to have grown more creamy, her beautiful eyes softer, her carriage, always graceful, more assured. There was no woman in the county more admired than she — certainly no one less spoiled. She was absolutely and entirely contented with our simple country life. I sometimes think that, if she had had her way, she would never have wandered at all outside our little domain. More than once, when I had broached the subject, she had evaded the question of a visit to London or Paris, but, curiously enough, it was only at that moment that I realised the truth. She still feared Michael.

" There is just the one possibility, " I remarked, " that I might not be able to evade the challenge. If I do not go after Michael, he may come after me. "

It was precisely at this moment that the amazing event happened. We were a party of twelve at dinner, seated at a round table in the centre of the large banquetting hall of Kindersley Court. The room was rather dimly lit, except for the heavily shaded lamps upon the table and the shaded electric lights over some of the old Masters around the walls, lights which had been turned on during the meal at the request of one of the guests. The two footmen had left the room, presumably to fetch the coffee, and the butler standing behind Lord Kindersley's chair was the only servant in attendance. Suddenly every light in the place went out and we were plunged into the most complete darkness. Conversation was broken off for a moment, then there was the usual little medley of confused exclamations.

" Never knew such a thing happen before, " our host declared, in an annoyed tone. " Somebody must have been tinkering with the power house. Fetch some candles, Searle. "

The butler turned to grope his way towards the door but he was not allowed to reach it. A further sensation was in store for us. From various parts of the shadowy spaces on every side of us, little pinpoints of fire blazed out and steadily approached, without sound. One of them came to a standstill immediately behind Lord Kindersley's chair. Wielded by some unseen hand, the dazzling brilliancy of a high-powered electric torch was flashed round upon twelve amazed faces. Then a strange voice broke the spellbound silence, a voice still and cold and perfectly

modulated. Every word seemed to have the crispness
of a pistol shot.

"Ladies and gentlemen," the intruder said, "there
is no need for any particular alarm. This is, to use
a slang phrase, a 'hold-up.' If you all sit still and
keep still and obey orders, you will be moderately safe.
If any one attempts to leave his chair or to strike a
match I, or one other of my four friends, will shoot.
We have automatic pistols, and I trust that you will
realise the absurdity of resistance."

"God bless my soul!" Lord Kindersley exclaimed.
"Where are all my servants? How the devil did you
get in?"

"It is scarcely policy to let you into the secret of
our methods," the same cold voice continued, "but I
have no objection to telling you that we came in
through the front door, that your servants are locked
up and guarded in the servants' hall, very much as
you are, that your telephone wires are cut, your elec-
tric-light supply is in our hands, and the lodge gates
guarded. You ladies will kindly place all the jewellery
you are wearing upon the table in front of you. There
must be no delay, please, or any attempt at concealment. Madame," the voice continued, and there was
something terrible in its menacing quality, the torch
flashing at the same moment into the startled face of
a woman on the opposite side of the table, "if you
attempt to drop any of your jewellery upon the floor,
or to conceal it in any way, you will force us to adopt
measures which we should regret."

"What shall I do?" the woman next to me whispered hoarsely. " I am wearing my emeralds — Jack implored me not to — they are worth a hundred thousand pounds. "

" You will have to do as the others are doing, " I told her. " The first act of this little drama must be played out according to orders. "

She unclasped the necklace with trembling fingers, and the unseen figure behind Lord Kindersley's chair spoke again.

" Will it be Sir Norman Greyes who struts across the stage in the second act? " he asked mockingly.

Then I knew who was there, and I remembered that Michael had sworn to take my life when and how the opportunity offered. I was an easy mark for him, sitting there, but somehow the idea of assassination never had any terrors for me.

" I may occupy the stage for a little time, " I answered, feeling for my wine through the darkness. " But, after all, it will be the third act that counts. Which will you choose, I wonder, Michael — the gallows at Wandsworth Gaol or the electric chair at Sing Sing? "

This, of course, was sheer bravado, a touch of melodrama of which I repented as soon as I had indulged in it. I heard the click of a weapon, and in the steady glare of that small circle of light I saw the flash upon its barrel as it drew level with my head. There was a silence as poignant as it was hysterical, then a cry from Janet rang through the room. All this time the business of collecting the jewellery was proceeding without interruption.

"A familiar voice, I fancy," Michael said coldly, as he lowered his weapon. "You do well to intervene, dear lady. Some day or other, I think that your husband will kill me or I him, but, unless he hunts me with a posse of policemen, it will be when we are both armed and the odds are even."

There was a little sobbing sigh from somewhere in the background. Then the silence was broken again in less dramatic fashion.

"May I speak, please?" Beatrice Kindersley asked.

Instantly the light flashed upon her face. I was amazed at her composure. Her eyes were bright and sparkling and her cheeks full of colour. She had the air of being one of a vitally interested audience following the mazes of some fascinating drama. I heard the voice from the darkness answer her. It was no longer the voice I recognised.

"Say what you have to say as quickly as possible, please."

"I have put my rings and bracelets upon the table. I am wearing around my neck a miniature set with brilliants. It is not really very valuable but it was left me by a relative. May I keep it?"

The light flashed for a moment upon the pendant which she seemed to be holding forward for examination, flashed on the little heap of her jewellery upon the table.

"Pray keep your miniature," the voice conceded. "Do me the further honour, if you will, of replacing your jewellery upon your fingers and your wrists. We are not here to rob children of their baubles."

Beatrice's laugh was a most amazing thing. It was perfectly natural and full of amused enjoyment.

" I don't like the reflection upon my jewellery, " she complained. " However, since you are so generous, I will accept your offer. "

" Look here, " Lord Kindersley exclaimed, finding a certain courage from his niece's complete composure, " is this a practical joke? Because, if so, it has gone d — d well far enough! "

" You will discover if it is a practical joke or not, if you attempt to leave your seat! " was the instant reply.

" These fellows can't think they're going to get away with a thing like this, " muttered Lord Harroden, the Lord Lieutenant of the County, from the other end of the table.

" Your lordship is mistaken, " was the confident reply from the unseen figure who was directing the proceedings. " I will lay you five to one in hundreds that we do, payment to be made through the Personal Column of the *Times* in thirty days' time. "

" Gad, he's a cool hand! " chuckled Anstruther, the Master of Hounds, who was seated next but one to me, " I wish I could see his face for a moment. "

" It would be your last on earth if you did, " he was promptly told.

" What if I strike a match? " a young man who was seated next to Beatrice Kindersley, enquired.

" I should put it out with one bullet and you with the next, " Michael assured him grimly. " Now, ladies and gentlemen, " he went on, after a brief pause,

" our business seems to be over. Any one who leaves
his seat before we reach the door will be shot. As
soon as we get there we shall lock you in, and then you
can commence your part of the fun as soon as you like.
If you care for suggestions, why not leave it to Mr.
Anstruther to organise a midnight steeplechase, every
one to choose his own mount, motor car, hunter or
bicycle. We sha'n't leave much of a trail, but for once
in a while you'll be worrying something to death that
can spit death back. Why don't you come and try?
You'll all be welcome. "

No one attempted a single word of reply. The little points of fire were kept turned upon us whilst our
visitors slowly retreated. We heard the door unlocked, heard it slammed, heard it locked again — the
signal for our emancipation. Very nearly simultaneously, we all started to our feet. Two of the women
were sobbing and shrieking. The woman whose emerald necklace had gone was the least discomposed of
any.

" I wouldn't have missed this show for the world, "
she declared.

" I'm all for the steeplechase, " Anstruther proposed. " Gad! that fellow would be worth hunting! "

" I'll sack every servant in the house, " Lord Kindersley growled. " Curse them all, why doesn't some
one come! "

Every one was talking at once, without much result.
We rang bells that made no sound and battered at the
door, a somewhat futile proceeding, as it was several
inches thick. Some one found a box of matches and,

illuminated by the fitful flame, the faces of the little company were a Holbein-like study. With the help of some chairs, I mounted to the windows, but they were too narrow to allow the passage of even the slimmest of us. Finally Lord Kindersley groped his way back to the table from the sideboard with a fresh decanter of port in his hand.

" Dash it all, " he exclaimed, " let's have another glass of wine! I don't mind telling you that I'm shaking all over. It was like having the Lord High Executioner behind one's chair. His pistol was real enough, too. I felt it once against my neck. Ugh! "

Anstruther asked me a question from somewhere in the shadows.

" Greyes, " he said, " you were speaking of a famous criminal, a man named Michael. You called that fellow —— "

" That was the man, " I told him.

The drama of it all was curiously poignant. We sat around in the match-lit darkness, talking in disjointed fashion, waiting until such time as the servants might find their way to our relief.

" Greyes seems to me to be the lucky man, " Lord Harroden remarked. " He could have settled scores with you, all right — potted you like a sitting rabbit any moment he wanted to. "

" Quite true, " I admitted, " but the one thing which has made the pursuit of Michael so fascinating is that he is the sort of man who would never shoot a sitting rabbit. He spoke the truth when he said that the end would come when one or the other of us was

driven into a corner and both were armed. So far as
I am concerned, " I added, glancing across at Janet,
" I am rather inclined to let it be a drawn battle. The
hunting of men is a great sport but the zest for it
passes with the years. "

Release came at last; another key to the apartment where we were imprisoned was found, the door
was thrown open and a stream of servants with lamps
and candles entered. A few minutes of incoherent exclamations followed. It seemed that the servants' hall
had been locked at both ends and guarded in the same
way as the banqueting hall, the guests' bedrooms had
been systematically ransacked, and it became clear
that the marauders must have numbered at least fifteen
or twenty. The orders which Lord Kindersley roared
out were almost pitifully ineffective. In due course
we discovered that the telephone wires had indeed been
cut, that every motor car in the garage had been rendered useless, the stables emptied and every horse
driven out into the Park. We were seventeen miles
from a market town and five miles from a village, and
the moor which stretched from the park gates led
across the loneliest part of England. The more we
discussed it, the more we realised that it was, without
a doubt, a most amazing coup.

Naturally, the Press devoted a great deal of attention to a robbery of such sensational magnitude,
and several journalists and photographers travelled
down specially from London in search of material.
The fact that I was one of the guests at Kindersley

Court, and my wife amongst the victims of the robbery, gave a certain piquancy to the affair of which the facile pens of some of my literary acquaintances took full advantage. Rimmington himself came down from Scotland Yard with two of his shrewdest assistants, but, as he acknowledged to me upon the third night after their arrival, the whole affair had been carried out with such amazing foresight that it seemed impossible to lay hold anywhere of a clue. A large reward was offered for the recovery of any portion of the jewels, the total value of which was estimated at something over two hundred thousand pounds, and every outlet from the country was carefully watched; but neither in Paris, London nor Amsterdam was there the slightest movement amongst the known dealers in stolen gems. The little company of robbers seemed, indeed, to have driven away in their cars, and, within a mile and a half of the front door of Kindersley Court, to have vanished from the face of the earth. No shepherd upon the moors had seen them pass, none of the inhabitants of the small hamlets around had been awakened from their slumbers by the rushing through the night of those mysterious automobiles. Even Rimmington, who had more optimism than any man of my acquaintance in the profession, returned to London a saddened and disappointed man.

Janet and I stayed on at Kindersley Court for the last Meet of the Stag Hounds — a day which we are neither of us likely ever to forget. We motored over to Exford, where our host had sent all his available horses two days before. Janet, Beatrice Kindersley and I were amongst those of the house party who rode, Beatrice looking remarkably well on a fine, Dartmoor-bred chestnut, a present from her uncle within the last few days. We had one short hunt and a great deal of waiting about. Early in the afternoon we found ourselves on the fringe of the hunt, on the southern slope of Hawksley Down. Below us, at the bottom of the coombe, hounds were being put through a thick jungle of dwarf pines, through which, if a stag were found, he was almost certain to make for Dooneley Barrow, on our right. Suddenly Beatrice, who had been looking over her shoulder, gave a little exclamation. A man, riding a dark bay horse, whom I had noticed once or twice always on the outskirts of the hunt, came round the side of a piled-up mass of stones and boulders and rode straight up to us. I must confess that at first the incident possessed no significance for me. In his well-cut and well-worn riding clothes, and possessing the assured seat of a practised rider, there was nothing to distinguish this man from half a dozen of Lord Kindersley's neighbours with whom we had exchanged greetings during the day. It was not, in fact, until he suddenly wheeled his horse round to within a yard or two of us, and I saw something glitter in his right hand, that I realised who he was.

"Norman Greyes," he said, "I call an armistice for five minutes. You will admit," he added, glancing downward at his right hand, "that I am in a position to call the game."

"Let it be an armistice Michael," I agreed. "What do you want with me?"

"With you, nothing," he answered. "I came to speak to Miss Kindersley."

He looked full at Beatrice as he spoke, and his voice seemed for the moment to have gained a strange new quality.

"I find that my confederate misunderstood me the other night," he continued, "and that after all he took your jewellery from the table. I have stayed in the neighbourhood to return it."

He leaned over and placed a sealed box in Beatrice's hand. I could have sworn that I saw her fingers clutch passionately at his as he drew away.

"I knew that it was a mistake," she said softly, looking across at him, as though striving to call him back to her side. He kept his face, however, turned steadily away. His expression had changed. The old mocking smile was back upon his lips.

"Upon reflection, Janet," he continued, "especially when I considered the richness of our haul, I felt a certain impulse of distaste towards robbing you of your newly acquired splendours. Permit me."

He handed her also a little packet. Then he backed his horse a few paces, but he still lingered, and I knew that he had something else to say.

"So our friend Rimmington has given up the chase and gone back to London," he observed. "Give him a hint from me some day. Tell him not to take it for granted that the first impulse of the malefactor is to place as great a distance as possible between himself and the scene of his misdemeanours. Sometimes the searching hand passes over what it seeks to grasp. "

" I will remember your message, " I promised. " You realise, of course, that I shall report your being still in the neighbourhood? "

" If you did not, " was the cool reply, " the next few hours would be empty of interest to me. Even if you yourself take a hand in the game, Greyes, and I will do you the credit to admit that you are the cleverest of the lot, I promise you that I shall make my way to safety as easily as I shall canter across this moor. "

He leaned towards me.

" Send the women on for a moment, " he begged. " I have a word for you alone. "

Janet turned her horse at once in obedience to my gesture. Beatrice, however, lingered. She was gazing across at my companion. I saw their eyes meet and it seemed to me a strange thing that such a look should pass between those two. Then I saw Michael shake his head.

" I must speak to Greyes alone, " he insisted. " Every moment that I linger here makes my escape more difficult. "

She turned and rode slowly after Janet, but reined in her horse scarcely twenty paces away. Michael rode up to my side. He had dropped his weapon back into the loose pocket of his riding coat. He was at my mercy and he knew it. Yet, rightly enough, he had no fear.

" Norman Greyes, " he said, " this is the end of our

duel, for I have finished with life as you and I understand life. Fate has made us enemies. Fate might more than once have given either of us the other's life. Those things are finished. "

" You speak as though you were making a voluntary retirement, — yet how can you hope to escape? " I asked him. " There is a price upon your head wherever you turn. Even though my day has passed, there are others who will never rest until they have brought you to justice. "

" I am not here to speak about myself, " he answered indifferently. " I want a word with you about that girl. "

" About Beatrice Kindersley? "

" Yes. "

" What can you have to say about her, " I demanded, puzzled, although the memory of that look was still with me.

" Never mind — you know life, Greyes, although you walk on the wrong side of the fence. You know that the greatest of us are great because of our follies. That girl is the folly of my later life. There is a touch of romance in her, a sentiment — for God's sake, Greyes, don't sit and look at me like a graven image! Be a human being and say that you understand. "

I remembered that look and I nodded.

" I understand, " I said. " Go on. "

" Tell her, then, for the love of heaven, who and what I am. Tell her that I have wives living, women whom I have deceived in every quarter of the globe.

Tell her that a policeman's hand upon my shoulder would mean the gallows in England or the electric chair in America. Tell her what manner of life I have lived. Strip off the coverings. Show her the raw truth. Tell her that I am a criminal at heart from the sheer love of crime. "

" I will tell her what you say, " I promised.

" Damn it, man! " he answered passionately, as he turned his head to windward for a moment and swung round his horse. " Tell her nothing from me, tell her from yourself. You know the truth, if any man does. Give her pain, if you must. Show her the ugly side. As man to man, Greyes, enemy to enemy, swear that you will do this. "

" I swear, " I answered.

He must have touched his horse with his whip, unseen by me, for the words had scarcely left my lips before he was galloping away, making for the loneliest and bleakest part of the moor. I heard a stifled cry from Beatrice, a cry that was almost a sob.

" Why did you let him go, Norman? I wanted to say good-by!"

" He left some message for you, " I answered, a little grimly.

MICHAEL

I lunched one Sunday morning at the Café de Paris, with my friend Gaston Lefèvre, the well-known insurance agent of the Rue Scribe, — a luncheon specially planned to celebrate the winding-up of one of the greatest coups of our partnership. We had a table in the far corner of the restaurant, and we were able by reason of its isolation to speak of intimate things.

" You must now be a very wealthy man, my friend, " Lefèvre said to me, a trifle enviously, for all Frenchmen worship money, " a very wealthy man indeed. "

" I have enough, " I answered. " As a matter of fact, that is one of the reasons why I have decided to levy no more contributions upon the fools of the world. "

" You are not going to retire? " Lefèvre cried, in a tone of alarm.

" Absolutely, " I assured him. " I have burned all my boats in England, destroyed all ciphers, sealed up my secret places of refuge and said good-by to all my friends. I have said good-by even to Younghusband, the cleverest rascal who ever successfully carried out the bluff of being a respectable Lincoln's Inn solicitor for over fifteen years. The rascal is actually getting new clients every week. Genuine clients, I mean. He is almost as wonderful as you. "

" As for me, " my companion confessed, sipping his wine, " my position has never been so difficult as yours. I have run no risks like you. I have never stolen a penny in my life, or raised my hand in anger or strife against any of my fellow creatures. "

I laughed softly. After all, the hypocrites of the world are amongst the essential things.

" You have made a million or so by those who have, " I reminded him.

" Money which has been thoroughly well earned, "

was the confident reply. "Under the shelter of my name and position, many things have been rendered possible which could not otherwise have been even attempted. Take this last business, for instance. Could you ever have smuggled a quarter of a million pounds' worth of jewellery out of the country without my aid?"

"It is agreed," I assented. "In such matters you have genius."

M. Lefèvre waved his hand.

"It is a trifle, that," he declared. "Let us speak of yourself, my friend. You are in the prime of life, excitement is as necessary to you as his sweetheart to a Frenchman or his golf to an Englishman. You have just brought off one of the finest coups which has ever been planned. A hundred and fifty thousand pounds to divide for the sale of these jewels, and not a single clue left behind. It was genius indeed. What is going to take the place of these things to you in life?"

I shrugged my shoulders, for indeed I had asked myself the same question.

"There is plenty of amusement to be found," I answered.

Monsieur Lefèvre had his doubts.

"That is all very well," he pointed out, "but if you destroy for yourself, as you say you have done, all the hundred and one means of escape which our ingenuity has evolved, you will have to step warily for the next few years. Neither London nor New York will forget you easily."

"My disappearance," I replied, "will be your task.

To-day we divided the last instalments of our recent profits, amounting, I think, to a little over two million francs. Half a million I have placed in this envelope. They will be yours in return for the service you are about to render me. "

My companion's eyes glistened.

" It is a difficult matter, this, then, my friend? " he asked anxiously.

" On the contrary, it will give you very little trouble indeed, " I assured him. " You have, I think, amongst your other very useful connections, a friendly one with a certain French hospital. I will mention no names. "

" That is, in a measure, true, " Monsieur Lefèvre assented cautiously.

" Your task, then, is simple, " I explained. " In the bag which I left at your office yesterday are clothes, jewellery, papers and other trifles of apparent insignificance. The next unknown man who dies in the hospital, of my height and build, will be wearing these clothes, and will have in his possession the other trifles I have spoken of, which have been all carefully chosen to establish my identity. The authorities will notify the French and New York police, Scotland Yard and the Press. You, also, will assist in making it publicly known that a well-known criminal has passed away. "

" I see no difficulty, " my companion admitted thoughtfully.

" There is no difficulty, " I assured him.

" And afterwards? "

I shook my head.

" There is no person breathing, " I told him, " to whom I shall confide my plan. I am in no hurry. I think you will agree that for a certain length of time, I could move about Paris without fear of being recognised. "

" It is, without doubt, true, " my companion assented, leaning back in his place and studying me thoughtfully. " I passed you on the Boulevard and here, in the entrance, without a single impulse of recognition. I did not know you even when you spoke to me. You look precisely what I took you to be, an elderly Frenchman of good birth, retired from some profession, rather an elegant, something of a *boulevardier*, nothing whatever of an Englishman. I tell you, Michael, " my companion concluded, with some enthusiasm, " that no artist upon the stage or off it, in our day, is such a master of human disguise as you. "

" I will not attempt to say that you flatter me, Lefèvre, " I replied, " because, as a matter of fact, I believe that what you say is the truth. Very well, then, just as I am, I commence so much as may be left to me of the aftermath of life. Within a week I shall leave Paris. You may never see or hear of me again. On the other hand I may feel the call. I make no rash promises or statements. "

" It would interest me strangely to be in the secret of your whereabouts, " Lefèvre persisted.

I shook my head, as I called for the bill.

" I have a fancy, " I told him, " for stepping off

the edge of the world. Let us take an automobile and
watch the beautiful women at Auteuil. "

A fortnight later I read my obituary notice in a
dozen papers. The *New York Herald* devoted a column to me, and the Continental *Daily Mail* followed
suit. The *Times* dismissed me with half a dozen lines
of small print, which seemed unkind when one considered the quantity of free sensational material I
had afforded them. The *Daily Telegraph* seemed to
think that Scotland Yard was at fault in having allowed me to slip out of the world according to my own
time and inclination. The *Morning Post* thought that
Society at large must breathe a sigh of relief at the
passing away of one of the world's greatest criminals.
Only one French paper reported a little incident
which for a single moment brought the fires of madness into my blood — madness and a weakness of
which I shall not speak. Some one in England, a woman, had wired to a Paris florist and there were flowers sent to the hospital on the morning of the
funeral, with no hypocritical message, just the
name " Beatrice " on a card. Well, it was my choice.

JANET

It was chance which brought us to St. Jean de Luz,
chance and Norman's desire to escape from the pande-
monium of an overcrowded golf course. We sat out
on the verandah of the Golf Club on the late afternoon
of our arrival, watching the pink and mauve outlines

of the lower hills and the sombre majesty of the snow-capped mountains beyond. There had been a wind earlier in the day, but the stillness here was almost incredible. The trees which crowned the summit of the grassy slopes were silent and motionless; the cypresses beyond, against the background of the pink-fronted farmhouses they sheltered, seemed darker than ever; the poplars leading to the villas on the south side of the valley stood like silent sentinels. I was conscious of a curious sense of tranquillity, inspired a little, no doubt, by my surroundings. Norman, after a few words of appreciation, looked longingly at his golf clubs and suggested a game to the secretary, who had come out to welcome us.

" Sorry, but I've had two rounds already, " the latter regretted. " There's a man named Benisande out there, practising. He's a Frenchman, but a thundering good player. Would you care about a round with him? "

" I should like a round with any one, " Norman declared enthusiastically.

The secretary strolled across towards the man who was practising mashie shots on to the last green, a slim man with a slight but graceful stoop, silver-grey hair and clean-cut, weather-beaten features. He was dressed in tweed golf clothes of English fashion, and was attended by his own manservant, who was carrying his clubs. He apparently accepted the secretary's suggestion with alacrity, and the two men came over . to us at once. A few words of introduction were spoken and we all made our way to the first tee. The

Frenchman, discovering that Norman's handicap was the same as his own, insisted upon the latter taking the honour. Norman drove an average ball straight down the course — and then came the great moment. Monsieur Benisande glanced curiously at us both, handed his cap to his servant, swung his club and addressed the ball. I gave a little cry. Norman stood as though he were turned to stone. In that moment we had both recognised him. Unmoved, Michael drove straight and far up the course and watched his ball for the length of its run. Afterwards, we three stood and looked at one another upon the tee. The secretary had disappeared in the clubhouse, the caddies had already started after the balls; we were practically alone.

" This is an interesting coincidence, " Michael remarked, with a smile that seemed to have lost all its cynicism. ' " Our acquaintance, Sir Norman, if I remember rightly, commenced with a game of golf at Woking. "

" We thought that you were dead, " I gasped.

Michael sighed.

" I took great pains to insure your thinking so, " he declared. " It is my misfortune to have run up against the two people who were bound to recognise me. Still, I have had a very pleasant four years. "

" Is it so long? " I murmured, for Norman seemed still incapable of speech.

" Four years and a few months, " Michael continued. " It is a great deal to have snatched from a life which should have been ended. I have a charming little

villa, a converted farmhouse — you can see it through
the trees there; a delightful garden — my violets and
carnations are famous — and there are very few English flowers which I have not managed to grow. I play
a round of golf whenever I feel like it and when the
wander hunger comes I vanish up there into the Pyre-
nées. Antoine, my servant, is a Basque, and an accomplished mountaineer. To-day I can follow him
anywhere. "

" What are we going to do about this? " Norman
muttered.

" That remains with you, " Michael replied.

We started to walk slowly towards where the two
balls were lying almost side by side. I passed my
arm through my husband's and looked into his face.
It was obvious that he perfectly well realised the crisis
with which he had to deal. During the last four years,
wonderful years they had been, we had spent scarcely
more than a month or two in London. We had travelled
in Italy and Egypt, wintered twice in the South of
France and the remainder of the time had been devoted
to Greyes Manor. I had my two babies to look after,
and Norman his farms. The ties which had bound him
to his old profession had naturally weakened, yet I
knew now how his mind was working. Here, by his
side, was a man whom he had sworn to bring to justice, a notorious criminal, a man whom, by every code
of ethics and citizenship, he ought promptly to de-
nounce. And I knew that, for some reason, he hated
the task almost as much as I hated it for him. They
drew near to their balls and Norman came to a stand-

still. He had arrived at his decision. I, at any rate, awaited it breathlessly.

"Michael," he said, "you shall have your chance. You know my duty. You know that I am a man who generally tries to do it. Yet, to be candid with you, I have a conviction that your career as a criminal is over, and my personal inclination is to leave you alone. We will let Fate decide it. We are as nearly equal at this game as two men can be. Fate made you my partner this evening. I will play you this round for your liberty and my silence."

I saw Michael's eyes glitter and I knew that the idea appealed to him. He looked towards the green and swung his cleek lightly backwards and forwards.

"Let us understand one another," he insisted. "If I win, I am free of you for the rest of my life. If I lose, I am to face the end."

"If you lose," Norman said, "I shall send a telegram to Scotland Yard, and another to the Chief of the Police at Marseilles."

"The terms are agreed," Michael declared, taking up his stance. "My life against your bruised conscience."

So the match started. The first hole was halved in four, and from then onwards commenced a struggle which I can hardly think of, even now, without a shiver of excitement. Neither was ever more than two up but, towards the sixteenth hole, I began to realise that another factor besides skill was at work. Norman topped his second shot but jumped the bunker and lay upon the green. Michael carried the bunker with

a perfectly played mashie shot, but pitched upon a
mowing machine and came back to an almost unplay-
able place in the long grass. He lost the hole. Norman, who was as nearly nervous as I have ever seen
him, muttered something about bad luck, but his adversary only shrugged his shoulders. At the seventeenth hole, Norman drove fairly well but was still
sixty yards short of the green. It was the old Michael
who took his stand afterwards on the tee, hard and
dogged. I saw his teeth gleam for a moment, and the
whitening of the flesh· around his knuckles as he
gripped his club fiercely. He hit the most wonderful
drive I have ever seen, long and low and straight. It
carried on and on whilst we watched it breathlessly.
Finally it ran on to the green and ended within a
couple of clubs' lengths of the hole. I gave a little
gasp of relief, for, from the first, I had prayed that
my husband might lose. But I had reckoned without
that unseen force. Norman topped his mashie shot,
which bumped along the ground on to the green, passed
Michael's ball and, to my horror, dropped in the hole.
Even Norman himself seemed to have no words. He
stood looking at the spot where his ball had disappeared, his face averted from his opponent.

" Sorry, " he said gruffly. " My second fluke in
two holes, I'm afraid. "

Michael made no remark. He studied his putt long
and carefully, hit it with a musical little click and we
all watched it run straight for the hole. At the last
moment some trifling irregularity of surface seemed
to deflect it, it caught the corner of the hole, swung

round inside and came out again. It rested on the
very edge and we stood there waiting. Nothing,
however, happened. Michael turned away and I
fancied that I saw a little quiver upon his lips.

"We are now all square," he said. "I scarcely
expected to lose the last two holes."

"I have been lucky," Norman admitted, a little
brusquely, "but I can't help it. It might have been
the other way."

At the eighteenth, a strong wind was against them.
Norman, pulling a little, escaped the bunkers, but
Michael, hitting a far better ball, carried them with
a few yards to spare. Norman played a fine second
and reached the green, four or five yards from the
hole. When Michael reached his ball, I saw him stop
and look at it. His servant gave an exclamation. It
was lying where a huge clod of earth had been knocked
away by some beginner and never replaced, without a
blade of grass around it and on a downward slope. I
looked across towards my husband.

"It isn't fair," I whispered hoarsely. "Move it
with your foot. Norman can't see. Besides, I'm in
the way."

Michael, who was choosing a club, just glanced up
at me for a moment, and I felt as though I had said
something sacrilegious.

"We don't play games that way," he rejoined
quietly. "I am afraid this is going to be rather a
forlorn hope, though."

He took a niblick, and against the wind he was only

able to get about halfway to the green. This time, however, his ball was lying well.

"I play the odd," he murmured, as he selected a running-up cleek. We waited breathlessly for the shot. Norman's caddy and Michael's servant, although they had no idea, of course, of the significance of the match, had gathered from our tense air that it was of no ordinary interest. We all watched Michael's ball, when at last he played it, spellbound. It was a low shot, beautifully straight for the flag, and I could scarcely keep back a little cry of joy when I saw it land on the green and run slowly two or three yards past the hole.

"A fine recovery," Norman said thickly. "My turn now to play the like."

He took his putter and my heart sank as I saw him strike the ball well and firmly. For a moment it seemed as though he had holed it and the match was over. It came to a standstill about eighteen inches short.

"This for a half," Michael remarked, as he went towards his ball.

I saw him half close his eyes as he took up his stance, and I wondered for a moment what he was thinking of. He took the line carefully and struck the ball straight for the back of the hole. I gave a little gasp. It seemed as though the half were assured. Then a cry of dismay from Michael's caddy startled me. The ball, although it had seemed to hit the back of the hole, spun round and came out again. Again it lay within a foot or so of the hole. Michael

stood quite still looking at it. He glanced up and our
eyes met.

" The fates, " he said quietly, " are against me. "

Norman took out his putter and I scarcely dared to
watch. He was only a few inches from the hole. The
result seemed certain. Then as I forced myself to
watch him, a strange thought came to me. He seemed
to be taking unusual care, but he was holding his
putter differently and he seemed to have lost his confidence.

" This for the match, " he said, looking across at
his opponent.

" For the match, " Michael repeated hopelessly.

Norman struck the ball with a little stab and I
could scarcely believe my eyes. It missed the hole,
passing it on the left-hand side and coming to a standstill at least two feet away. Norman looked down at
the ground in a puzzled manner.

" This is the rottenest green on the course, " he
muttered. " Whose play, caddy? "

The caddy considered the matter for a moment and
pointed to Michael. This time there was no mistake.
The ball went well and truly to the bottom of the hole.
Norman again surprised me. He studied his ridiculous
little putt with exaggerated care, brushed away some
fancied impediment and reproved his caddy sharply
for talking. When he hit the ball, he hit it crisply
enough but again with that little stab which drew it
once more to the wrong side of the hole. There was a
little murmur.

" I never saw such filthy putting in my life! " Norman exclaimed, looking exactly like a normal man who has lost an important match by a moment's carelessness. " Your match, Monsieur Benisande. I think perhaps you deserved it. You had all the worst of the luck until my putting paralysis set in. "

Michael took off his hat and I saw great beads of perspiration upon his forehead.

" I am thankful for my win, " he said quietly, " but I scarcely expected it. "

We all walked back to the clubhouse together.

" Janet and I will leave St. Jean de Luz at once, " Norman announced.

" It will not be necessary, " Michael rejoined quickly. " To-morrow I start for the mountains. I shall be gone for a week or more. I beg that you will not hurry your departure. May I speak to you for a moment, Janet? "

Norman made his way, without remark, to the clubhouse. He neither spoke to nor looked towards Michael again. Men are strange beings. This was the passing of the feud which left them both foresworn.

I spared Michael the question which I knew was upon his lips.

" Beatrice is well, " I told him. " She is still unmarried. "

There was a light in Michael's face which I pretended not to see. It was gone in a moment, and when he spoke his voice was quite steady.

" I am sorry to hear that she is unmarried, " he said, " although no man in the world could be worthy of her. I am going to entrust you with a mission. If ever the truth concerning me should come to light, I want her to know this."

He drew from his pocket a letter case of black silk with platinum clasps, a simple but very elegant trifle for a man. Out of it he drew what appeared to be its sole contents, a crumpled card, upon which was written, in Beatrice's handwriting, her own name. The card was smeared as though with the stain of crushed flowers.

"I planned my death," he continued, with a faint return to his old cynical smile, "very much as I have lived my life — with my tongue in my cheek. Then I read in some French paper that Beatrice had sent flowers to the hospital for my funeral and I felt all the bitter shame of a man who has done an ugly thing. I made what atonement I could. After having reached absolute safety, I risked my life in almost foolhardy fashion. I attended my own funeral. I stole that card and one of the flowers from the grave. If ever she should learn the truth," he added, his face turned away towards the mountains, "I should like her to know that. She may reckon it as atonement."

I laid my hand upon his arm. Speech of any sort seemed to have become extraordinarily difficult. When I had found the words I wanted, Michael had gone.

The last we saw of Michael was, in its way, allegorical. As we climbed one of the grassy slopes of the Golf Club on the following morning, we saw two men on the other side of the river, walking steadily away from us along the path which led across the lower chain of hills towards the mountains. They carried knapsacks on their backs and long staves in their hands. They had, somehow, at that distance the air of pilgrims.

"There goes Benisande, off on one of his mountain expeditions," the secretary, who was playing with Norman, remarked, pointing them out. "They say that he has made up his mind to climb that further peak beyond the Pass. Even the Basque guides call him foolhardy."

I watched the two figures. I waved my hand in futile farewell. But Michael never once turned back.

www.ingramcontent.com/pod-product-compliance
Lightning Source LLC
Chambersburg PA
CBHW031237090426
42742CB00007B/230